THE 100+ SERIES™

Reproducible Activities

Pre-Algebra

Grades 5-8

By
Mary Lee Vivian
and
Margaret Thomas

Instructional Fair
An imprint of Carson-Dellosa Publishing LLC
Greensboro, North Carolina

Instructional Fair

Authors: Mary Lee Vivian and Margaret Thomas
Editor: Jerry Aten

Instructional Fair
An imprint of Carson-Dellosa Publishing LLC
PO Box 35665
Greensboro, NC 27425 USA

ISBN 978-0-74241-787-8
02-152127784

Note to Teacher: Each activity in this book has been linked to the related NCTM Standards listed below. The numbers of the related Standards for each activity are indicated in the Table of Contents.

1. Number and Operations – Understand numbers, ways of representing numbers, relationships among numbers, and number systems. Understand meanings of operations and how they relate to one another. Compute fluently and make reasonable estimates.

2. Algebra – Understand patterns, relations, and functions. Represent and analyze mathematical situations and structures using algebraic symbols. Use mathematical models to represent and understand quantitative relationships. Analyze change in various contexts.

3. Geometry – Analyze characteristics and properties of two- and three-dimensional geometric shapes and develop mathematical arguments about geometric relationships. Specify locations and describe spatial relationships using coordinate geometry and other representational systems. Apply transformations and use symmetry to analyze mathematical situations. Use visualization, spatial reasoning, and geometric modeling to solve problems.

4. Measurement – Understand measurable attributes of objects and the units, systems, and processes of measurement. Apply appropriate techniques, tools, and formulas to determine measurements.

5. Data Analysis and Probability – Formulate questions that can be addressed with data and collect, organize, and display relevant data to answer them. Select and use appropriate statistical methods to analyze data. Develop and evaluate inferences and predictions that are based on data. Understand and apply basic concepts of probability.

6. Problem Solving – Build new mathematical knowledge through problem solving. Solve problems that arise in mathematics and in other contexts. Apply and adapt a variety of appropriate strategies to solve problems. Monitor and reflect on the process of mathematical problem solving.

7. Reasoning and Proof – Recognize reasoning and proof as fundamental aspects of mathematics. Make and investigate mathematical conjectures. Develop and evaluate mathematical arguments and proofs. Select and use various types of reasoning and methods of proof.

8. Communication – Organize and consolidate their mathematical thinking through communication. Communicate their mathematical thinking coherently and clearly to peers, teachers, and others. Analyze and evaluate the mathematical thinking and strategies of others. Use the language of mathematics to express mathematical ides precisely.

9. Connections – Recognize and use connections among mathematical ideas. Understand how mathematical ideas interconnect and build on one another to produce a coherent whole. Recognize and apply mathematics in contexts outside of mathematics.

10. Representation – Create and use representations to organize, record, and communicate mathematical ideas. Select, apply, and translate among mathematical representations to solve problems. Use representations to model and interpret physical, social, and mathematical phenomena.

Table of Contents

Name ______________________ Date ______________________

Adding and Subtracting Fractions

Use the common denominator. Add or subtract the numerators. Reduce to lowest terms.

$\frac{1}{8} + \frac{3}{8} = \frac{4}{8} = \frac{1}{2}$ Add same

1. $\frac{2}{9} + \frac{5}{9} =$

2. $\frac{3}{4} - \frac{1}{4} =$

3. $\frac{9}{15} + \frac{5}{15} =$

4. $\frac{19}{20} - \frac{14}{20} =$

5. $\frac{27}{38} + \frac{13}{38} =$

6. $\frac{35}{60} - \frac{17}{60} =$

7. $\frac{17}{20} + \frac{23}{20} =$

8. $\frac{25}{13} - \frac{12}{13} =$

9. $\frac{11}{18} + \frac{16}{18} =$

10. $\frac{17}{48} - \frac{14}{48} =$

11. $\frac{7}{45} + \frac{8}{45} =$

12. $\frac{33}{50} - \frac{17}{50} =$

13. $\frac{16}{33} + \frac{21}{33} =$

14. $\frac{43}{56} - \frac{19}{56} =$

15. $\frac{12}{42} + \frac{31}{42} =$

16. $\frac{29}{52} - \frac{13}{52} =$

17. $\frac{15}{18} + \frac{8}{18} =$

18. $\frac{43}{65} - \frac{28}{65} =$

0-7424-1787-5 *Pre-Algebra*

Name ______________________ Date ______________________

More Adding and Subtracting Fractions

Hint: Remember to re-write fractions.

$$\frac{7}{9} - \frac{1}{4} = \frac{28}{36} - \frac{9}{36} = \frac{19}{36}$$

36 is the least common multiple

1. $\frac{2}{3} + \frac{5}{9} =$

2. $\frac{4}{5} - \frac{3}{4} =$

3. $\frac{5}{6} + \frac{7}{12} =$

4. $\frac{11}{15} - \frac{2}{5} =$

5. $\frac{11}{12} + \frac{5}{8} =$

6. $\frac{1}{2} - \frac{4}{9} =$

7. $\frac{13}{36} + \frac{5}{12} =$

8. $\frac{7}{8} - \frac{3}{10} =$

9. $\frac{5}{12} - \frac{5}{18} =$

10. $\frac{5}{9} + \frac{3}{8} =$

11. $\frac{5}{12} - \frac{3}{15} =$

12. $\frac{3}{4} + \frac{7}{12} =$

13. $\frac{8}{19} - \frac{1}{3} =$

14. $\frac{7}{15} + \frac{3}{25} =$

15. $\frac{30}{36} - \frac{5}{18} =$

16. $\frac{4}{5} + \frac{12}{13} =$

Name ______________________ Date ______________________

Words to the Wise

Write each sum or difference in lowest terms. Cross out the answers below to reveal the "Words to the Wise."

1. $\frac{4}{9} + \frac{13}{15} =$
2. $\frac{5}{6} + \frac{7}{32} =$
3. $\frac{13}{15} - \frac{1}{3} =$
4. $\frac{3}{11} + \frac{6}{7} =$
5. $\frac{5}{9} - \frac{1}{15} =$
6. $\frac{7}{9} + \frac{1}{6} =$
7. $\frac{9}{10} - \frac{3}{20} =$
8. $\frac{11}{42} + \frac{1}{7} =$
9. $\frac{8}{9} - \frac{1}{12} =$
10. $\frac{7}{12} + \frac{31}{42} =$
11. $\frac{11}{12} - \frac{1}{18} =$
12. $\frac{7}{23} - \frac{1}{7} =$
13. $\frac{8}{21} + \frac{36}{49} =$
14. $\frac{7}{9} - \frac{1}{4} =$
15. $\frac{11}{30} + \frac{2}{25} =$
16. $\frac{27}{35} - \frac{11}{30} =$
17. $\frac{7}{8} + \frac{13}{14} =$
18. $\frac{76}{81} - \frac{22}{63} =$
19. $\frac{1}{3} + \frac{2}{3} =$
20. $\frac{23}{45} - \frac{1}{3} =$

$\frac{19}{36}$ CAN	$\frac{17}{24}$ PUT	$\frac{17}{18}$ IT	$\frac{334}{567}$ PLACE	$\frac{7}{8}$ FORTH	1 IS	$1\frac{14}{45}$ WAS	$1\frac{17}{147}$ WHOLE	$\frac{29}{36}$ IT	$\frac{5}{27}$ HALF	$1\frac{5}{96}$ PROPER
$\frac{3}{8}$ THE	$\frac{26}{161}$ THIS	$\frac{17}{42}$ ON	$\frac{31}{36}$ TRY	$1\frac{35}{68}$ EFFORT	$\frac{31}{80}$ AND	$\frac{8}{15}$ SUM	$\frac{9}{30}$ YOU	$\frac{11}{45}$ GET	$\frac{1}{4}$ A	$1\frac{47}{147}$ FRACTION
$\frac{8}{45}$ IF	$\frac{17}{42}$ ARE	$\frac{22}{45}$ IN	$\frac{13}{55}$ OF	$1\frac{10}{77}$ TOTAL	$\frac{67}{150}$ HAS	$\frac{3}{5}$ THE	$1\frac{45}{56}$ VALUE	$1\frac{9}{28}$ TO	$\frac{3}{4}$ ALL	$1\frac{7}{47}$ RESULTS

_______ _______ _______ _______ _______ _______

_______ _______ _______ _______ _______ _______ _______

Name ______________________ Date ______________________

Adding and Subtracting Mixed Numbers

$$3\frac{7}{8} + 5\frac{11}{24} = 3\frac{21}{24} + 5\frac{11}{24} = 8\frac{32}{24} = 9\frac{8}{24} = 9\frac{1}{3}$$

add

add

1. $1\frac{1}{4} + 2\frac{1}{2} =$

2. $5\frac{7}{10} - 1\frac{1}{6} =$

3. $8\frac{3}{8} + 9\frac{2}{3} =$

4. $6 - 2\frac{8}{11} =$

5. $2\frac{1}{16} + 2\frac{1}{3} =$

6. $7\frac{7}{8} - 7\frac{5}{12} =$

7. $4\frac{1}{2} + 6\frac{2}{5} =$

8. $5\frac{1}{2} - \frac{11}{15} =$

9. $1\frac{5}{6} + 4 =$

10. $6\frac{7}{9} - 6\frac{1}{2} =$

11. $7\frac{1}{4} + 1\frac{7}{9} + 2\frac{5}{6} =$

12. $8\frac{1}{6} - 7\frac{3}{4} =$

13. $5 + 3\frac{3}{11} =$

14. $3\frac{5}{8} - 1\frac{6}{7} =$

15. $4\frac{3}{7} + 5\frac{5}{14} =$

16. $6\frac{3}{12} - 3\frac{9}{36} =$

Name ______________________ Date ______________________

Pair Them Up!

Each problem in the first column has the same answer as a problem in the second column. Solve the problems and determine the matches.

1. $7\frac{3}{5} + 2\frac{1}{2} =$

A. $8\frac{1}{3} + 12\frac{1}{2} =$

2. $10\frac{3}{5} - 4 =$

B. $2\frac{5}{18} - \frac{11}{24} =$

3. $5\frac{2}{9} + 7\frac{1}{3} =$

C. $5\frac{2}{9} - 3\frac{7}{9} =$

4. $11\frac{5}{6} - 3\frac{3}{4} =$

D. $13 - 6\frac{2}{5} =$

5. $4\frac{7}{12} + 4\frac{3}{14} =$

E. $3\frac{5}{6} + 8\frac{13}{18} =$

6. $8 - 6\frac{5}{9} =$

F. $17\frac{5}{12} - 4\frac{7}{12} =$

7. $17\frac{14}{15} + 2\frac{9}{10} =$

G. $7\frac{11}{12} + \frac{1}{6} =$

8. $1\frac{17}{18} - \frac{1}{8} =$

H. $10\frac{13}{14} - 2\frac{11}{84} =$

9. $6\frac{1}{12} + 6\frac{3}{4} =$

I. $5\frac{1}{5} + 4\frac{9}{10} =$

10. $8\frac{2}{9} - 6\frac{17}{18} =$

J. $9\frac{1}{6} - 7\frac{8}{9} =$

0-7424-1787-5 *Pre-Algebra*

Name ______________________ Date ______________________

Multiplying Fractions

Multiply numerators. Multiply denominators. Reduce to lowest terms.
Hint: Rewrite mixed numbers as improper fractions.

$$2\frac{1}{4} \bullet 1\frac{2}{3} = \frac{9}{4} \bullet \frac{5}{3} = \frac{\overset{3}{\cancel{9}}}{4} \bullet \frac{5}{\underset{1}{\cancel{3}}} = \frac{15}{4} = 3\frac{3}{4}$$

(rewrite) (rewrite)

1. $\frac{1}{2} \bullet \frac{5}{6} =$

2. $3 \bullet \frac{1}{2} =$

3. $\frac{2}{5} \bullet \frac{1}{3} =$

4. $\frac{16}{5} \bullet \frac{25}{27} =$

5. $\frac{8}{21} \bullet 2\frac{7}{16} =$

6. $1\frac{5}{7} \bullet 2\frac{1}{4} =$

7. $5\frac{7}{8} \bullet 4 =$

8. $\frac{5}{7} \bullet \frac{7}{5} =$

9. $3\frac{2}{3} \bullet \frac{17}{22} =$

10. $\frac{5}{6} \bullet 2 =$

11. $8\frac{1}{3} \bullet \frac{3}{4} =$

12. $4\frac{1}{4} \bullet 3\frac{1}{5} =$

13. $2\frac{1}{6} \bullet \frac{18}{20} =$

14. $\frac{21}{35} \bullet 3\frac{4}{7} =$

15. $1\frac{3}{5} \bullet 2\frac{3}{16} =$

16. $6\frac{3}{4} \bullet 1\frac{5}{9} =$

17. $3\frac{1}{3} \bullet 1\frac{3}{18} =$

18. $\frac{1}{2} \bullet \frac{6}{11} \bullet \frac{3}{5} =$

0-7424-1787-5 *Pre-Algebra*

Name ______________________ Date ______________________

Mort's Multiplication

Mort did not understand multiplying mixed numbers when he completed the quiz below. Find and correct the 10 errors Mort made. Explain how to multiply mixed numbers.

FRACTIONS QUIZ

Name *Mort*

1. $5\frac{3}{5} \bullet 3\frac{4}{7} = 15\frac{12}{35}$
2. $2\frac{1}{12} \bullet 2\frac{2}{15} = 4\frac{4}{9}$
3. $1\frac{1}{15} \bullet 3\frac{3}{7} = 3\frac{69}{105}$
4. $8\frac{2}{9} \bullet 2\frac{7}{8} = 16\frac{7}{36}$
5. $16 \bullet 4\frac{1}{4} = 68$
6. $6\frac{2}{3} \bullet 1\frac{15}{16} = 12\frac{11}{12}$
7. $5\frac{1}{3} \bullet 4\frac{1}{2} = 20\frac{1}{6}$
8. $9\frac{1}{3} \bullet 8\frac{1}{10} = 75\frac{3}{5}$
9. $2\frac{1}{12} \bullet 3\frac{5}{9} = 7\frac{11}{27}$
10. $3\frac{5}{6} \bullet 8 = 24\frac{5}{6}$
11. $9\frac{1}{3} \bullet 1\frac{5}{7} \bullet \frac{3}{4} = 9\frac{15}{84}$
12. $6\frac{8}{9} \bullet 3\frac{6}{7} = 26\frac{4}{7}$
13. $8\frac{2}{5} \bullet 3\frac{1}{3} = 24\frac{2}{15}$
14. $9\frac{3}{5} \bullet 2\frac{1}{12} = 20$
15. $2\frac{1}{2} \bullet 2\frac{8}{9} = 4\frac{4}{9}$
16. $5\frac{3}{7} \bullet 2\frac{3}{16} = 10\frac{9}{112}$
17. $2\frac{1}{4} \bullet 6 \bullet 1\frac{1}{9} = 15$
18. $4\frac{1}{2} \bullet 2\frac{2}{5} = 8\frac{1}{5}$
19. $7\frac{1}{2} \bullet 7\frac{1}{3} = 55$
20. $3\frac{1}{8} \bullet \frac{1}{9} \bullet \frac{9}{10} = 3\frac{1}{80}$

Name ____________________ Date ____________________

Dividing Fractions

Invert and multiply

$$1\frac{1}{2} \div 3\frac{3}{7} = \frac{3}{2} \div \frac{24}{7} = \frac{3}{2} \bullet \frac{7}{24} = \frac{\overset{1}{\cancel{3}}}{2} \bullet \frac{7}{\underset{8}{\cancel{24}}} = \frac{7}{16}$$

rewrite the mixed numbers

1. $\frac{3}{7} \div \frac{1}{2} =$

2. $\frac{17}{9} \div \frac{8}{9} =$

3. $6\frac{2}{3} \div 5 =$

4. $1\frac{7}{9} \div 4\frac{2}{9} =$

5. $\frac{15}{4} \div \frac{5}{14} =$

6. $\frac{11}{12} \div \frac{13}{8} =$

7. $4 \div 4\frac{2}{5} =$

8. $3\frac{1}{4} \div 4\frac{3}{8} =$

9. $\frac{6}{15} \div \frac{9}{10} =$

10. $\frac{7}{8} \div 2\frac{1}{3} =$

11. $9\frac{3}{8} \div 3\frac{3}{4} =$

12. $5\frac{1}{6} \div \frac{31}{6} =$

13. $\frac{7}{8} \div \frac{3}{4} =$

14. $\frac{7}{12} \div \frac{7}{4} =$

15. $4\frac{6}{7} \div \frac{1}{3} =$

16. $5\frac{1}{2} \div \frac{7}{4} =$

17. $2\frac{2}{9} \div 4\frac{2}{6} =$

18. $5\frac{5}{12} \div 3\frac{1}{3} =$

Name ______________________ Date ______________________

Division Magic

In a Magic Square, each row, column and diagonal has the same sum - Magic Sum. Complete the problems and determine the magic Sum.

$\frac{5}{12} \div \frac{1}{2}$	$1\frac{1}{2} \div 1\frac{1}{3}$	$\frac{5}{6} \div 5$	$\frac{11}{12} \div 2$	$1\frac{1}{2} \div 2$
$6\frac{1}{2} \div 6$	$\frac{3}{4} \div \frac{9}{4}$	$\frac{5}{6} \div 2$	$2\frac{1}{8} \div 3$	$1\frac{7}{12} \div 2$
$\frac{7}{8} \div 3$	$\frac{6}{7} \div 2\frac{2}{7}$	$\frac{2}{5} \div \frac{3}{5}$	$2\frac{7}{8} \div 3$	$\frac{5}{12} \div \frac{2}{5}$
$\frac{13}{48} \div \frac{1}{2}$	$\frac{5}{32} \div \frac{1}{4}$	$\frac{2}{3} \div \frac{8}{11}$	$\frac{7}{8} \div \frac{7}{8}$	$\frac{1}{2} \div 2$
$1\frac{1}{2} \div 2\frac{4}{7}$	$1\frac{3}{4} \div 2$	$\frac{7}{18} \div \frac{1}{3}$	$\frac{1}{3} \div 1\frac{3}{5}$	$\frac{3}{4} \div 1\frac{1}{2}$

Magic Sum = ____________

If every row and column in a Magic Square of problems has the same sum except for the last row and the last column, what do you know?

____

Name ______________________ Date ______________________

Confused Calculations

Cal Q. Late was very confused about fractions when he completed the quiz below. Find and correct the ten errors Cal made.

FRACTIONS QUIZ

Name *Cal*

1. $\frac{3}{5} + \frac{1}{3} = \frac{2}{5}$
2. $\frac{3}{4} + \frac{3}{4} = \frac{6}{8}$
3. $4\frac{2}{3} + 6\frac{3}{4} = 10\frac{5}{7}$
4. $2\frac{1}{2} + 3\frac{1}{2} = 6$
5. $\frac{7}{8} - \frac{2}{3} = \frac{5}{24}$
6. $\frac{6}{7} - \frac{2}{7} = \frac{4}{7}$
7. $2\frac{4}{5} - 1\frac{2}{3} = 1\frac{2}{15}$
8. $6\frac{1}{4} - 2\frac{3}{4} = 4\frac{1}{2}$
9. $\frac{3}{4} \bullet \frac{6}{7} = \frac{1}{14}$
10. $\frac{1}{3} \bullet \frac{1}{3} = \frac{1}{6}$
11. $1\frac{2}{3} \bullet 2\frac{1}{2} = 2\frac{1}{3}$
12. $4\frac{1}{2} \bullet 3\frac{1}{3} = 12\frac{1}{6}$
13. $\frac{3}{4} \div \frac{1}{2} = 1\frac{1}{2}$
14. $\frac{2}{3} \div \frac{3}{4} = \frac{8}{9}$
15. $2\frac{4}{5} \div 1\frac{2}{5} = 2\frac{2}{5}$
16. $5\frac{1}{4} \div 3\frac{1}{2} = 15\frac{1}{8}$

What rules for computing with fractions would you share with Cal?

Addition ______________________

Subtraction ______________________

Multiplication ______________________

Division ______________________

Name ____________________ Date ____________________

... More Mixed Practice with Fractions

1. $8\frac{1}{15} - 5\frac{11}{20} =$

2. $3\frac{1}{9} + 8\frac{3}{7} + 1\frac{1}{3} =$

3. $1\frac{7}{8} \bullet 3\frac{3}{5} =$

4. $4\frac{4}{5} \div 2\frac{8}{10} =$

5. $3\frac{5}{12} + 5\frac{1}{4} - 2\frac{7}{20} =$

6. $(\frac{16}{21} \bullet 3\frac{1}{4}) + 6\frac{1}{3} =$

7. $5\frac{7}{10} - (\frac{25}{27} \div 3\frac{1}{3}) =$

8. $(2\frac{15}{24} + 3\frac{11}{12}) \bullet 6\frac{1}{2} =$

9. $7\frac{3}{12} - 2\frac{8}{9} =$

10. $1\frac{1}{6} \bullet 3\frac{5}{7} \bullet 2\frac{2}{9} =$

11. $8\frac{7}{12} + 11\frac{3}{4} =$

12. $7 - (3\frac{7}{9} \div 4\frac{2}{3}) =$

13. $2\frac{1}{2} \bullet 3\frac{3}{15} =$

14. $5\frac{2}{9} - 2\frac{17}{18} + 1\frac{2}{3} =$

15. $(3\frac{6}{8} \div 4\frac{2}{4}) - \frac{13}{16} =$

16. $4\frac{2}{3} \bullet 1\frac{3}{4} \bullet 3\frac{3}{4} =$

17. $3\frac{4}{15} + 8\frac{3}{45} =$

18. $12\frac{1}{2} - 7\frac{15}{16} =$

19. $(1\frac{12}{13} \bullet 7\frac{3}{5}) - 3 =$

20. $2\frac{1}{8} + (6\frac{2}{3} \div 8\frac{4}{9}) =$

21. $3\frac{1}{3} \bullet 7\frac{5}{6} \bullet 2\frac{2}{5} =$

22. $1\frac{15}{16} + 3\frac{7}{24} + 3\frac{11}{12} =$

Name ______________________ Date ______________________

Problems with Fractions

1. If $1\frac{1}{4}$ pounds of bananas sell for 80¢ and $1\frac{1}{3}$ pounds of apples sell for 90¢, which fruit is cheaper?

2. A cake recipe calls for $\frac{2}{3}$ teaspoons of salt, $1\frac{1}{2}$ teaspoons baking powder, 1 teaspoon baking soda and $\frac{1}{2}$ teaspoon cinnamon. How many total teaspoons of dry ingredients are used?

3. A baseball team played 35 games and won $\frac{4}{7}$ of them.

   How many games were won?

   How many games were lost?

4. During 4 days, the price of the stock of PEV Corporation went up $\frac{1}{4}$ of a point, down $\frac{1}{3}$ of a point, down $\frac{3}{4}$ of a point and up $\frac{7}{10}$ of a point. What was the net change?

5. Janie wants to make raisin cookies. She needs $8\frac{1}{2}$ cups of raisins for the cookies. A 15-ounce box of raisins contains $2\frac{3}{4}$ cups. How many boxes must Janie buy to make her cookies?

6. A one-half gallon carton of milk costs \$1.89. A one-gallon carton of milk costs \$2.99. How much money would you save if you bought a one-gallon carton instead of 2 one-half gallon cartons?

Name ______________________ Date ______________________

Changing Fractions to Decimals

$$\frac{7}{20} \rightarrow 20\overline{\smash{)}7.00}\ (\text{quotient } .35) \rightarrow \frac{7}{20} = 0.35$$

$$\begin{array}{r} .35 \\ 20\overline{)7.00} \\ \underline{6.0} \\ 1.00 \\ \underline{1.00} \\ 0 \end{array}$$

terminating

$$\frac{5}{12} \rightarrow 12\overline{\smash{)}5.00000}\ (\text{quotient } .41666) \rightarrow \frac{5}{12} = 0.41\overline{6}$$

$$\begin{array}{r} .41666 \\ 12\overline{)5.00000} \\ \underline{4.8} \\ 20 \\ \underline{12} \\ 80 \\ \underline{72} \\ 80 \\ \underline{72} \\ 80 \end{array}$$

repeating

1. $\frac{3}{5} =$

2. $\frac{11}{25} =$

3. $\frac{7}{15} =$

4. $2\frac{1}{9} =$

5. $\frac{23}{33} =$

6. $1\frac{5}{16} =$

7. $\frac{12}{25} =$

8. $\frac{1}{3} =$

9. $\frac{5}{33} =$

10. $2\frac{5}{16} =$

11. $\frac{25}{37} =$

12. $3\frac{13}{15} =$

13. $\frac{17}{22} =$

14. $3\frac{11}{12} =$

0-7424-1787-5 *Pre-Algebra*

Name ______________________ Date ______________________

Terminators

Change each of the following fractions into decimal equivalents. Indicate whether the decimal terminates (T) or repeats (R).

Fraction	Decimal	T or R	Fraction	Decimal	T or R
1. $\frac{3}{8}$			11. $2\frac{3}{8}$		
2. $\frac{8}{15}$			12. $2\frac{15}{37}$		
3. $\frac{27}{32}$			13. $\frac{67}{90}$		
4. $\frac{23}{30}$			14. $1\frac{19}{33}$		
5. $\frac{4}{7}$			15. $\frac{124}{333}$		
6. $5\frac{1}{8}$			16. $5\frac{7}{10}$		
7. $1\frac{4}{5}$			17. $2\frac{11}{16}$		
8. $\frac{10}{35}$			18. $7\frac{31}{40}$		
9. $\frac{9}{15}$			19. $3\frac{9}{16}$		
10. $2\frac{7}{8}$			20. $11\frac{3}{4}$		

BONUS: For fractions in lowest terms, what are the prime factors of the denominators that terminate?

____

Give a rule for determining whether a fraction will be a terminating or repeating decimal.

____

Name ____________________ Date ____________________

Rounding Decimals

Rounding Decimals

Round 8.135 to the nearest tenth.

$8.1\underline{3}5 \rightarrow 8.1$

less than 5

Round 32.56713 to the nearest hundredth.

$32.56\underline{7}13 \rightarrow 32.57$

greater than 5

Round to the nearest whole number.

1. 41.803 =	2. 119.63 =	3. 20.05 =	4. 3.45 =
5. 79.531 =	6. 8.437 =	7. 29.37 =	8. 109.96 =

Round to the nearest tenth.

9. 33.335 =	10. 1.861 =	11. 99.96 =	12. 103.103 =
13. 16.031 =	14. 281.05 =	15. 8.741 =	16. 27.773 =

Round to the nearest hundredth.

17. 69.713 =	18. 5.569 =	19. 609.906 =	20. 247.898 =
21. 5.535 =	22. 67.1951 =	23. 14.0305 =	24. 6.9372 =

0-7424-1787-5 *Pre-Algebra*

Name ______________________ Date ______________________

Multiplying and Dividing by 10, 100, etc.

When multiplying by a power of 10, move the decimal to the right:

34.61 x 1<u>0</u> → move 1 place → 346.1

6.77 x 1<u>00</u> → move 2 places → 677

When dividing by a power of 10, move the decimal to the left:

7.39 ÷ 1<u>00</u> → move 2 place → 0.0739

105.61 ÷ 1<u>000</u> → move 3 places → 0.10561

1. 4.81 x 100 =
2. 37.68 ÷ 10 =
3. 0.46 x 1,000 =
4. 7.12 ÷ 10,000 =
5. 5.4 x 10 =
6. 27,500 ÷ 1,000 =
7. 4.395 x 100,000 =
8. 0.0075 ÷ 100 =
9. 2.274 x 10 =
10. 90,000 ÷ 100 =
11. 0.000618 x 1,000 =
12. 39.006 ÷ 1,000 =
13. 16 x 100 =
14. 28.889 ÷ 10,000 =
15. 36.89 x 10,000 =
16. 0.091 ÷ 100 =
17. 0.0336 x 100,000 =
18. 1,672 ÷ 100,000 =

Name ______________________ Date ______________________

Adding and Subtracting Decimals

13.6 + 7.12 =	$\begin{array}{r} 13.6 \\ +\ 7.12 \\ \hline 20.72 \end{array}$	12 - 3.78 =	$\begin{array}{r} 12 \\ -\ 3.78 \\ \hline 8.22 \end{array}$

1. 3.5 + 8.4 =
2. 43.57 + 104.6 =
3. 15.36 + 29.23 + 7.2 =
4. 2.304 + 6.18 + 9.2 =
5. $12.91 + $6.99 =
6. 0.08 + 19 =
7. 22.63 + 1.694 =
8. 362.1 + 8.888 + 0.016 =
9. 1392.16 + 16.16 =
10. 83.196 + 0.0017 =
11. 17.6 – 9.3 =
12. 32.3 – 12.72 =
13. 23.96 – 19.931 =
14. $29.98 – $16.09 =
15. 63.36 – 0.007 =
16. 16.22 – 0.039 =
17. 44.44 – 16.1 =
18. $75.02 – $3.99 =
19. 575.021 – 65.98 =
20. 394.6 – 27.88 – 0.0933 =

Name ____________________ Date ____________________

More or Less

Compute the sums and differences. Cross out each answer below. The remaining letters spell out an important rule.

1. 6.2 + 0.25 = __________
2. 3.3 – 0.33 = __________
3. 0.26 + 0.4 = __________
4. 8.76 – 5.43 = __________
5. 19.9 + 1.1 = __________
6. 9.53 – 5.3 = __________
7. 0.22 + 2.2 = __________
8. 77.7 – 7 = __________
9. 7.8 + 64.2 = __________
10. 9.25 – 2.5 = __________
11. 36 + 6.3 = __________
12. 37.2 – 32 = __________
13. 0.23 + 3.7 = __________
14. 28.55 – 20.5 = __________
15. 27.8 + 2.2 – 3.5 + 0.5 – 20.5 = __________

20	3.33	34	70.7	71	6.75	0.3	6.45	0.66	9	42.3	3.93	8.7	8.05
RE	AL	ME	WA	MB	YS	ER	CO	UN	TO	AD	DU	LI	PT
9.9	2.42	4.4	5.2	4.49	77	72	0.6	21	4.23	9	2.97	6.5	3.07
NE	HE	UP	PL	TH	EP	AC	OI	ES	TO	NT	AD	D.	S.

Write the remaining letters, one letter to space.

___ ___ ___ ___ ___ ___ ___ ___   ___ ___

___ ___ ___ ___   ___ ___   ___ ___ ___

___ ___ ___ ___ ___ ___

Name ______________________ Date ______________________

Multiplying Decimals

The number of decimal places in a product equals the sum of decimal places in the factors.

(0.7)	(0.04)	=	0.028
1	+ 2	=	3
place	places		places

1. (0.003) (6) =
2. (0.051) (0.003) =
3. (260) (0.01) =
4. (9.6) (5) =
5. (7) (3.42) =
6. (5.29) (11.3) =
7. (0.017) (6.2) =
8. (0.3) (0.03) (0.003) =
9. (1.5) (0.096) (4.3) =
10. (0.05) (0.16) (0.001) =
11. (8) (0.217) (0.01) =
12. (18) (0.08) =
13. (16.01) (0.5) (0.31) =
14. (1.06) (0.005) =
15. (4.802) (11.11) =
16. (10.25) (0.331) =
17. (5) (1.102) =
18. (12.8) (0.05) (3.09) =

Name ______________________ Date ______________________

Get to the Point

For each multiplication problem, locate the decimal point in the product. Insert zeros if needed.

1. $\begin{array}{r} 2.2 \\ \times 0.011 \\ \hline 242 \end{array}$

2. $\begin{array}{r} 12.8 \\ \times\ 0.12 \\ \hline 1536 \end{array}$

3. $\begin{array}{r} 1.8 \\ \times\ 6.03 \\ \hline 10854 \end{array}$

4. $\begin{array}{r} 34.1 \\ \times\ 1.4 \\ \hline 47.74 \end{array}$

5. $\begin{array}{r} 7.21 \\ \times\ 22.2 \\ \hline 160062 \end{array}$

6. $\begin{array}{r} 55 \\ \times\ 0.033 \\ \hline 1815 \end{array}$

7. $\begin{array}{r} 6.9 \\ \times\ 11 \\ \hline 759 \end{array}$

8. $\begin{array}{r} 6.7 \\ \times\ 0.801 \\ \hline 5.3667 \end{array}$

9. $\begin{array}{r} 4.04 \\ \times\ 4.04 \\ \hline 163216 \end{array}$

10. $\begin{array}{r} 32.1 \\ \times\ 2.02 \\ \hline 64842 \end{array}$

11. $\begin{array}{r} 0.005 \\ \times\ 0.011 \\ \hline 55 \end{array}$

12. $\begin{array}{r} 66.2 \\ \times\ 1.1 \\ \hline 7282 \end{array}$

13. $\begin{array}{r} 0.84 \\ \times\ 0.07 \\ \hline 588 \end{array}$

14. $\begin{array}{r} 8.2 \\ \times\ 0.1 \\ \hline 82 \end{array}$

15. $\begin{array}{r} 0.6 \\ \times\ 1.7 \\ \hline 102 \end{array}$

16. (5.7) (0.2) (0.07) = 798
17. (9.8) (2.8) (1.8) = 49392
18. (10.6) (4.3) (0.8) = 36464
19. (0.13) (8.5) (0.5) = 5525
20. (6.7) (1.2) (0.03) = 2412

HINT:
The sum of the number of all decimal places in your products equals 64.

Name ______________________________ Date ______________________________

Dividing Decimals

HINT:
Move the decimal points the number of places needed to make the divisor a whole number.

0.03652 ÷ .88 =

$$
\begin{array}{r}
.0415 \\
.88\overline{)\,.036520} \\
\underline{352} \\
132 \\
\underline{88} \\
440 \\
\underline{440} \\
0
\end{array}
$$

1. 0.128 ÷ 0.8 =
2. 2.45 ÷ 3.5 =
3. 0.5773 ÷ 5.02 =
4. 39.78 ÷ 0.195 =
5. 4.2016 ÷ 5.2 =
6. 1.45 ÷ 0.08 =
7. 0.1716 ÷ 5.2 =
8. 3.906 ÷ 1.2 =
9. 6.56 ÷ 0.16 =
10. 0.0135 ÷ 4.5 =
11. 0.0483 ÷ 0.21 =
12. 0.5418 ÷ 0.3 =
13. 16.83 ÷ 0.11 =
14. 0.1926 ÷ 32.1 =

0-7424-1787-5 *Pre-Algebra*

Name ______________________ Date ______________________

Mixed Practice with Decimals

1. 12.16 – 8.72 =
2. 119.7 + 11.97 =
3. (3.4) (8) =
4. 2960 ÷ 0.37 =
5. 1.21 ÷ 1.1 =
6. 7 + 6.91 =
7. 18.91 – 11.857 =
8. (1.35) (21.4) =
9. 21.2 – 9.03 =
10. 0.7 + 0.02 + 4 =
11. (0.25) (2.5) (25) =
12. 95.6 – 87.81 +12.21 =
13. (0.8) (1.3) (0.62) =
14. 37.92 ÷ 1.2 =
15. 0.1007 ÷ 5.3 =
16. 329.82 + 6.129 =
17. 893.631 – 11.09 =
18. 18.332 + 82.82 =
19. 132.03 ÷ 8.1 =
20. (16.1) (3.66) =
21. 1093.62 – 10.993 =
22. 6.963 ÷ 2.11 =

0-7424-1787-5 *Pre-Algebra*

Name ______________________ Date ______________________

Going Around the Block

Start at 0.5. Move clockwise. Fill the blank spaces with +, –, x , or ÷ to make true math statements. End back at 0.5.

Start

0.5		0.2	=	0.1		0.5	=	0.2		0.8	=	0.25
=												
0.3												0.75
												=
0.15												1
=												
0.1												0.6
												=
1.5												0.4
=												
3												0.3
												=
4.5	=	2.5		2	=	1.4		0.6	=	5		0.12

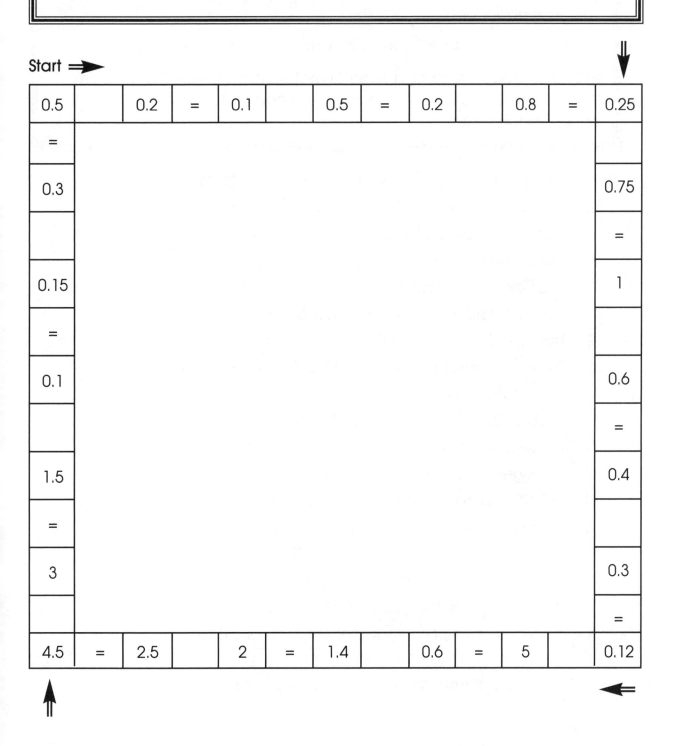

Name ______________________ Date ______________________

Scientifically Speaking

Scientific notation is used to write very large and very small numbers. A number in scientific notation is the product of a number between 1 and 10 and a power of 10.

Examples: $45{,}000{,}000 = 4.5 \times 10^{7}$ $0.00000625 = 6.25 \times 10^{-6}$

write each measurement in scientific notation; then write the problem letter above the value of the exponent to complete the statement at the bottom of the page.

C The population of China is greater than 1,250,000,000.

E Scientists at Oak Ridge National Laboratory have sent an electric current of 2,000,000 amperes/cm^2 down a wire.

E The diameter of an electron is 0.0000000000011 cm.

E In an election in India, more than 343,350,000 people voted.

E The Earth's mass is 5,980,000,000,000,000,000,000 metric tons.

G The Greenland–Canada boundary is about 1,700 miles long.

I The isotope lithium 5 decays in 0.0000000000000000000044 seconds.

I The isotope tellurium 128 has a half-life of 1,500,000,000,000,000,000,000,000 years.

M A microbe strain of H39 has a diameter of 0.0000003 m.

N A nugget of platinum found in 1843 weighed 340 ounces.

N In 1996 the United States national debt was $5,129,000,000,000.

O A Saudi Arabia oil field contains about 82,000,000,000 barrels.

P The fastest planet Mercury travels at 107,000 mph.

R Sales of the record "White Christmas" exceeded 30,000,000.

V In 1973, a vulture flying at 37,000 ft. collided with an aircraft.

X The wavelength of an X ray is about 0.0000000015 m.

What the decimal point said about scientific notation:

"It's a ___ ___ ___ ___ ___ ___ ___ ___ ___ ___ ___ ___ ___ ___ ___ ___ !"

–7	10	4	–22	2	3	6	–9	5	–12	7	24	8	12	9	21

Name ______________________ Date ______________________

Problems with Decimals

1. Jim's gas credit card bill was $80.97 for June, $41.35 for July and $65.08 for August. What were his total charges for the summer?

2. One cup of hot chocolate can be made with .18 ounces of hot chocolate mix. How many cups can be made from a 6.48 ounce canister of mix?

3. Karl's car payments are $215.37 per month for the next three years. What will be the total amount he will pay for his car?

4. The dress Sally wants cost $85.15. If the price was reduced by $12.78, how much will she pay?

5. Melissa went to the mail and noticed that the price of a coat she wanted was cut in half! The original price was $58.22. What is the sales price?

6. Tyler decided that he wanted a dog. He went to the pet store and bought one for $42.95. Tyler also bought three bags of food for $12.55 a bag. How much did Tyler spend altogether?

7. Christopher decided to make his grandmother a birdhouse instead of buying her one. The materials for the birdhouse totaled $21.99. the cost of a new birdhouse is $37.23. How much did Christopher save?

8. Jim thinks that snow skiing looks like lots of fun. He decided he wants to try it. First he needs equipment. He bought a pair of skis for $129.78, a pair of boots for $62.22, poles for $12.95, a hat for $2.50, a coat for $49.95, ski pants for $27.50 and gloves for $11.25. How much did Jim spend altogether?

Name ______________________________ Date ______________________________

Changing Decimals to Fractions

Terminating Decimals

$0.25 = \frac{25}{100} = \frac{1}{4}$

$0.132 = \frac{132}{1000} = \frac{33}{250}$

Repeating Decimals

$N = 0.\overline{12} = 0.121212\ldots$

$100\,N = 12.1212\ldots$
$^{-}N = {}^{-}0.1212\ldots$

$\frac{99N}{99} = \frac{12}{99}$

$N = \frac{4}{33}$

or $0.12 = \frac{4}{33}$

1. $0.125 =$

2. $0.\overline{6} =$

3. $0.36 =$

4. $0.\overline{46} =$

5. $0.6875 =$

6. $0.91\overline{6} =$

7. $0.625 =$

8. $0.\overline{27} =$

9. $0.3\overline{8} =$

10. $0.55 =$

11. $0.5625 =$

12. $0.775 =$

Name ______________________ Date ______________________

Ratios

Write each ratio as a fraction in simplest form.

$3 \text{ to } 12 \rightarrow \frac{3}{12} = \frac{1}{4}$ $65 : 35 \rightarrow \frac{65}{35} = \frac{13}{7}$

$6 \text{ out of } 40 \rightarrow \frac{6}{40} = \frac{3}{20}$

1. 196 to 7
2. 19 : 76
3. 18 out of 27
4. $\frac{3}{8}$ to $\frac{3}{4}$
5. 0.11 : 1.21
6. 140 : 112
7. 18 to 27
8. 54 out of 87
9. 112 : 140
10. 88 to 104
11. 65 out of 105
12. 65 : 117
13. 165 to 200
14. 168 : 264

0-7424-1787-5 *Pre-Algebra*

Name ______________________ Date ______________________

Proportions

Solve each proportion.

$$\frac{3}{7} = \frac{x}{49} \qquad 3 \bullet 49 = 7x$$

$$\frac{147}{7} = \frac{7x}{7} \qquad 21 = x$$

1. $\frac{8}{6} = \frac{m}{27}$

2. $\frac{z}{3} = \frac{8}{15}$

3. $\frac{16}{40} = \frac{24}{c}$

4. $\frac{9}{p} = \frac{5}{2}$

5. $\frac{1.8}{x} = \frac{3.6}{2.4}$

6. $\frac{4}{5} = \frac{0.8}{y}$

7. $\frac{x}{2} = \frac{15}{5}$

8. $\frac{18}{12} = \frac{24}{x}$

9. $\frac{18}{15} = \frac{6}{x}$

10. $\frac{121}{x} = \frac{220}{100}$

11. $\frac{1.6}{x} = \frac{14}{21}$

12. $\frac{x}{168} = \frac{66\frac{2}{3}}{100}$

13. $\frac{x}{32} = \frac{37\frac{1}{2}}{100}$

14. $\frac{16}{48} = \frac{x}{100}$

15. $\frac{0.12}{.25} = \frac{x}{100}$

16. $\frac{1.5}{x} = \frac{0.07}{0.14}$

Name ______________________ Date ______________________

Problems Using Proportions

Three loaves of bread cost $3.87. How much do 2 loaves cost?

$\frac{\text{number of loaves}}{\text{cost}}$

$$\frac{3}{3.87} = \frac{2}{x}$$

$$3x = 2 \bullet 3.87$$

$$\frac{3x}{3} = \frac{7.74}{3}$$

$$x = 2.58$$

2 loaves cost $2.58

1. If 64 feet of rope weigh 20 pounds, how much will 80 feet of the same type of rope weigh?

2. If a 10 pound turkey takes 4 hours to cook, how long will it take a 14 pound turkey to cook?

3. An 18 ounce box of cereal costs $2.76. How many ounces should a box priced at $2.07 contain?

4. Mike and Pat traveled 392 miles in 7 hours. If they travel at the same rate, how long will it take them to travel 728 miles?

5. If 2 pounds of turkey costs $1.98, what should 3 pounds cost?

6. If 2 liters of fruit juice cost $3.98, how much do 5 liters cost?

7. A 12 ounce box of cereal costs $.84. How many ounces should be in a box marked $.49?

8. Janie saw an advertisement for a 6 ounce tube of toothpaste that costs $.90. How much should a 4 ounce tube cost?

Name ______________________________ Date ______________________________

Percents

Percent (%) means:	per hundred out of a hundred hundredths 2 decimal places	$\frac{3}{4} \rightarrow \frac{3}{4} = \frac{x}{100}$ $300 = 4x$ $75 = x$ $\frac{3}{4} = 75\%$ $0.375 \rightarrow 37.5$ hundredths $= 37.5\%$

1. $\frac{4}{5}$

2. $\frac{4}{7}$

3. 0.22

4. 2.5

5. $\frac{3}{8}$

6. 0.006

7. 1.125

8. $\frac{1}{2}$

9. $\frac{9}{40}$

10. 11.3

11. $\frac{11}{20}$

12. 0.086

13. $\frac{7}{8}$

14. 16.688

15. $\frac{7}{16}$

16. 621.9

17. $\frac{5}{16}$

18. 3.9932

Name ______________________ Date ______________________

Working with Percents

> 80% of 30 =
>
> $\frac{80}{100} = \frac{x}{30}$
>
> $100x = 2400$
>
> $x = 24$

1. 20% of 10 = ________
2. 25% of 45 = ________
3. 88% of 15 = ________
4. $9\frac{1}{2}$% of 20 = ________
5. 25% of 39 = ________
6. 16% of 90 = ________

> ____% of 40 = 10
>
> $\frac{x}{100} = \frac{10}{40}$
>
> $40x = 1000$
>
> $x = 25$ 25%

1. ________% of 25 = 15
2. ________% of 30 = 10
3. ________% of 4 = 7
4. ________% of 75 = 33
5. ________% of 15 = 6
6. ________% of 80 = 40

> 50% of ____ = 65
>
> $\frac{50}{100} = \frac{65}{x}$
>
> $50x = 6500$
>
> $x = 130$

1. 20% of ________ = 15
2. 80% of ________ = 56
3. 25% of ________ = 19
4. $33\frac{1}{3}$% of ________ = 41
5. 80% of ________ = 16
6. 30% of ________ = 15

Name ______________________________ Date ______________________________

Problems with Percents

1. In a group of 60 children, 12 have brown eyes. What percent have brown eyes?

   $\frac{12 \div 2}{60 \div 2} = \frac{6 \div 2}{30 \div 2} = \frac{3}{15}$

2. A salesman makes a 5% commission on all he sells. How much does he have to sell to make $1500?

3. A sales tax of $5\frac{3}{4}$% is charged on a blouse priced at $42. How much sales tax must be paid?

4. A baby weighed 7.6 pounds at birth and $9\frac{1}{2}$ pounds after 6 weeks. What was the percent increase?

5. A scale model of a building is 8% of actual size. If the model is 1.2 meters tall, how tall is the building?

6. The purchase price of a camera is $84. The carrying case is 12% of the purchase price. Find the total cost including the carrying case.

7. The regular price of a record cost is $15. Find the discount and the new price if there is a 20% discount.

8. A basketball team played 45 games. They won 60% of them. How many did the team win?

9. A test had 50 questions. Joe got 70% of them correct. How many did Joe get correct?

10. Diet soda contains 90% less calories than regular soda. If a can of regular soda contains 112 calories, how many calories does a can of diet soda contain?

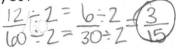

Name ______________________ Date ______________________

Can You Decode this Puzzle?

Decipher the code and perform the indicated operations.

.3	$\frac{1}{20}$	2.1
3.1	2.8	$\frac{8}{25}$
4	.1	$\frac{1}{2}$

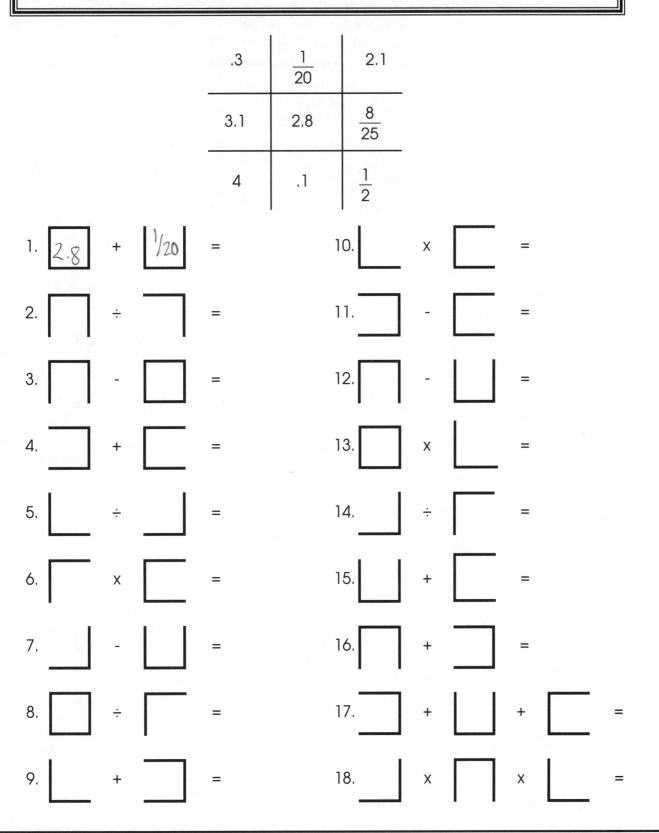

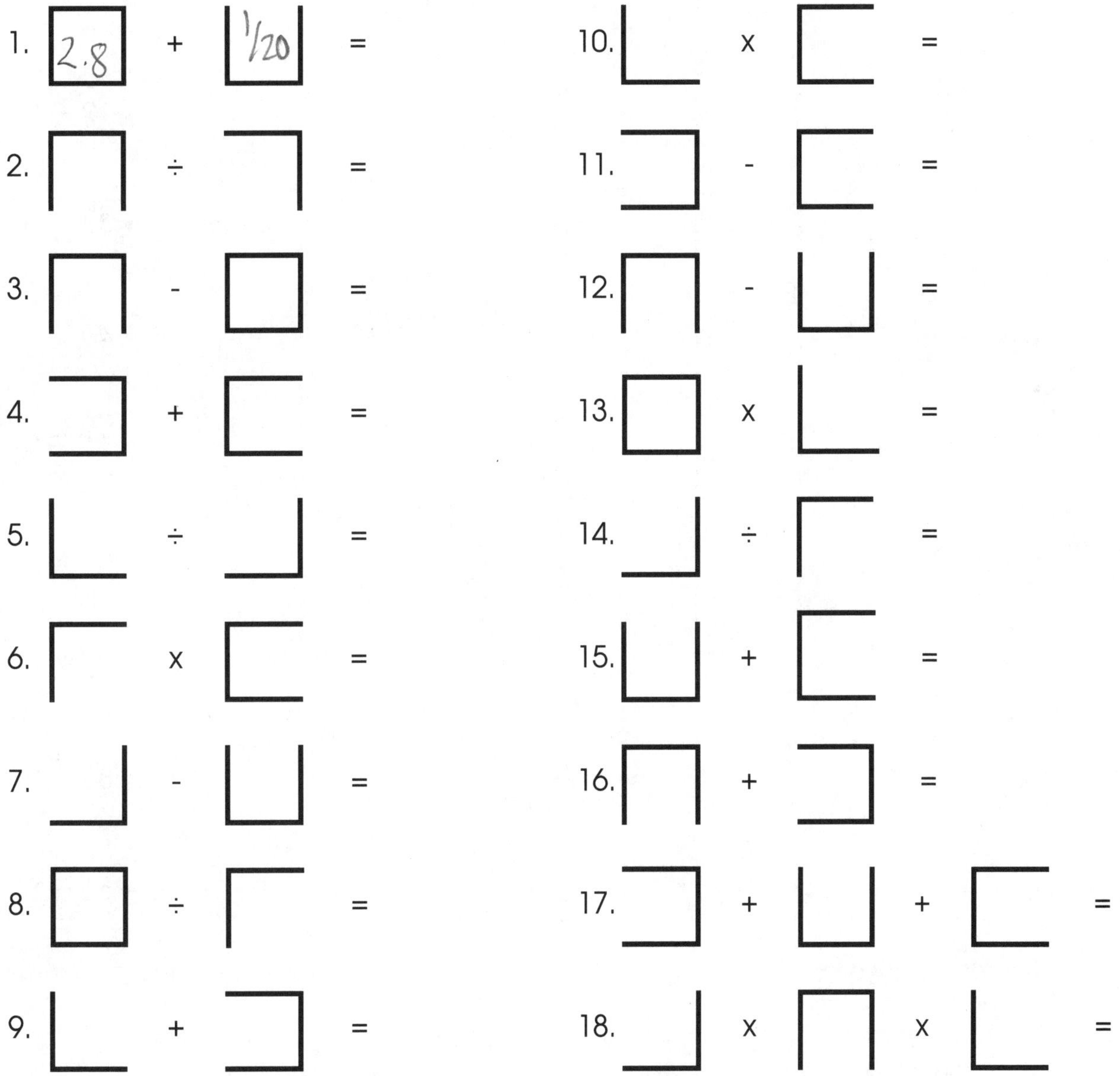

Name ______________________________ Date ______________________________

Triple Match

Use a ruler to connect each decimal to its fraction equivalent. Then draw a line connecting the fraction to its percent equivalent. Each path (decimal → fraction → percent) will pass through a letter and a number. Write the letter on the blank above the corresponding number at the bottom of the page.

$0.3\overline{3}$ •		• $\frac{3}{8}$ •	10	• 25 %
	H			
0.25 •	N	• $\frac{3}{4}$ •	9	• $37\frac{1}{2}$ %
0.75 •	S	• $\frac{1}{8}$ •		• 75 %
			11	
0.125 •	A	• $\frac{5}{6}$ •	2	• $12\frac{1}{2}$ %
0.375 •	P	• $\frac{1}{3}$ •	8	• $33\frac{1}{3}$ %
	E		7	
$0.6\overline{6}$ •		• $\frac{1}{4}$ •	4	• 40 %
$0.8\overline{3}$ •	R Y	• $\frac{2}{5}$ •		• $16\frac{2}{3}$ %
			1	
0.4 •		• $\frac{1}{6}$ •		• 50 %
0.7 •	O	• $\frac{7}{10}$ •	3	• 70 %
	g			
0.5 •		• $\frac{2}{3}$ •	6	• $83\frac{1}{3}$ %
	T		5	
$0.1\overline{6}$ •		• $\frac{1}{2}$ •		• $66\frac{2}{3}$ %

Secret society of mathematicians that studied geometric ratios such as the golden ratio:

___	___	___	___	___	___	___	___	___	___	___	___
2	4	6	8	10	1	3	5	7	10	9	11

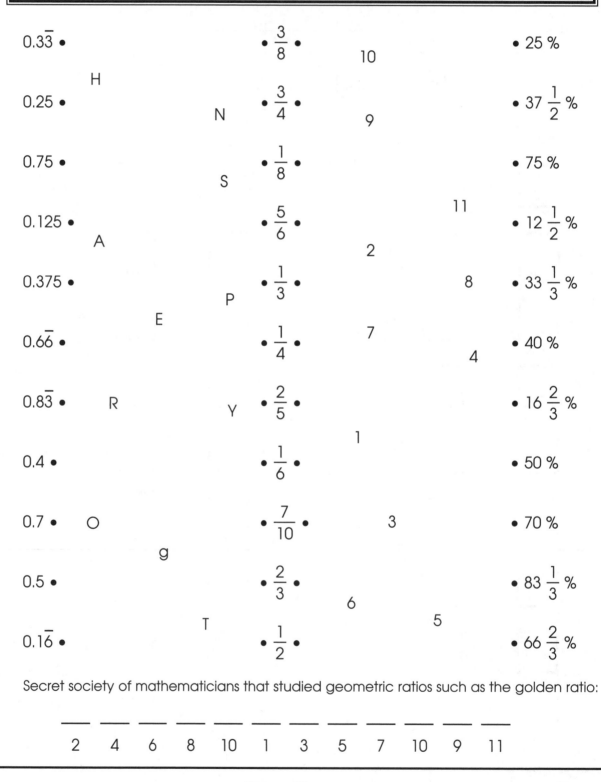

Name ______________________ Date ______________________

Adding Integers (Number Line)

Label each arrow. Write the resulting expression.

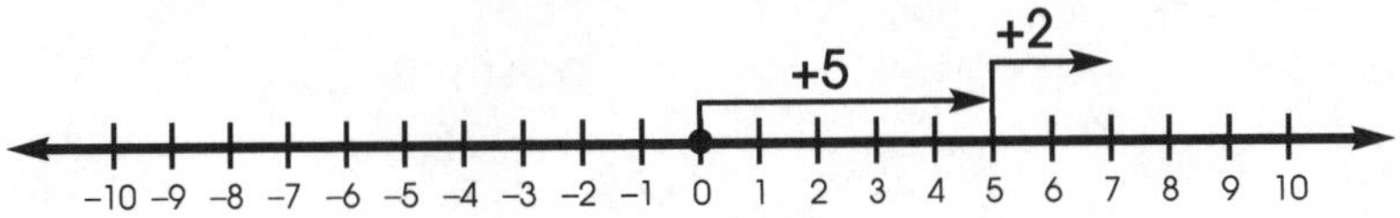

5 + 2 = 7

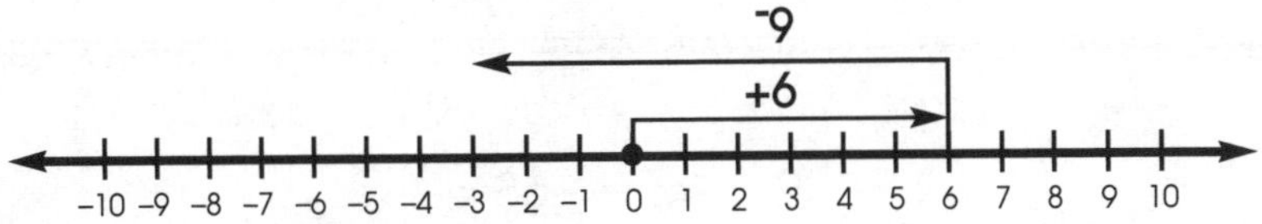

6 + ⁻9 = ⁻3

1.

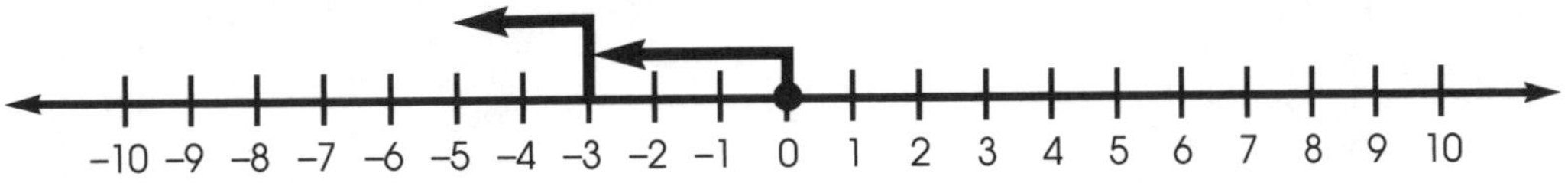

2.

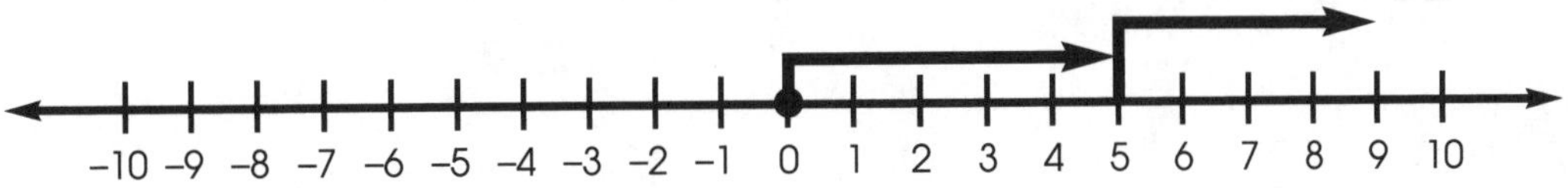

3.

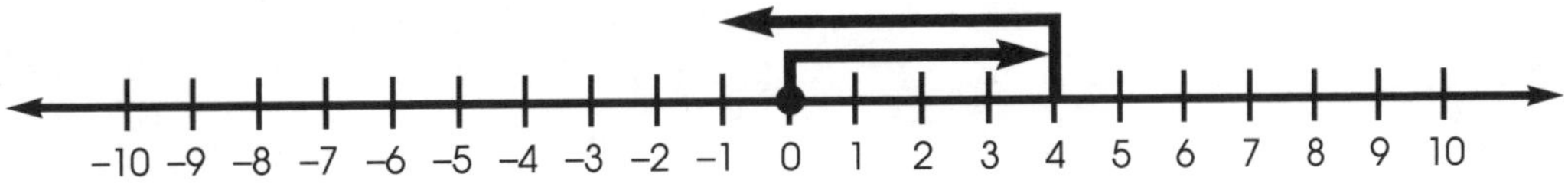

4.

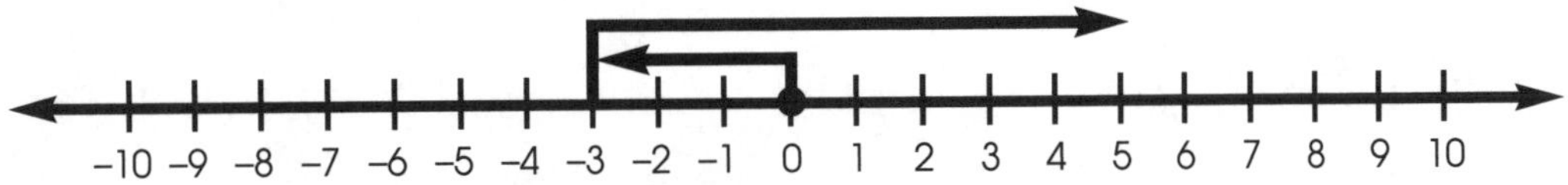

5.

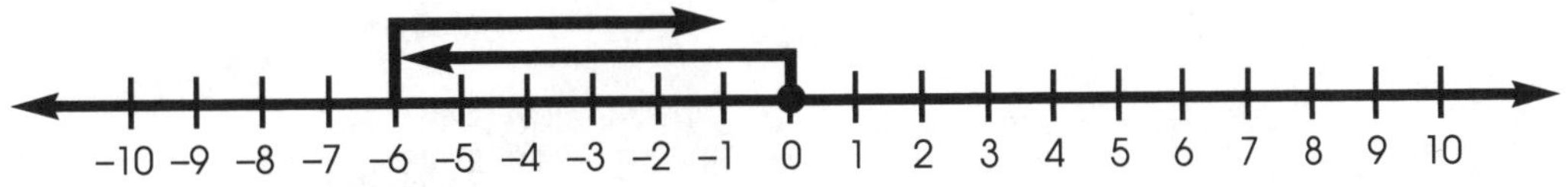

6.

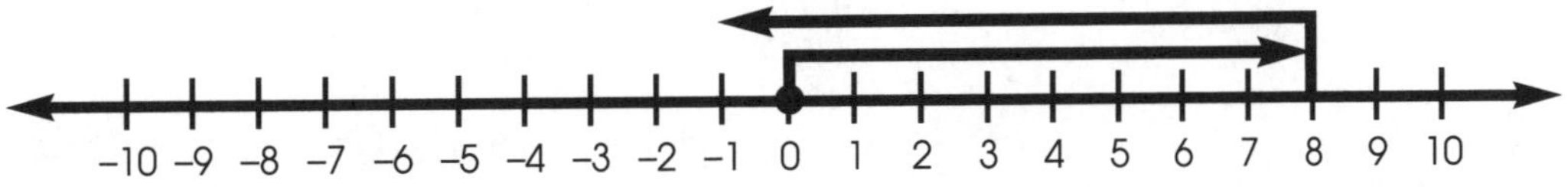

Name ______________________ Date ______________________

Adding Integers with Like Signs

$5 + 5$	=	10
2 positives		positive
$^{-}3 + {}^{-}12$	=	$^{-}15$
2 negatives		negative

1. $6 + 8 =$

2. $^{-}9 + {}^{-}23 =$

3. $25 + 37 =$

4. $^{-}85 + {}^{-}19 =$

5. $132 + 899 =$

6. $^{-}104 + {}^{-}597 =$

7. $^{-}642 + {}^{-}33 =$

8. $88 + 298 =$

9. $^{-}45 + -68 =$

10. $^{-}12 + {}^{-}18 + {}^{-}35 =$

11. $21 + 108 + 111 =$

12. $^{-}62 + {}^{-}33 + {}^{-}12 =$

13. $17 + 39 + 44 =$

14. $^{-}18 + {}^{-}18 + {}^{-}18 =$

15. $19 + 42 + 647 =$

16. $^{-}29 + {}^{-}108 + {}^{-}337 + {}^{-}503 =$

Name ______________________ Date ______________________

Adding Integers with Unlike Signs

To add integers with different signs:

Use the sign of the number farther from zero.

Find the difference of the two numbers.

(sign) → ↓	(sign) → ↓
18 + $^{-}23$ = $^{-}5$	$^{-}16$ + 19 = +3
(23 – 18) → ↑	(19 – 16) → ↑

1. 21 + $^{-}87$ =
2. $^{-}63$ + 59 =
3. 12 + $^{-}12$ =
4. $^{-}28$ + 82 =
5. $^{-}32$ + 97 =
6. $^{-}53$ + 74 =
7. 132 + $^{-}87$ =
8. 212 + $^{-}99$ =
9. $^{-}331$ + 155 =
10. $^{-}413$ + 521 =
11. 8,129 + $^{-}6,312$ =
12. $^{-}11,332$ + 566 =
13. 1,627 + $^{-}7,193$ =
14. 7,864 + $^{-}6,329$ =
15. $^{-}10,822$ + 6,635 =
16. 13,894 + $^{-}81,139$ =
17. $^{-}16,742$ + 65,524 =
18. $^{-}56,814$ + 73,322 =
19. 101,811 + $^{-}322,885$ =
20. 562,493 + $^{-}112,819$ =
21. 116,667 + $^{-}912,182$ =
22. $^{-}629,922$ + 81,962 =
23. $^{-}196,322$ + 422,899 =
24. 467,833 + $^{-}36,838$ =

Name ______________________ Date ______________________

Integer Grid

Fill in the blanks so that the last number of each row is the sum of the numbers in that row and the bottom number of each column is the sum of the numbers in that column.

3	-1	5		-3		0	4	-8	
2	6	0	-4	-8	2	-7	1		-3
-9		-8	1	4	7		-3	6	2
4	-8	1	-5	9	-6	2	-6	0	
-3		2	-6		7	-1		9	8
5	-8	1	-4	7		-5	9	-2	2
	0		3	-7	1	5	9	2	0
3	-7	4	-8		6	0	4	-9	-5
5	8	-2	6			6	-9	-2	9
	2	-4	-8		6	0	4		6

0-7424-1787-5 *Pre-Algebra*

Name ______________________ Date ______________________

Subtracting Integers

Re-write each problem as an addition problem and solve.

$6 - 11 = 6 + {}^{-}11 = {}^{-}5$ (add the opposite)

$26 - {}^{-}67 = 26 + 67 = 93$ (add the opposite)

1. $19 - 23 =$
2. ${}^{-}8 - 7 =$
3. $35 - 20 =$
4. ${}^{-}46 - {}^{-}18 =$
5. ${}^{-}118 - 12 =$
6. $7 - {}^{-}103 =$
7. $211 - 108 =$
8. ${}^{-}9 - {}^{-}16 =$
9. $63 - 72 =$
10. ${}^{-}93 - 117 =$
11. $45 - {}^{-}50 =$
12. ${}^{-}18 - {}^{-}12 =$
13. $21 - 82 =$
14. ${}^{-}831 - 616 =$
15. ${}^{-}632 - {}^{-}714 =$
16. $1{,}192 - {}^{-}983 =$

Name ______________________ Date ______________________

More Subtracting Integers

1. $7 - 13 =$

2. $^{-}17 - 9 =$

3. $^{-}11 - 7 =$

4. $^{-}24 - {}^{-}23 =$

5. $2 - 25 =$

6. $0 - {}^{-}14 =$

7. $^{-}3 - {}^{-}7 =$

8. $^{-}8 - {}^{-}27 =$

9. $^{-}29 - 36 =$

10. $^{-}72 - {}^{-}84 =$

11. $63 - 94 =$

12. $77 - {}^{-}27 =$

13. $^{-}23 - {}^{-}96 =$

14. $^{-}70 - 18 =$

15. $318 - {}^{-}864 =$

16. $^{-}626 - 118 =$

17. $553 - {}^{-}764 =$

18. $^{-}832 - 1{,}129 =$

19. $6{,}793 - {}^{-}8{,}329 =$

20. $^{-}7{,}624 - 11{,}652 =$

21. $108{,}719 - {}^{-}96{,}989 =$

22. $^{-}832{,}629 - {}^{-}163{,}864 =$

23. $^{-}629{,}299 - 532{,}106 =$

24. $735{,}300 - {}^{-}800{,}919 =$

Name ______________________ Date ______________________

Adding and Subtracting Integers

1. ${}^{-}6 + {}^{-}8 =$

2. ${}^{-}10 - 3 =$

3. ${}^{-}14 + 20 =$

4. $31 - {}^{-}9 =$

5. ${}^{-}17 + 9 =$

6. ${}^{-}8 - {}^{-}27 =$

7. ${}^{-}33 - 36 =$

8. $19 + {}^{-}32 =$

9. $112 - {}^{-}52 =$

10. $8 - {}^{-}7 =$

11. $24 + {}^{-}24 =$

12. $508 - 678 =$

13. ${}^{-}23 - {}^{-}28 =$

14. $0 - 31 =$

15. ${}^{-}40 - 35 =$

16. $73 + {}^{-}19 =$

17. ${}^{-}231 - {}^{-}231 =$

18. ${}^{-}107 + {}^{-}293 =$

19. $52 + {}^{-}41 - 60 =$

20. ${}^{-}85 - {}^{-}106 + 18 =$

21. $81 - 165 - {}^{-}75 =$

22. ${}^{-}16 + 312 + {}^{-}621 =$

23. ${}^{-}121 + {}^{-}632 - {}^{-}11 =$

24. ${}^{-}553 - {}^{-}632 + {}^{-}85 =$

0-7424-1787-5 *Pre-Algebra*

Name ______________________________ Date ______________________________

Multiplying Integers

$(4)\,(4) = 16$
$+ \bullet + \; = +$

$(^-8)\,(^-6) = 48$
$- \bullet - \; = +$

Like Signs ⟶ Positive

$(^-5)\,(10) = {}^-50$
$- \bullet + \; = -$

Unlike Signs ⟶ Negative

1. $(^-3)\,(^-6) =$

2. $(14)\,(^-4) =$

3. $(25)\,(2) =$

4. $(20)\,(^-49) =$

5. $(75)\,(15) =$

6. $(^-30)\,(^-30) =$

7. $(^-17)\,(23) =$

8. $(^-218)\,(^-32) =$

9. $(801)\,(^-37) =$

10. $(^-89)\,(^-321) =$

11. $(31)\,(^-31)\,(31) =$

12. $(^-4)\,(^-18)\,(28) =$

13. $(^-53)\,(^-14)\,(^-7) =$

14. $(32)\,(125)\,(11) =$

15. $(^-37)\,(^-18)\,(^-5)\,(2) =$

16. $(111)\,(^-63)\,(19) =$

17. $(20)\,(^-7)\,(35)\,(^-3) =$

18. $(16)\,(^-8)\,(^-10)\,(^-1) =$

19. $(^-9)\,(^-29)\,(32)\,(2) =$

20. $(^-18)\,(^-6)\,(^-21)\,(^-30) =$

0-7424-1787-5 *Pre-Algebra*

Name ______________________ Date ______________________

Dividing Integers

$\frac{^-24}{^-8} = 3$

$\frac{-}{-} = +$

Like Signs ⟹ Positive

$^-32 \div 4 = {}^-8$

$- \div + = -$

Unlike Signs ⟹ Negative

1. $^-49 \div 7 =$
2. $100 \div {}^-4 =$
3. $^-75 \div {}^-15 =$
4. $^-84 \div 21 =$
5. $^-120 \div 5 =$
6. $57 \div {}^-19 =$
7. $^-288 \div {}^-4 =$
8. $804 \div 67 =$
9. $\frac{17}{^-17} =$
10. $\frac{^-72}{^-18} =$
11. $\frac{^-195}{13} =$
12. $\frac{^-23}{^-1} =$
13. $\frac{200}{10} =$
14. $\frac{270}{^-45} =$
15. $\frac{^-343}{7} =$
16. $\frac{^-1125}{^-45} =$

Name ____________________ Date ____________________

Divide and Conquer

Compute. Substitute the values into the problem below.

A. $^{-}81 \div {}^{-}9 =$

B. $13 \div {}^{-}13 =$

C. $^{-}60 \div 10 =$

D. $^{-}88 \div {}^{-}11 =$

E. $^{-}104 \div 8 =$

F. $^{-}147 \div {}^{-}21 =$

G. $80 \div {}^{-}5 =$

H. $52 \div 4 =$

I. $^{-}150 \div {}^{-}6 =$

J. $\frac{^{-}102}{17} =$

K. $\frac{^{-}75}{^{-}5} =$

L. $\frac{196}{^{-}14} =$

M. $\frac{1378}{^{-}26} =$

N. $\frac{^{-}468}{^{-}26} =$

O. $\frac{253}{11} =$

P. $\frac{^{-}465}{^{-}31} =$

Q. $\frac{^{-}552}{^{-}23} =$

R. $\frac{^{-}1824}{^{-}48} =$

William I of Normandy conquered England in → → → ↓

(A+B+C+D+E+F) – (G+H) – (I÷(J+K+L)) – M•N + (O+P+Q+R) = 1066

(_ + _ + _ + _ + _ + _) – (_ + _) – (_ ÷ (_ + _ + _)) – _ • _ + (_ + _ + _ + _)

Name ____________________ Date ____________________

Mixed Practice with Integers

1. ${}^{-}41 + {}^{-}125 =$

2. $79 - 88 =$

3. ${}^{-}3 \bullet {}^{-}4 =$

4. $\frac{{}^{-}125}{5} =$

5. $19 \bullet {}^{-}24 =$

6. $\frac{{}^{-}123}{41} =$

7. $82 + {}^{-}95 =$

8. $27 - {}^{-}46 =$

9. ${}^{-}31 - {}^{-}32 =$

10. $\frac{{}^{-}825}{{}^{-}33} =$

11. ${}^{-}34 + 52 + {}^{-}18 =$

12. $14 \bullet {}^{-}12 \bullet 3 =$

13. $\frac{{}^{-}185}{5} \bullet - 4 =$

14. $76 - 19 + {}^{-}60 =$

15. $17 - {}^{-}12 - 22 =$

16. $100 \bullet {}^{-}4 \bullet 40 =$

17. $\frac{54}{{}^{-}9} + \frac{33}{11} + \frac{24}{8} =$

18. ${}^{-}51 \div 17 =$

19. $4 - 8 + {}^{-}9 =$

20. $-\frac{98}{49} \bullet {}^{-}10 =$

21. $(256 \div {}^{-}16) \bullet {}^{-}3 =$

22. $({}^{-}18 - {}^{-}26 + {}^{-}13) \bullet {}^{-}2 =$

23. $(202 + {}^{-}196 - 321) \div {}^{-}5 =$

24. $(\frac{{}^{-}575}{23} - 18) \bullet {}^{-}11 =$

Name ______________________ Date ______________________

Problems with Integers

1. An elevator started at the first floor and went up 18 floors. It then came down 11 floors and went back up 16. At what floor was it stopped?

2. At midnight, the temperature was 30° F. By 6:00 a.m., it had dropped 5° and by noon, it had increased by 11°. What was the temperature at noon?

3. Some number added to 5 is equal to $^{-}11$. Find the number.

4. From the top of a mountain to the floor of the valley below is 4,392 feet. If the valley is 93 feet below sea level, what is the height of the mountain?

5. During one week, the stock market did the following: Monday rose 18 points, Tuesday rose 31 points, Wednesday dropped 5 points, Thursday rose 27 points and Friday dropped 38 points. If it started out at 1,196 on Monday, what did it end up on Friday?

6. An airplane started at 0 feet. It rose 21,000 feet at takeoff. It then descended 4,329 feet because of clouds. An oncoming plane was approaching, so it rose 6.333 feet. After the oncoming plane passed, it descended 8,453 feet, at what altitude was the plane flying?

7. Some number added to $^{-}11$ is 37. Divide this number by $^{-}12$. Then, multiply by $^{-}8$. What is the final number?

8. Jim decided to go for a drive in his car. He started out at 0 miles per hour (mph). He then accelerated 20 mph down his street. Then, to get on the highway he accelerated another 35 miles per hour. A car was going slow in front of him so he slowed down 11 mph. He then got off the highway, so he slowed down another 7 mph. At what speed is he driving?

Name ______________________ Date ______________________

Adding and Subtracting Rational Numbers

$$^{-}3 + {}^{-}2 + 2\frac{1}{2} = {}^{-}5 + 2\frac{1}{2} = {}^{-}4\frac{2}{2} + 2\frac{1}{2} = {}^{-}2\frac{1}{2}$$

1. $^{-}1.6 + 1\frac{7}{10} =$

   (Hint: $1\frac{7}{10} = 1.7$)

2. $0 - 6\frac{1}{2} + {}^{-}3 =$

3. $\frac{^{-}3}{4} + 5 - \frac{1}{2} =$

4. $9 - 10.2 + {}^{-}8.6 =$

5. $\frac{1}{2} + 1\frac{1}{2} - 1\frac{1}{3} =$

6. $6.75 - 3\frac{1}{2} + 2.55 =$

   (Hint: $3\frac{5}{10} = 3.5$)

7. $3\frac{3}{7} - {}^{-}1\frac{1}{7} + \frac{3}{7} =$

8. $^{-}7 - {}^{-}2\frac{3}{4} + {}^{-}5\frac{1}{4} =$

9. $7\frac{1}{10} + {}^{-}7.25 - 11.39 =$

10. $^{-}8\frac{1}{4} + {}^{-}3\frac{3}{12} - 7\frac{2}{3} =$

11. $^{-}5 - 7\frac{1}{8} + {}^{-}3\frac{5}{12} =$

12. $3\frac{3}{10} + {}^{-}3.38 - 6\frac{6}{10} =$

Name ____________________ Date ____________________

More Adding and Subtracting Rational Numbers

1. $^{-}3\frac{5}{10} + 8 =$

2. $^{-}5\frac{3}{7} + {^{-}3}\frac{3}{14} =$

3. $6\frac{1}{6} - 6\frac{3}{10} =$

4. $^{-}8 + 15.32 =$

5. $^{-}8\frac{3}{10} - {^{-}5.9} =$

6. $13 - 5\frac{3}{5} =$

7. $12\frac{1}{9} + {^{-}5}\frac{2}{3} =$

8. $^{-}11.03 - {^{-}21.6} =$

9. $^{-}7\frac{3}{10} - 16.53 =$

10. $31\frac{8}{9} + {^{-}27}\frac{27}{81} =$

11. $11 - 18.6 + {^{-}3}\frac{3}{10} =$

12. $^{-}5\frac{2}{10} + 16.7 - 3\frac{1}{5} =$

13. $13\frac{1}{3} + {^{-}12} + {^{-}7}\frac{7}{12} =$

14. $41.32 + {^{-}18.7} - 16.21 =$

15. $^{-}18.75 - 5\frac{3}{4} - 7\frac{5}{12} =$

16. $^{-}15 - 21\frac{1}{7} + 18\frac{2}{49} =$

17. $7\frac{2}{3} + {^{-}8}\frac{4}{9} - {^{-}16}\frac{1}{6} =$

18. $^{-}31.5 - {^{-}3}\frac{7}{10} + 21 =$

19. $25\frac{1}{5} - 17.3 + {^{-}11}\frac{2}{11} =$

20. $19.25 - {^{-}6}\frac{3}{4} + 12\frac{5}{12} =$

0-7424-1787-5 *Pre-Algebra*

Name ______________________ Date ______________________

Multiplying and Dividing Rational Numbers

$$^{-}4 \cdot 5 \cdot \frac{1}{2} = {}^{-}20 \cdot \frac{1}{2} = -\frac{\overset{10}{\cancel{20}}}{1} \cdot \frac{1}{\underset{1}{\cancel{2}}} = -\frac{10}{1} = {}^{-}10$$

$$5\frac{1}{4} \cdot 1\frac{2}{7} \div 1\frac{1}{2} = \frac{21}{4} \cdot \frac{9}{7} \div \frac{3}{2} = \frac{\overset{3}{\cancel{21}}}{\underset{2}{\cancel{4}}} \cdot \frac{\overset{3}{\cancel{9}}}{\underset{1}{\cancel{7}}} \cdot \frac{\overset{1}{\cancel{2}}}{\underset{1}{\cancel{3}}} = \frac{9}{2} \text{ or } 4\frac{1}{2}$$

1. $^{-}1\frac{2}{3} \bullet {}^{-}3\frac{1}{5} =$

2. $4\frac{5}{9} \div -\frac{10}{27} =$

3. $4\frac{1}{4} \bullet 3\frac{1}{5} =$

4. $^{-}9\frac{3}{8} \div {}^{-}3\frac{9}{12} =$

5. $-\frac{3}{8} \bullet 4 \bullet \frac{4}{9} =$

6. $^{-}9\frac{3}{5} \div \frac{12}{5} \bullet {}^{-}4 =$

7. $^{-}4.1 \bullet {}^{-}5.2 \div 4 =$

8. $6.2 \bullet 3 \bullet -\frac{1}{2} =$

9. $({}^{-}2\frac{1}{2})({}^{-}2\frac{1}{2}) \div 0.5 =$

10. $-\frac{6}{7} \bullet -\frac{5}{12} \bullet -\frac{2}{15} =$

11. $5\frac{2}{3} \bullet 9.81 \bullet 0 =$

12. $12 \bullet 3\frac{1}{4} \bullet {}^{-}2\frac{2}{3} =$

0-7424-1787-5 *Pre-Algebra*

Name ______________________ Date ______________________

More Multiplying and Dividing Rational Numbers

1. $^{-}9\frac{3}{5} \bullet \frac{5}{12} =$

2. $-\frac{16}{7} \div \frac{12}{35} =$

3. $4\frac{1}{2} \bullet {}^{-}2\frac{2}{7} =$

4. $^{-}5\frac{5}{6} \div 2\frac{1}{3} =$

5. $^{-}8\frac{1}{3} \bullet {}^{-}2\frac{2}{5} =$

6. $16\frac{1}{8} \div 14\frac{1}{3} =$

7. $^{-}37.6 \bullet 0.03 =$

8. $^{-}16.188 \div {}^{-}4.26 =$

9. $^{-}1.75 \bullet {}^{-}3.4 =$

10. $^{-}3.45 \div 1\frac{1}{2} =$

11. $^{-}8 \div {}^{-}1\frac{1}{3} \bullet {}^{-}5 =$

12. $4.498 \div {}^{-}1.73 \bullet {}^{-}1.2 =$

13. $-\frac{5}{7} \div -\frac{1}{14} \bullet -\frac{1}{2} =$

14. $^{-}6\frac{2}{3} \bullet 2.75 \div {}^{-}1\frac{2}{3} =$

15. $-\frac{3}{8} \div {}^{-}3 \bullet \frac{4}{5} =$

16. $12\frac{3}{8} \bullet {}^{-}2\frac{2}{3} \div 2.5 =$

17. $-\frac{5}{6} \bullet 4\frac{1}{4} \bullet -\frac{3}{5} =$

18. $^{-}3\frac{1}{5} \div 4\frac{2}{5} \div {}^{-}1\frac{1}{7} =$

19. $3\frac{3}{5} \bullet {}^{-}1.46 =$

20. $4\frac{2}{3} \div -\frac{6}{7} \bullet \frac{9}{10} =$

Name ______________________ Date ______________________

Order of Operations with Rational Numbers

Order of operations: Perform operations within parenthesis.
Compute exponents.
Multiply or divide in order from left to right.
Add or subtract in order from left to right.

$2 + {}^{-}3 \bullet 5 = 2 + {}^{-}15$
$= {}^{-}13$

$7 - 6^2 \div 2 \bullet 5 = 7 - 36 \div 2 \bullet 5$
$= 7 - 18 \bullet 5$
$= 7 - 90$
$= {}^{-}63$

1. ${}^{-}28 \div 7 + 2\frac{1}{3} =$

2. $\frac{1}{2}({}^{-}16 - 4) =$

3. ${}^{-}9 \div {}^{-}3 + 4 \bullet -\frac{1}{4} - 20 \div 5 =$

4. $\frac{1}{3}(({}^{-}18 + 3) + (5 + 7) \div {}^{-}4) =$

5. $(8\frac{1}{3} + 3\frac{2}{3}) \div 4 - {}^{-}16 =$

6. $\frac{(80 \bullet \frac{1}{2}) + 35}{{}^{-}10 + 25} =$

7. $2\ ({}^{-}6\ (3 - 12) - 17) =$

8. $\frac{1}{4}\ (20 + 72 \div {}^{-}9) =$

9. $3 \bullet 2\ (4 + (9 \div 3)) =$

10. $50 \div ((4 \bullet 5) - (36 \div 2)) + {}^{-}91 =$

Name ______________________ Date ______________________

Calculator Order

Use a scientific calculator to solve each problem. Turn the calculator around to determine the word answer.

Problem	Solution	Clue	Word
1. 501 x 7		To not win	
2. $10^3 - 3 \times 131$		Type of cabin	
3. $17^2 + 7^2$		It buzzes.	
4. 67,077 ÷ 87		Sick	
5. 2 • (2 • 1900 + 3 • 23)		It rings.	
6. $2^9 + 2$		Not hers	
7. $279^2 - (500 - 4)$		Nautilus ________	
8. $3^3 \times 100 + 3 \times 115$		Worn on foot	
9. $22{,}416 \div 2^2$		Big pigs	
10. 473,720 – 12,345		Snow vehicle	
11. 3 x 5 x 246 +15		Bottom of shoe	
12. 4,738 – 1,234		Fire equipment	
13. $60^2 + 4 \times 26$		Center of a donut	
14. 11 x (60 – 2)		To plead	
15. 5787 ÷ 9 x 12		Fish organ	
16. 12,345 + 23,456 – 465		They "honk".	
17. 8 x 100 + 8 – 1		Tennis shot	
18. $50 \times 700 + 3 \times 6^2$		Capital of Idaho	
19. 50 x 110 + (10 – 3)		Not a win	
20. $64{,}118 - 80^2$		Ducks' beaks	

A googol is 10^{100} or 1 followed by 100 zeros.
What number would result in the "calculator word" googol? ______________

Name ______________________ Date ______________________

Comparing Rational Numbers

Use <, > or = to make you a true sentence.

5.68	____	5.7	$^{-}7\frac{3}{10}$	____	$^{-}7.29$
5.68	<	5.70	$^{-}7.30$	<	$^{-}7.29$

1. 2.5 ______ $2\frac{17}{34}$
2. 1.049 ______ 1.49
3. $^{-}0.\overline{3}$ ______ $^{-}0.3$
4. 15.62 ______ 1.562
5. 8156.6 ______ 8166.6
6. $^{-}7\frac{4}{5}$ ______ $^{-}7\frac{24}{30}$
7. $^{-}8\frac{7}{8}$ ______ $^{-}8.857$
8. 329.93 ______ 32.993
9. 982.61 ______ 7662.8
10. $13\frac{5}{8}$ ______ 13.6

$5\frac{1}{2}, 5\frac{3}{5}, 5.4$ → 5.5, 5.6, 5.4 → $5\frac{3}{5}, 5\frac{1}{2}, 5.4$

Rewrite — Descending Order

1. 6.41, 6.411, 6.4111
2. $^{-}2\frac{9}{14}, ^{-}2\frac{5}{8}, ^{-}2\frac{4}{7}$
3. 11.6, $11\frac{2}{3}$, $11\frac{14}{25}$
4. $^{-}0.030$, $-\frac{33}{100}$, $^{-}0.003$
5. $7\frac{5}{8}$, $7\frac{3}{4}$, 7.775
6. $^{-}10\frac{3}{4}, ^{-}10.82, ^{-}10\frac{2}{3}$
7. 3.08, $3\frac{4}{5}$, $3\frac{3}{5}$
8. $^{-}1.35, ^{-}1\frac{1}{8}, ^{-}1\frac{1}{4}$

Name ______________________ Date ______________________

Flip Trip

Perform each of the following operations on your calculator. Then flip your calculator and find the "word answer" to the questions.

1. What did Amelia Earhart's father say the first time he saw her fly an air plane?
   0.115 x 3 + 10141 x 5 = ______________________
   Flip Trip ______________________

2. What did Farmer Macgregor throw at Peter Rabbit to chase him out of the garden?
   (27 x 109 + 4 – 0.027) 2 x 9 = ______________________
   Flip Trip ______________________

3. What did Snoopy add to his doghouse as a result of his dogfights with the Red Baron?
   7 (3 x 303 + 50) x 8 = ______________________
   Flip Trip ______________________

4. What kind of double does a golfer want to avoid at the end of a round of golf?
   4 (1956 x 4 +153) = ______________________
   Flip Trip ______________________

5. What did the little girl say when she was frightened by the ghost?
   0.07 x 0.111 x 5 + 0.00123 = ______________________
   Flip Trip ______________________

0-7424-1787-5 *Pre-Algebra*

Name ______________________________ Date ______________________________

Open Sentences

State the solution for each sentence.

$\frac{1}{2} \bullet {}^-10 = x$	$\frac{^-56}{^-7} - 4 = z$
$\frac{1}{\cancel{2}_{1}} \bullet \frac{\cancel{^-10}^{\,^-5}}{1} = x$	$8 - 4 = z$
${}^-5 = x$	$4 = z$

1. $\frac{18 + {}^-6}{2} = a$

7. $\frac{1}{3} \bullet {}^-15 + {}^-10 = r$

2. ${}^-3 \bullet 4 - 6 = c$

8. $1\frac{3}{5} \div \frac{16}{45} = d$

3. $4.5 - 6.2 = p$

9. $5 \bullet 7.32 - 18.19 = n$

4. $\frac{^-3}{8} \bullet {}^-4 - 1 = q$

10. $\frac{3}{4} \bullet {}^-16 + 8.12 = z$

5. $\frac{^-15 + {}^-27}{3} = x$

11. $\frac{^-40 + 15}{5} + 6 = b$

6. ${}^-8.1 \bullet 4.2 + 16 = g$

12. $-\frac{2}{5} \div \frac{4}{15} + {}^-2\frac{1}{2} = t$

0-7424-1787-5 *Pre-Algebra*

Name ______________________________ Date ______________________________

More Open Sentences

Using the given value, state whether each problem is true or false.

$$28 = r \cdot \frac{1}{4}, \text{ if } r = {}^{-}108$$

$$28 \stackrel{?}{=} {}^{-}108 \cdot \frac{1}{4}$$

$$28 \stackrel{?}{=} -27 \Longrightarrow \text{False}$$

1. $7 + x = 3\frac{1}{2}$, if $x = {}^{-}3\frac{1}{2}$

2. $y + 15 \div 6 = {}^{-}1\frac{1}{2}$, if $y = {}^{-}3$

3. $\frac{f}{13} + {}^{-}3 = 0$, if $f = 69$

4. $2x - 5.45 = 0.97$, if $x = 3.21$

5. $8\frac{1}{3} + a = 15\frac{8}{15}$, if $a = 7\frac{2}{5}$

6. $8 + (z - 32) = {}^{-}10$, if $z = 16$

7. $11.5 + c = 28\frac{1}{4}$, if $c = 16\frac{3}{4}$

8. $y(5 + 11) + 8 = 41$, if $y = 2$

9. $3g + 5.26 - 11.9 = 12.64$, if $g = {}^{-}3$

10. $5 + -\frac{16}{k} = {}^{-}3$, if $k = 2$

11. $7\frac{1}{9} \div w = \frac{1}{18}$, if $w = 2\frac{17}{32}$

12. $\frac{3(2q - q)}{8} + 29 = 32$, if $q = 8$

13. $\frac{16.8 - 91.6}{m}$ 37.4, if $m = 2$

14. $11\frac{1}{4} - f = 5\frac{1}{16}$, if $f = 16\frac{5}{16}$

Name ______________________________ Date ______________________________

Evaluating Expressions

Evaluate the following, if $a = \frac{1}{2}$, $x = 4$ and $y = {}^{-}2$

$$5x\,(2a - 5y) = 5 \bullet 4\,(2 \bullet \frac{1}{2} - 5 \bullet {}^{-}2) = 20\,(1 + 10) = 20\,(11) = 220$$

1. $4\,(a - 1) =$
2. $4a - 3y =$
3. $4\,(x - 3y) =$
4. $x\,(a + 6) =$
5. $6a + {}^{-}12a =$
6. $7\,(x + -y) =$
7. $6a\,(8a + 4y) =$
8. $3x + 2\,(a - y) =$
9. $x\,(ax + ay) =$
10. $ay + y - 5ax =$
11. $xy\,(2a + 3x - 2) =$
12. $4x - (xy + 2) =$
13. $5y - 8a + 6xy - 7x =$
14. $10x\,(8a + {}^{-}4y) + {}^{-}3y =$
15. $6xy - 2x\,(4a - 8y) =$
16. $(2a - x)\,(2x - 6) =$

Name ______________________ Date ______________________

Simplifying Expressions

Distributive Property

$$3(x + 2y) = 3x + 3 \bullet 2y$$
$$= 3x + 6y$$

1. $^{-}7(a + b) =$
2. $x(y - 4) =$
3. $-\frac{2}{3}(c - 12) =$
4. $^{-}8(\frac{t}{2} + 6) =$
5. $y(^{-}16 + 2x) =$
6. $3(2a - 8b) =$
7. $2x(3y + {}^{-}6) =$
8. $7(^{-}5x + 8z) =$
9. $^{-}5y(6z - 10) =$
10. $^{-}3x(^{-}7 + 8y) =$

Combining Like Terms

$$6m - 4m + 3p = (6 - 4)m + 3p$$
$$= 2m + 3p$$

same variable

1. $9y + 6y - 2 =$
2. $25x - x + 2y =$
3. $4a + 8b + 11a - 10b =$
4. $13xy + 18xy - 20xy =$
5. $^{-}2m + 16 - 13m =$
6. $4a + 7 + 3a - 8 - 3a =$
7. $16x + {}^{-}18y + 10x - 7y =$
8. $6c - 8ab + 9c - 10 =$
9. $18ab + {}^{-}6a + {}^{-}7b + 26ab + {}^{-}7b =$
10. $5x - 3x + 2xy + 31x + {}^{-}18xy =$

Name ______________________ Date ______________________

An Expression by Any Other Name

Simplify each expression. Cross out each box that contains an answer. The remaining words can be restated to make a familiar proverb.

1. $3(a + b) + 2b =$
2. $5a + 2a(5 - b) =$
3. $8 - 3(6 - 6a) =$
4. $4a + 6(a + 8) =$
5. $^{-}2a - 3(b - 4a) =$
6. $8(6a + 7b) - 11(2b + 8a) =$
7. $^{-}6(a + 5b) - 3(^{-}7b - a) =$
8. $2(a - b) + 3(a - b) - 4(a - b) =$
9. $4a + {}^{-}7(a + 2) =$
10. $6(a + 2b) + 8a - 16b =$
11. $3a + {}^{-}2(a + b) =$
12. $2(3a - 4b) - 6a =$
13. $^{-}5(2a - 3b) + 5(3b - 2a) =$
14. $4(11a - 9b) - 7(6a) =$
15. $^{-}3(4a - 5b) - (a - b) =$

$10 + 18a$ YOU	$^{-}10 + 18a$ ARE	$a - 2b$ SEE	$2a + 36b$ CANNOT	$3a + 5b$ LEAD	$12a - 8b$ INSTRUCT
$14a + 4b$ AN	$14a - 4b$ A	$40a + 34b$ ELDERLY	$^{-}40a + 34b$ HORSE	$3a - 14$ CANINE	$2a - 36b$ TO
$10a + 48$ WATER	$^{-}3a - 14$ BUT	$12a - 8b$ ON	$^{-}13a + 16b$ YOU	$^{-}3a - 9b$ CANNOT	$15a - 2b$ FRESH
$10a - 3b$ MAKE	$a - b$ HIM	$15a - 2ab$ DOWN	$^{-}20a + 30b$ DRINK	$20a - 30b$ PROCEDURES	$^{-}8b$ HOME

Write the familiar proverb.

______ ______ ______ ______ ______ ______ ______ ______

Name ______________________ Date ______________________

Solving Addition Equations

$$1.8 = {}^{-}2.1 + x$$
$$1.8 + 2.1 = {}^{-}2.1 + 2.1 + x$$
$$3.9 = 0 + x$$
$$3.9 = x$$

1. $a + {}^{-}7 = 8$

2. $y + 76 = {}^{-}93$

3. $4 + b = {}^{-}14$

4. ${}^{-}33 = z + 16$

5. ${}^{-}12 + x = 21$

6. $2.4 = m + 3.7$

7. ${}^{-}1\frac{1}{2} + n = {}^{-}1\frac{5}{8}$

8. ${}^{-}27 = c + 27$

9. $-\frac{5}{8} + x = -\frac{5}{8}$

10. $y + {}^{-}6.2 = 8.1$

11. $38 = x + {}^{-}19$

12. $a + {}^{-}2\frac{5}{9} = {}^{-}10\frac{5}{18}$

13. ${}^{-}1{,}129 + b = 3{,}331$

14. ${}^{-}3.5 = 7\frac{1}{2} + x$

Name ______________________ Date ______________________

Solving Subtraction Equations

$$24 = x - {}^{-}8$$
$$24 = x + 8$$
$$24 - 8 = x + 8 - 8$$
$$16 = x + 0$$
$$16 = x$$

1. $k - 36 = 37$

2. $^{-}22 = y - 8$

3. $x - {}^{-}7 = {}^{-}19$

4. $30 = b - {}^{-}2$

5. $a - 18 = {}^{-}32$

6. $^{-}1.7 = b - 9.3$

7. $^{-}4\frac{1}{3} = q - 3\frac{1}{3}$

8. $^{-}17 = q - 3$

9. $p - \frac{3}{5} = \frac{3}{5}$

10. $5.62 = m - 6$

11. $x - {}^{-}36.5 = {}^{-}2.563$

12. $^{-}1{,}132 = b - 6{,}339$

13. $7\frac{3}{4} = a - 16\frac{3}{16}$

14. $z - {}^{-}5.75 = {}^{-}8\frac{1}{4}$

Name ______________________ Date ______________________

Solving Addition and Subtraction Equations

1. $x + {}^{-}3 = -18$
2. $c - 11 = 43$
3. $12 + y = 32$
4. ${}^{-}26 = d - 7$
5. ${}^{-}62 = a + 16$
6. $q - {}^{-}83 = 121$
7. $t + {}^{-}101 = 263$
8. $w - 454 = {}^{-}832$
9. ${}^{-}332 = {}^{-}129 + s$
10. $665 = k - {}^{-}327$
11. ${}^{-}8.6 = m + 11.12$
12. $a - -\frac{1}{5} = \frac{3}{20}$
13. $-\frac{3}{4} + z = \frac{7}{18}$
14. $b - 17.8 = {}^{-}36$
15. $-\frac{13}{24} = -\frac{5}{16} + c$
16. $102.8 = g - {}^{-}66.09$
17. $f + \frac{3}{5} = \frac{3}{4}$
18. $b - \frac{5}{6} = -\frac{7}{8}$
19. $21.21 + p = {}^{-}101.6$
20. ${}^{-}762.46 = h - 32.061$

Name ______________________ Date ______________________

Solving Multiplication Equations

$$4y = {}^{-}28$$
$$\frac{4y}{4} = -\frac{28}{4}$$
$$1y = {}^{-}7$$

1. ${}^{-}6a = {}^{-}66$
2. ${}^{-}180 = 12b$
3. ${}^{-}13n = 13$
4. $42 = {}^{-}14p$
5. $1\frac{1}{2} = 3x$
6. ${}^{-}5.6 = {}^{-}0.8x$
7. $8 = {}^{-}32b$
8. $9a = {}^{-}3$
9. $0.25y = 1.5$
10. ${}^{-}0.0006 = 0.02x$
11. ${}^{-}11x = 275$
12. $45\frac{1}{2} = {}^{-}14c$
13. $61.44 = 12z$
14. ${}^{-}21y = {}^{-}756$

Name ______________________ Date ______________________

Solving Division Equations

$$\frac{x}{4} = {}^{-}6$$

$$4 \bullet \frac{x}{4} = {}^{-}6 \bullet 4$$

$$x = {}^{-}24$$

1. $^{-}18 = \frac{a}{6}$

2. $\frac{x}{6} = {}^{-}6$

3. $\frac{y}{^{-}2} = 231$

4. $\frac{1}{5}b = {}^{-}8$

5. $\frac{m}{0.6} = 0.3$

6. $35 = \frac{x}{^{-}7}$

7. $0.12 = \frac{y}{0.12}$

8. $3 = -\frac{1}{8}a$

9. $\frac{w}{^{-}2} = 0.04$

10. $\frac{u}{^{-}4} = {}^{-}14$

11. $\frac{x}{^{-}5.1} = {}^{-}16$

12. $-28 = \frac{a}{13}$

13. $\frac{1}{18}c = {}^{-}31$

14. $\frac{b}{^{-}0.29} = 5.5$

Name ______________________________ Date ______________________________

Solving Multiplication and Division Equations

1. ${}^{-}2p = {}^{-}38$

2. $\frac{b}{8} = {}^{-}24$

3. ${}^{-}85 = 17r$

4. ${}^{-}32 = \frac{c}{{}^{-}22}$

5. ${}^{-}13a = 52$

6. $\frac{1}{47}d = {}^{-}26$

7. ${}^{-}12f = {}^{-}180$

8. $\frac{1}{0.16}x = 0.7$

9. ${}^{-}77.4 = 9a$

10. $-\frac{1}{6}q = {}^{-}11$

11. $16 = \frac{n}{{}^{-}21}$

12. $0.7h = {}^{-}0.112$

13. ${}^{-}80 = \frac{p}{15}$

14. $792 = {}^{-}33y$

15. ${}^{-}5.2 = \frac{m}{30.1}$

16. ${}^{-}11.2x = {}^{-}60.48$

17. $\frac{1}{{}^{-}26}r = {}^{-}66$

18. $315 = 21s$

19. $\frac{z}{0.06} = {}^{-}7.98$

20. ${}^{-}14g = {}^{-}406$

0-7424-1787-5 *Pre-Algebra*

Name ______________________ Date ______________________

Mixed Up Pairs

Solve each equation. Each equation in column A has the same solution as an equation in Column B. Find the pairs.

Column A		Column B
______	1. $y + 12 = 8$	A. $y - 12 = {}^-12$
______	2. $\frac{y}{6} = {}^-2$	B. $2y = {}^-8$
______	3. ${}^-7y = {}^-84$	C. $y - 1 = {}^-7$
______	4. ${}^-42 = y - 20$	D. $y - {}^-12 = 24$
______	5. $92 + y = 92$	E. $\frac{y}{{}^-4} = 3$
______	6. $9 = 54y$	F. $y + 2 = 11$
______	7. ${}^-12 = y - 6$	G. $y + 11 = {}^-11$
______	8. ${}^-1 = \frac{y}{20}$	H. $12y = 2$
______	9. $27 = 3y$	I. $\frac{y}{{}^-2} = {}^-10$
______	10. ${}^-5 + y = 15$	J. ${}^-15 = y + 5$

Name ____________________ Date ____________________

Solving Equations with Two Operations

$$2y - 7 = {}^{-}29$$
$$2y - 7 + 7 = {}^{-}29 + 7$$
$$2y = {}^{-}22$$
$$\frac{2y}{2} = \frac{{}^{-}22}{2}$$
$$y = {}^{-}11$$

1. $13 + {}^{-}3p = {}^{-}2$

2. $\frac{{}^{-}5a}{2} = 75$

3. $6x - 4 = {}^{-}10$

4. $9 = 2y + 9$

5. ${}^{-}10 + \frac{a}{4} = 9$

6. $17 = 5 - x$

7. ${}^{-}7r - 8 = {}^{-}14$

8. $\frac{4y}{3} = 8$

9. $16 + \frac{x}{3} = {}^{-}10$

10. $\frac{{}^{-}4z}{5} = -12$

11. ${}^{-}22 = 3s - {}^{-}8$

12. $-\frac{a}{6} - {}^{-}31 = 64$

Name ______________________ Date ______________________

Solving Equations with Negative Variables

$$\frac{^-k}{6} + 1 = {^-5}$$

$$\frac{^-k}{6} + 1 - 1 = {^-5} - 1$$

$$\frac{^-k}{6} \cdot 6 = {^-6} \cdot 6$$

$$^-k = {^-36}$$

$$k = 36$$

1. $^-8 - y = 22$

2. $18 = {^-k} + 3$

3. $4 - \frac{x}{5} = {^-16}$

4. $-x - 15 = {^-15}$

5. $-z = 11$

6. $^-28 = \frac{-y}{4} - 12$

7. $^-82 = -a$

8. $\frac{-b}{3} + 50 = 100$

9. $^-6 - x\frac{1}{9} = {^-18}$

10. $^-3z + 5 = 38$

11. $-a\frac{1}{2} + 12 = {^-9}$

12. $^-5y - {^-7} = 52$

Name ______________________________ Date ______________________________

Magical Equations

Solve each equation. In a Magic Square, the sum of each row, column and diagonal is the same.

1. $\frac{x}{4} + 5 = 7$	2. $2x - 20 = 10$	3. $^{-}3x - 12 = 12$	4. $-x - 6 = -5$	5. $2 = 2x - 10$
6. $3x - 7 = 35$	7. $2 + 5x = {}^{-}18$	8. $4x + 5 = {}^{-}3$	9. $^{-}11x + 10 = {}^{-}45$	10. $5x - 6 = 29$
11. $^{-}4 = \frac{4x}{5}$	12. $^{-}2x + 7 = 13$	13. $\frac{5x}{4} + 2 = 7$	14. $^{-}64 = {}^{-}5x - 9$	15. $2x + 10 = 36$
16. $8x - 9 = {}^{-}1$	17. $12 = 3x + 3$	18. $^{-}4 = \frac{2x}{^{-}5}$	19. $9 + 4x = 57$	20. $\frac{x}{^{-}2} + 2 = 5$
21. $6 = \frac{x}{2} + 5$	22. $2x - 10 = 8$	23. $8 = \frac{x}{4} + 4$	24. $5x - 15 = {}^{-}50$	25. $3x - 9 = {}^{-}9$

The Magic Sum is ______________ .

0-7424-1787-5 *Pre-Algebra*

Name ______________________ Date ______________________

Solving Equations Using the Distributive Property

$$4(x - 3) = 20$$
$$4x - 12 = 20$$
$$4x - 12 + 12 = 20 + 12$$
$$\frac{4x}{4} = \frac{32}{4}$$
$$x = 8$$

1. $3(x + 8) = {}^{-}6$

2. $75 = {}^{-}5(a + 5)$

3. ${}^{-}8(y - 6) = {}^{-}16$

4. $20 = 4(\frac{t}{4} - 2)$

5. $17(x - 2) = {}^{-}34$

6. $63 = 9(2 - a)$

7. $6(2 - \frac{x}{6}) = 1$

8. ${}^{-}36 = 6(y - 2)$

9. ${}^{-}7(r + 8) = {}^{-}14$

10. $3(m + 5) = 42$

11. ${}^{-}54 = 3(2 + 5m)$

12. ${}^{-}3(x - 7) + 2 = 20$

Name ______________________ Date ______________________

Solving Equations - Variables on Both Sides

$$5x + 6 = 2x + 5$$
$$5x - 2x + 6 = 2x - 2x + 15$$
$$3x + 6 - 6 = 15 - 6$$
$$\frac{3x}{3} = \frac{9}{3}$$
$$x = 3$$

1. $20y + 5 = 5y + 65$

2. $13 - t = t - 7$

3. $^{-}3k + 10 = k + 2$

4. $^{-}9r = 20 + r$

5. $6m - 2\frac{1}{2} = m + 12\frac{1}{2}$

6. $18 + 4.5p = 6p + 12$

7. $5x - \frac{1}{4} = 3x - \frac{5}{4}$

8. $-x - 2 = 1 - 2x$

9. $3k + 10 = 2k - 21$

10. $8y - 6 = 5y + 12$

11. $-t + 10 = t + 4$

12. $4m - 9 = 5m + 7$

0-7424-1787-5 *Pre-Algebra*

Name ____________________ Date ____________________

Mixed Practice

1. $4x - 7 = 2x + 15$

2. ${}^{-}4 = {}^{-}4(f - 7)$

3. $5x - 17 = 4x + 36$

4. $3(k + 5) = {}^{-}18$

5. $y + 3 = 7y - 21$

6. ${}^{-}3(m - 2) = 12$

7. $18 + 4p = 6p + 12$

8. ${}^{-}8\,(\frac{a}{8} - 2) = 26$

9. ${}^{-}3k + 10 = k + 2$

10. $22 = 2\,(b + 3)$

11. $6a + 9 = {}^{-}4a + 29$

12. ${}^{-}22 = 11(2c + 8)$

13. $10p - 14 = 9p + 17$

14. ${}^{-}45 = 5(\frac{2a}{5} + {}^{-}3)$

15. $16z - 15 = 13z$

16. $36 + 19b = 24b + 6$

17. $144 = {}^{-}16\,(3 + 3d)$

18. $11h - 14 = 7 + 14h$

19. ${}^{-}3\,(\frac{2j}{3} - 6) = 32$

20. ${}^{-}43 - 3z = 2 - 6z$

0-7424-1787-5 *Pre-Algebra*

Name ______________________ Date ______________________

Equation Steps

Solve these equations.

1. $^{-}116 = -a$

2. $6m - 2 = m + 13$

3. $x + 2 = {}^{-}61$

4. $^{-}30 = {}^{-}6 - y$

5. $^{-}5t + 16 = {}^{-}59$

6. $4a - 9 = 6a + 7$

7. $\frac{^{-}3b}{8} = {}^{-}36$

8. $^{-}40 = 10\ (4 + s)$

9. $28 - \frac{k}{3} = 16$

10. $^{-}9r = 20 + r$

11. $114 = 11c - {}^{-}26$

12. $^{-}38 = 17 - 5z$

13. $^{-}5(2x - 5) = {}^{-}35$

14. $20c + 5 = 5c + 65$

15. $\frac{^{-}d}{5} - 21 = {}^{-}62$

16. $\frac{^{-}15c}{^{-}4} = {}^{-}30$

17. $384 = 12\ ({}^{-}8 + 5f)$

18. $3n + 7 = 7n - 13$

19. $^{-}8 - \frac{y}{3} = 22$

20. $^{-}5t - 30 = {}^{-}60$

HINT: The sum of the solutions equals the number of steps in the Statue of Liberty — 354

Name ______________________ Date ______________________

Writing Algebraic Expressions

The product of four and eleven	$4 \bullet 11$
A number increased by six	$x + 6$
The number divided by two	$y \div 2$ or $\frac{y}{2}$
Twice a number decreased by one	$2a - 1$

1. Five less than a number

2. Three times the sum of a number and twelve

3. Ten more than the quotient of c and three

4. Two increased by six times a number

5. Two-thirds of a number minus eleven

6. Twice the difference between c and four

7. The product of nine and a number, decreased by seven

8. Six times a number plus seven times the number

9. A number increased by twice the number

10. One-fourth times a number increased by eleven

11. The quotient of a number and three decreased by five

12. Twelve times the sum of a number and five times the number

0-7424-1787-5 *Pre-Algebra*

Name ______________________ Date ______________________

Solving One-Step Problems

Write an equation and solve

> Nine more than a number is 33.
> Find the number
> $9 + n = 33$
> $9 - 9 + n = 33 - 9$
> $n = 24$

1. A number decreased by 16 is $^-26$. Find the number.

2. One-fourth of a number is $^-60$. Find the number.

3. The product of negative eight and a number is 104. Find the number.

4. Twice a number is 346. Find the number.

5. A number increased by negative twenty-seven is 110. Find the number.

6. Tim weighs five pounds more than Mitchell. Find Mitchell's weight if Tim weighs ninety-three pounds.

7. The cost of five books is $71.00. What is the cost of each book?

8. The cost of a filter is $4.00. What is the cost of six filters?

Name ______________________________ Date ______________________________

Solving Two-Step Problems

Write an equation and solve

Ten more than 4 times a number is 6.
What is the number?

$$10 + 4n = 6$$

$$10 - 10 + 4n = 6 - 10$$

$$\frac{4n}{4} = \frac{^{-}4}{4}$$

$$n = {}^{-}1$$

1. Three-fifths of a number decreased by one is twenty-three. What is the number?

2. Seven more than six times a number is negative forty-seven. What is the number?

3. Nine less than twice a number is thirty-one. What is the number?

4. Three times the sum of a number and five times the number is thirty-six. What is the number?

5. The quotient of a number and four decreased by ten is two. What is the number?

6. Carol is sixty-six inches tall. This is twenty inches less than two times Mindy's height. How tall is Mindy?

7. In February, Paul's electric bill was three dollars more than one-half his gas bill. If the electric bill was ninety-two dollars, what was the gas bill?

0-7424-1787-5 *Pre-Algebra*

Name ______________________ Date ______________________

Solving Multi-Step Problems

Write an equation and solve

One number is seven times a second number.

Their sum is 112. Find the numbers.

$$n + 7n = 112$$

$$\frac{8n}{8} = \frac{112}{8}$$

$$n = 14 \text{ and } 98$$

1. One of two numbers is five more than the other. The sum of the numbers is 17. Find the numbers.

2. The sum of two numbers is twenty-four. The larger number is three times the smaller number. Find the numbers.

3. One of two numbers is two-thirds the other number. The sum of the numbers is 45. Find the numbers.

4. The difference of two numbers is 19. The larger number is 3 more than twice the smaller. Find the numbers.

5. 320 tickets were sold to the school play. There were three times as many student tickets sold as adult tickets. Find the number of each.

6. The first number is eight more than the second number. Three times the second number plus twice the first number is equal to 26. Find the numbers.

7. Dan has five times as many \$1 bills as \$5 bills. He has a total of 48 bills. How many of each does he have?

0-7424-1787-5 *Pre-Algebra*

Name ______________________ Date ______________________

Graphing Inequalities

$x > 2$

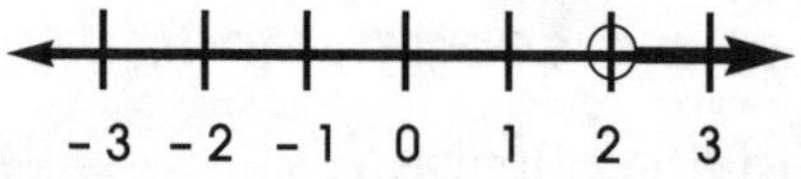

$y \leq 2$

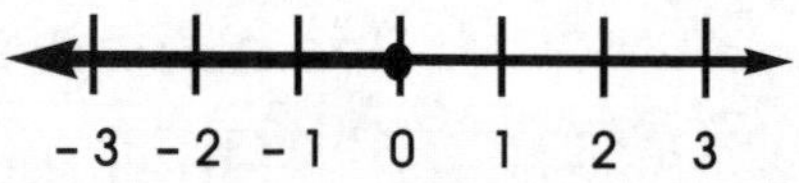

1. $x > 1$

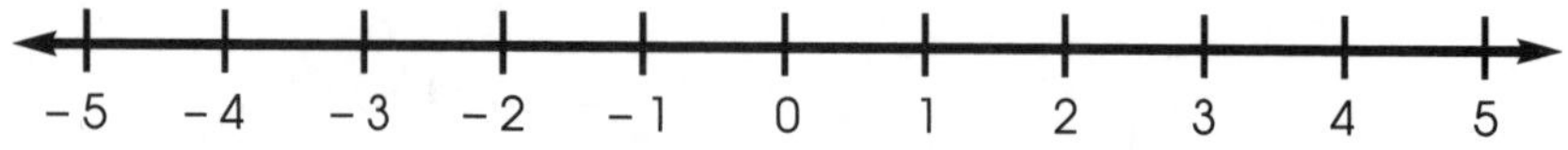

2. $a < {}^{-}1$

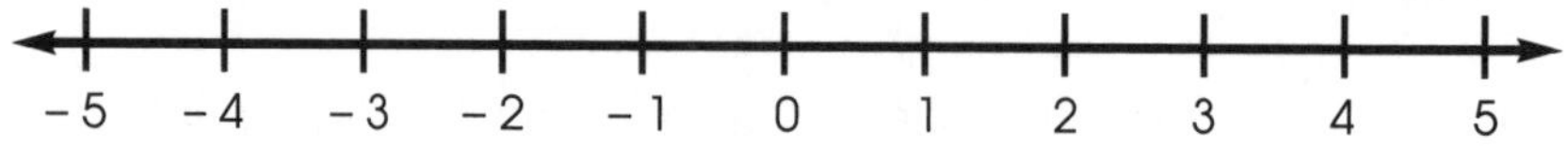

3. $y \leq 2$

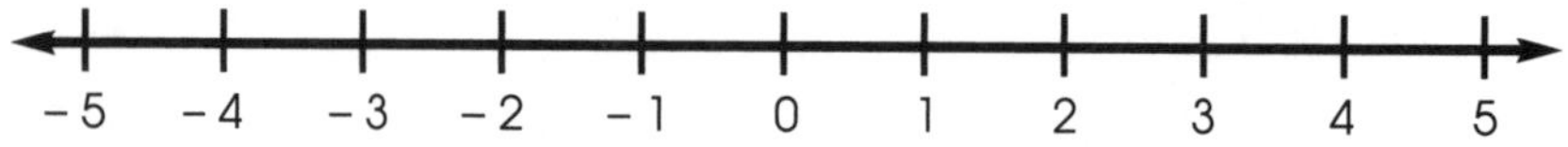

4. $b > {}^{-}4$

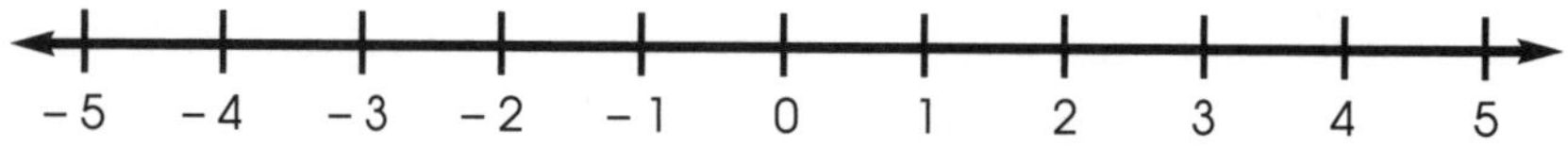

5. $p \geq 3$

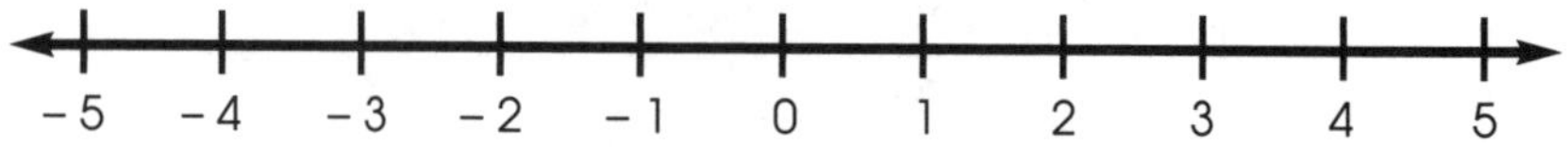

6. $x < \frac{1}{2}$

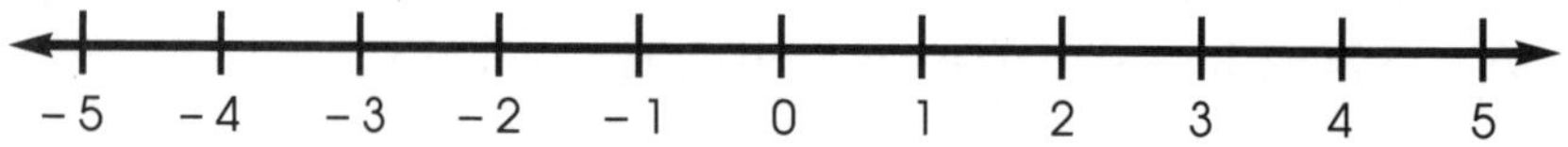

7. $y > {}^{-}1.5$

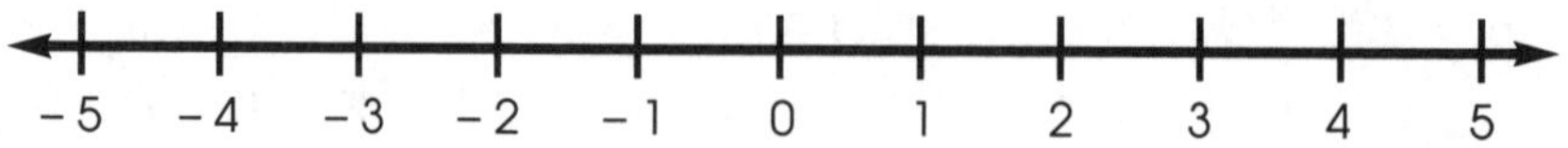

8. $m \leq 4\frac{1}{2}$

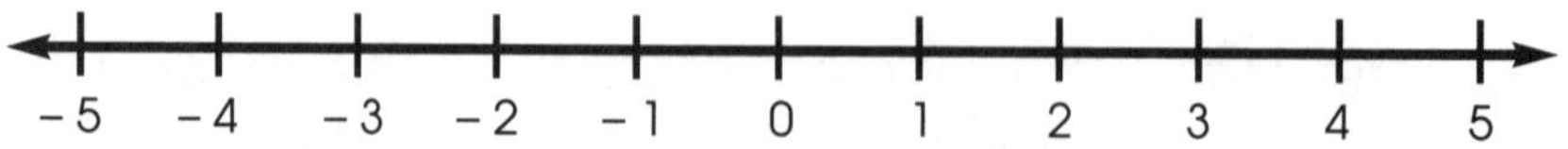

9. $c \leq \frac{{}^{-}10}{5}$

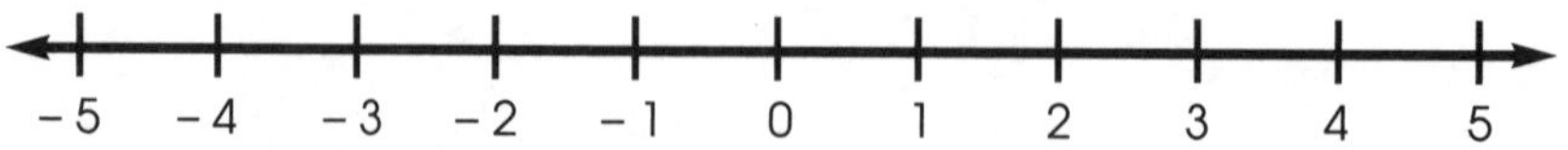

10. $d \geq 3.75$

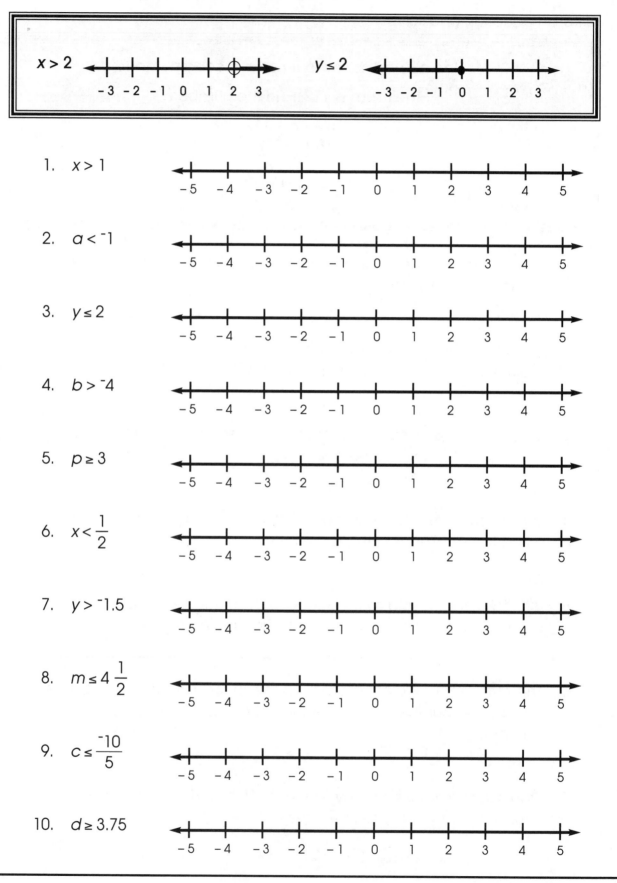

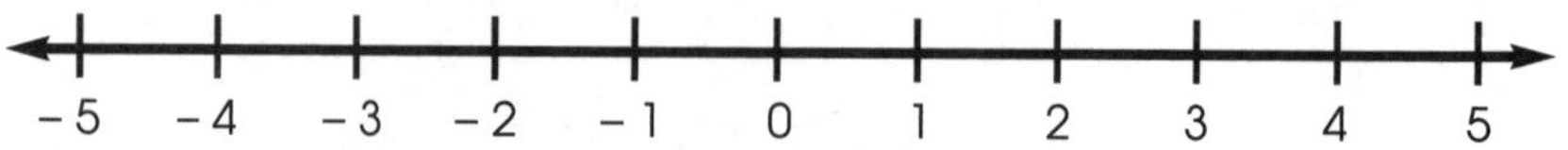

Name ______________________ Date ______________________

Solving Inequalities with Addition or Subtraction

$m + 9 > 5$

$m + 9 - 9 > 5 - 9$

$m > {}^{-}4$

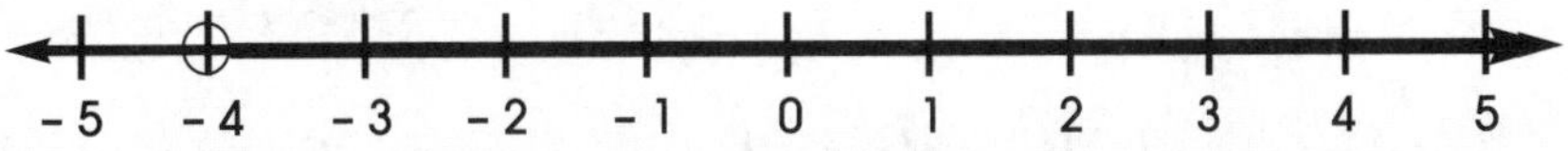

1. $g + 8 > 6$

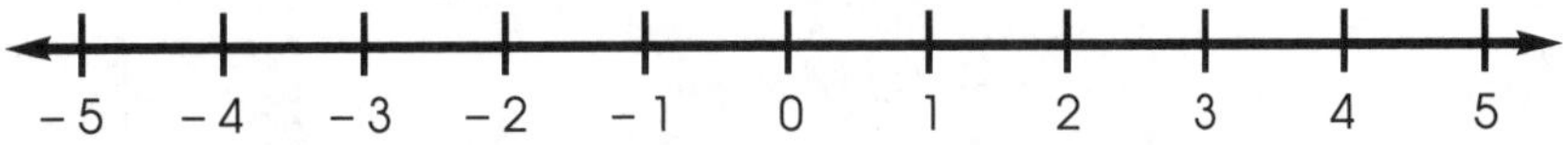

2. $d - 7 > {}^{-}3$

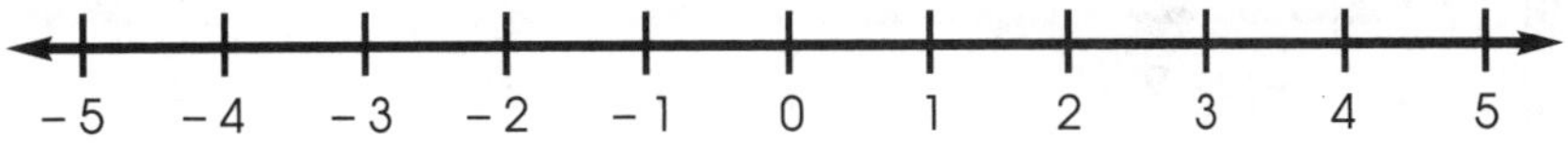

3. ${}^{-}3 > y + 1$

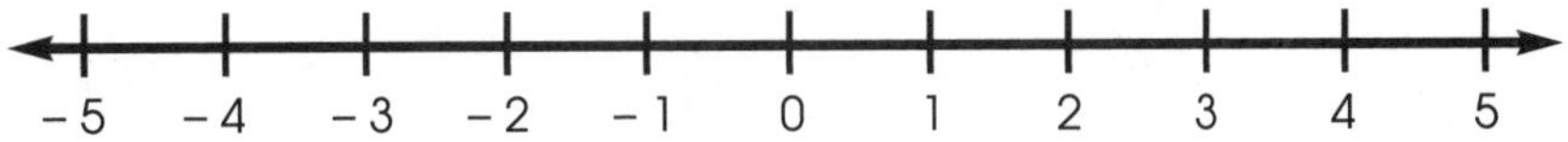

4. $a - 3 \leq 1$

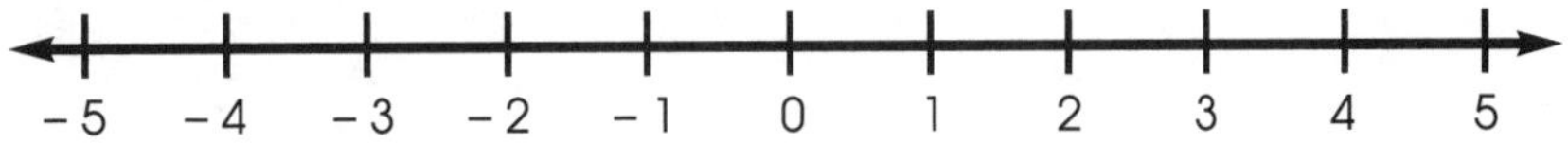

5. ${}^{-}4 \leq 1 + c$

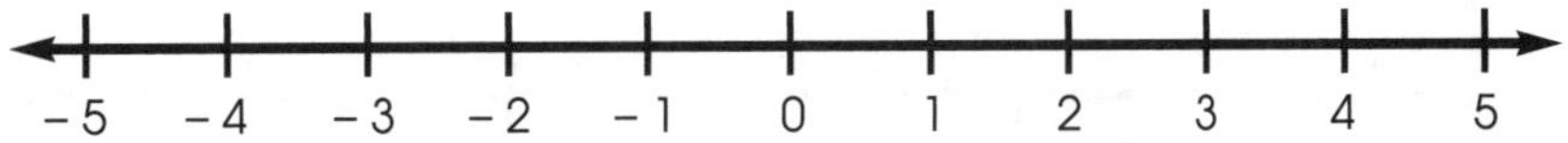

6. $x + \frac{1}{4} \geq 1\frac{1}{2}$

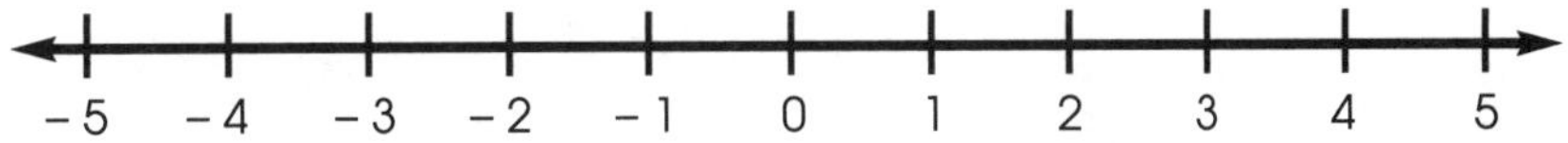

7. ${}^{-}2.4 < n - 0.6$

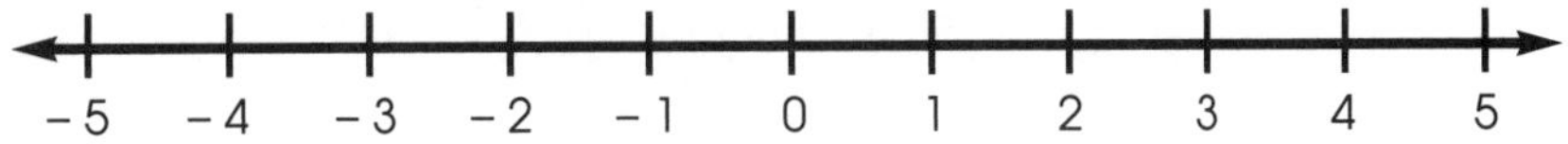

8. ${}^{-}20 + m \leq {}^{-}24$

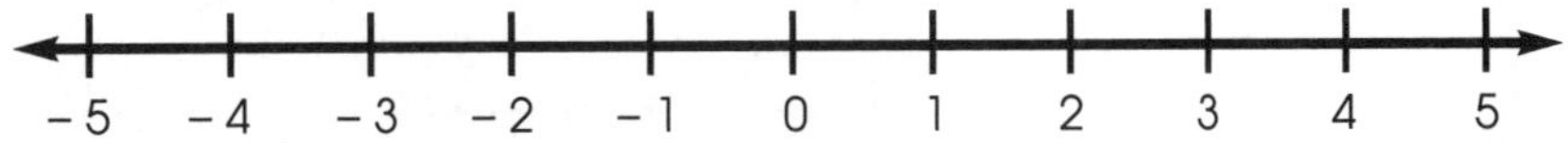

9. ${}^{-}7.5 + x \geq {}^{-}9$

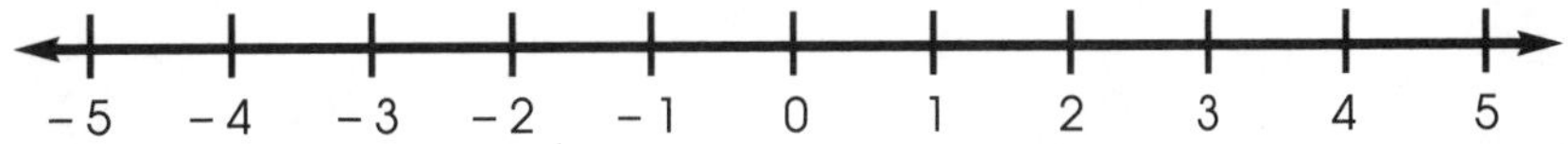

10. $3\frac{1}{3} \leq \frac{2}{9} + c$

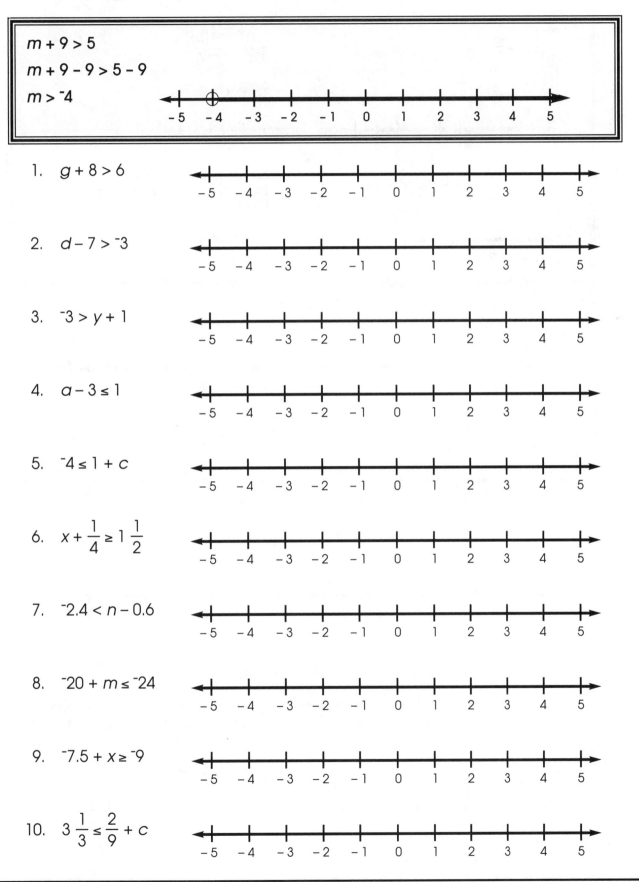

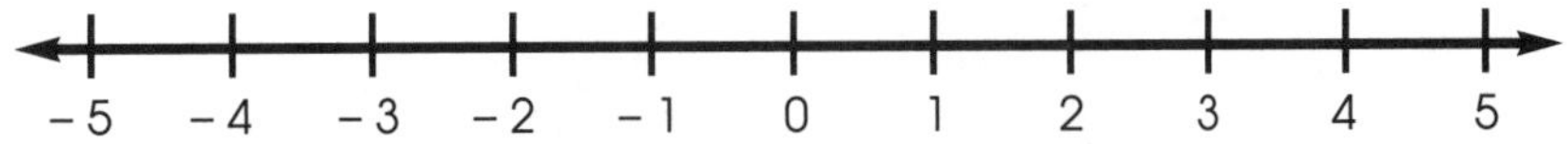

0-7424-1787-5 *Pre-Algebra*

Name ______________________________ Date ______________________________

Solving Inequalities with Multiplication or Division

$\frac{3y}{3} \leq \frac{9}{3}$

$y \leq 3$

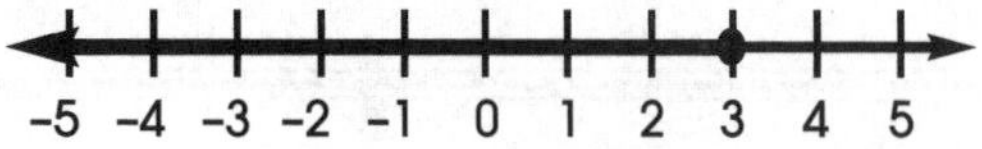

$\frac{40}{^{-}10} < \frac{^{-}10n}{^{-}10}$

$-4 \, (>) \, n$

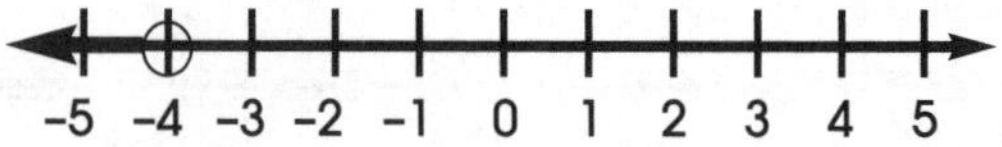

$-\frac{5}{2} \bullet -\frac{2}{5}x \geq {^{-}4} \bullet -\frac{5}{2}$

$x \, (\leq) \, 10$

Note: division or multiplication by a negative number switches the sign.

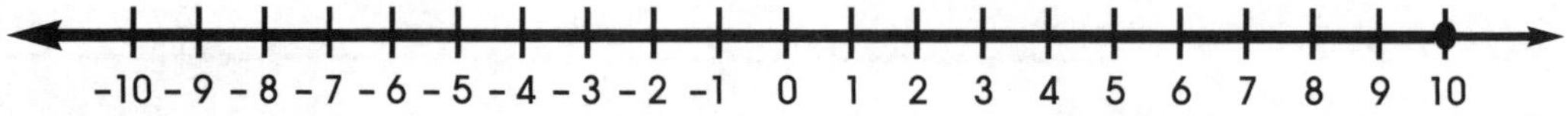

1. $11x > 22$

2. $^{-}15m \leq {^{-}75}$

3. $^{-}1 > \frac{b}{3}$

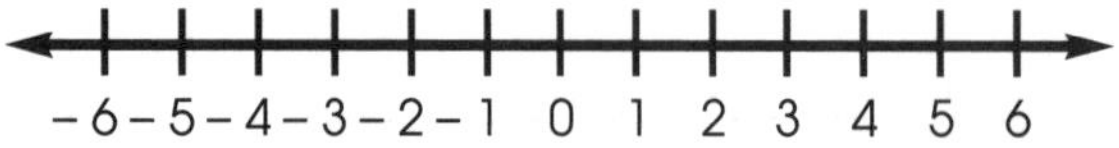

4. $1.9\,x \leq {^{-}7.6}$

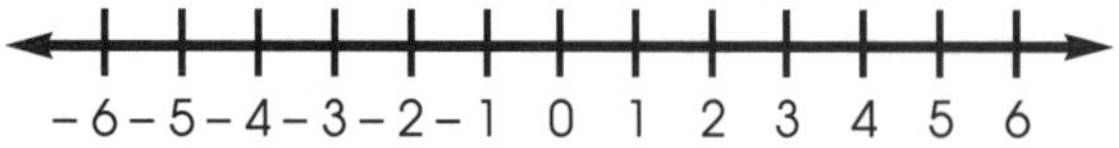

5. $\frac{3}{2}y < 6$

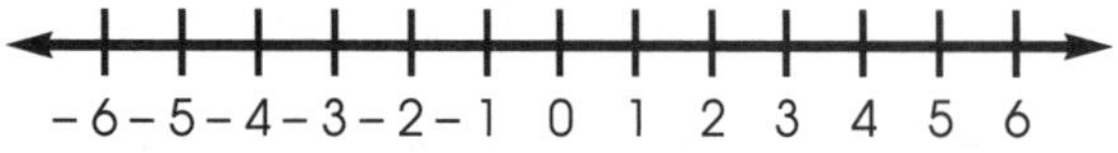

6. $^{-}26m \geq 13$

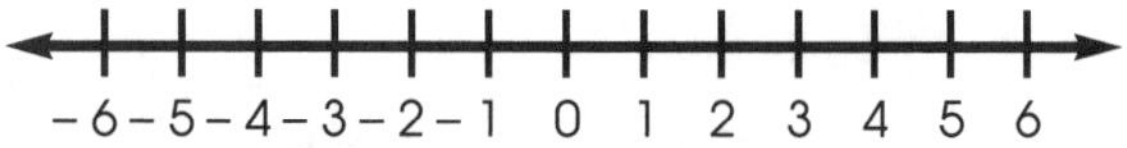

7. $^{-}4 \geq \frac{2}{3}x$

8. $^{-}2c < 2$

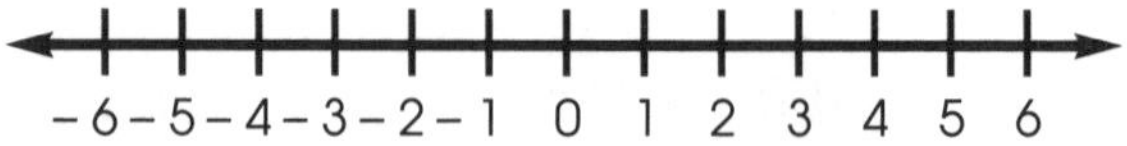

9. $^{-}3a \leq {^{-}9}$

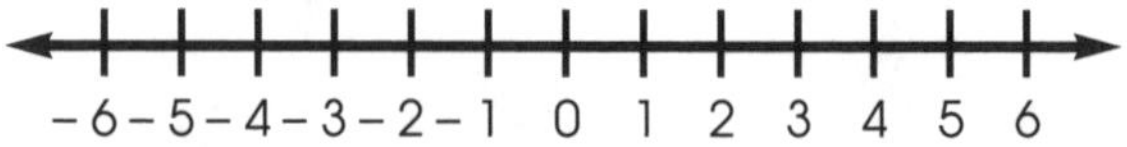

10. $-\frac{3}{4}x \geq {^{-}3}$

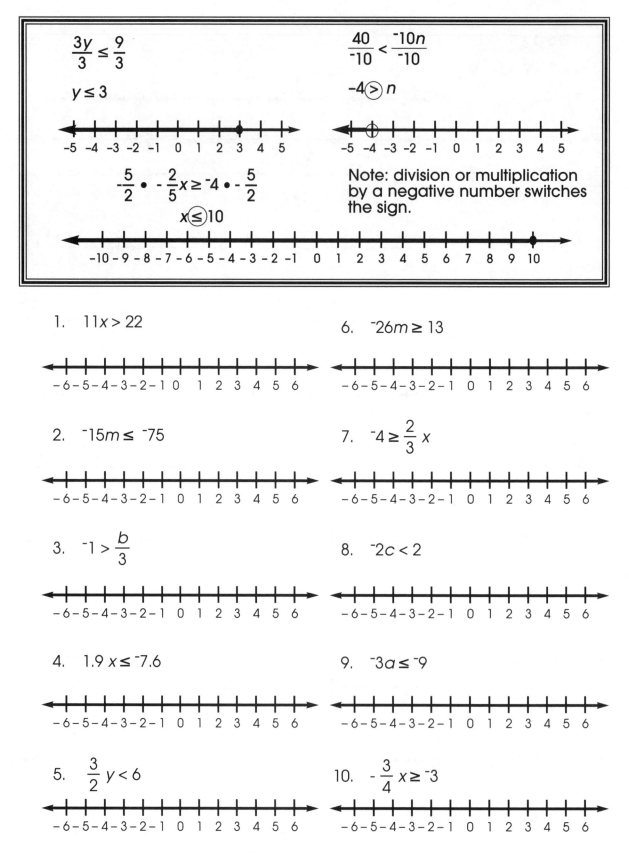

Name ______________________________ Date ______________________________

Mixed Practice: Solving One-Step Inequalities

1. $a + 8 > 16$

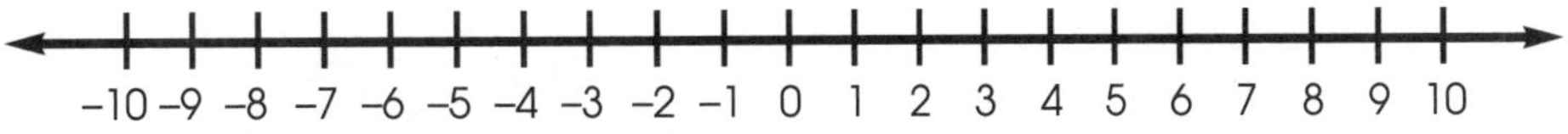

2. $^{-}7\frac{3}{5} \ge z - -\frac{1}{15}$

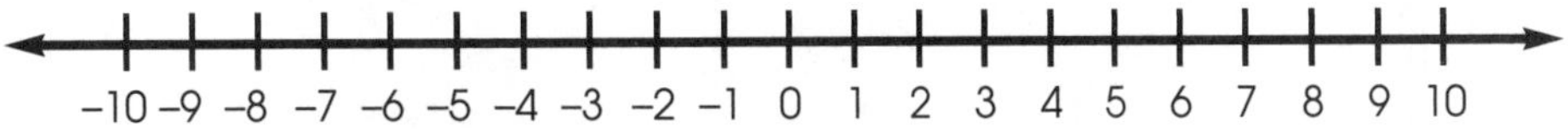

3. $^{-}28 < {}^{-}4x$

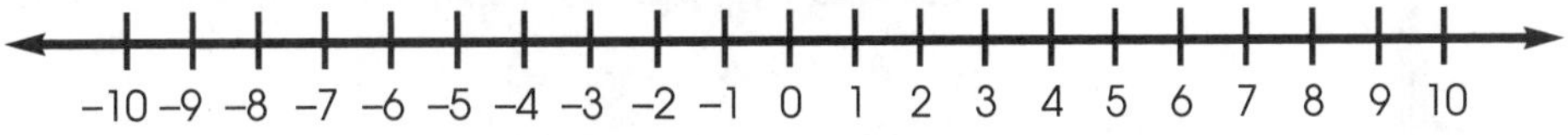

4. $^{-}28.5 \le c + {}^{-}19.6$

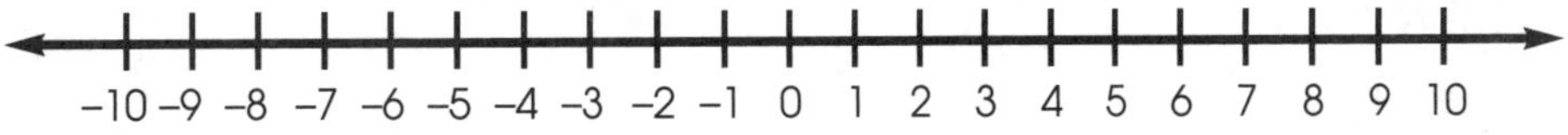

5. $\frac{^{-}4y}{3} > {}^{-}6$

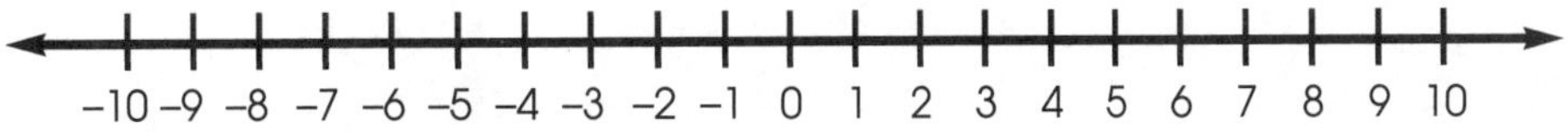

6. $6.3x < 7.56$

7. $-\frac{b}{3} \ge 3$

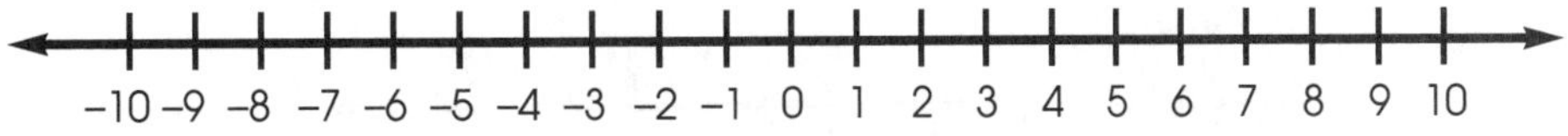

8. $^{-}18.2 < g - 13.7$

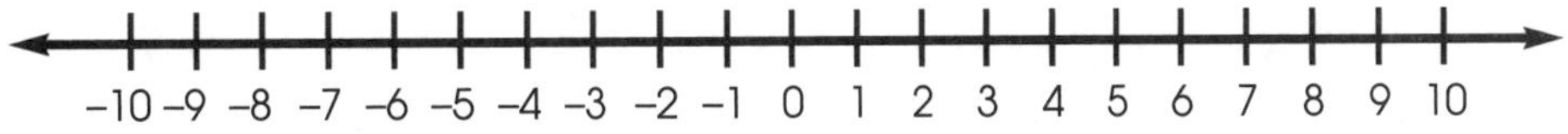

9. $b + 3\frac{1}{4} > {}^{-}2\frac{1}{8}$

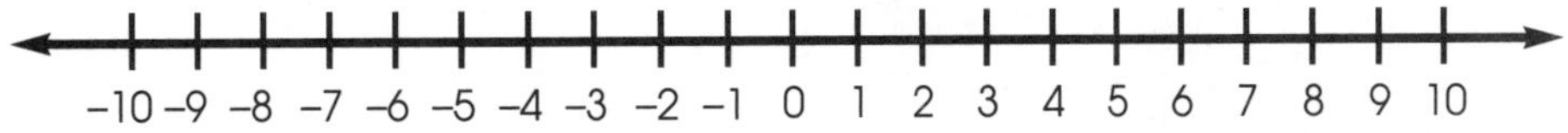

10. $\frac{z}{2} \le {}^{-}3$

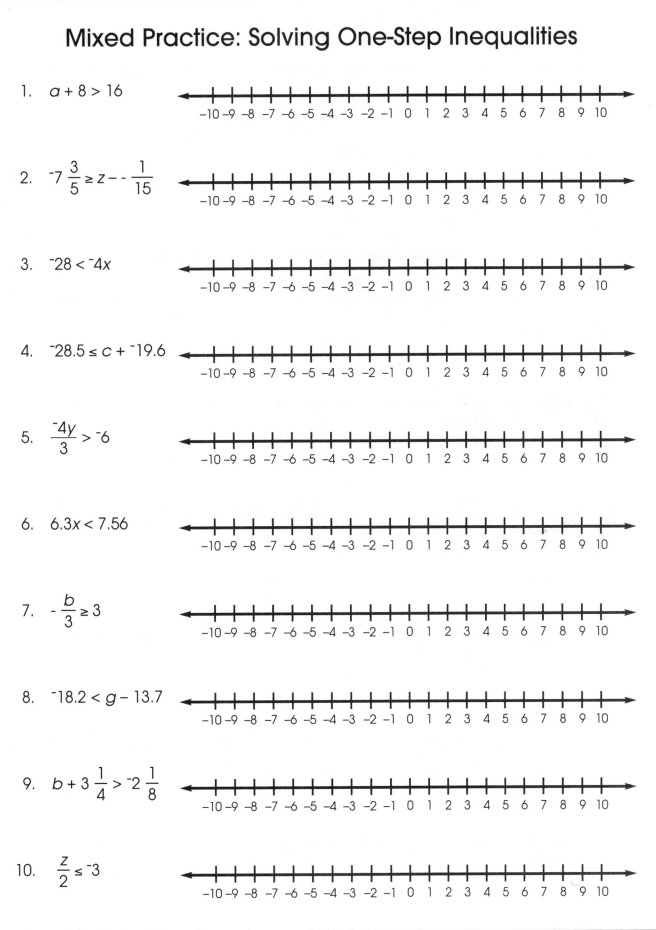

Name ______________________ Date ______________________

Solving Inequalities with More than One Operation

$$^{-}14x + 8 \le 64$$

$$^{-}14x + 8 - 8 \le 64 - 8$$

$$\frac{^{-}14x}{^{-}14} + 8 \le \frac{56}{^{-}14}$$

$$x \ge {^{-}4}$$

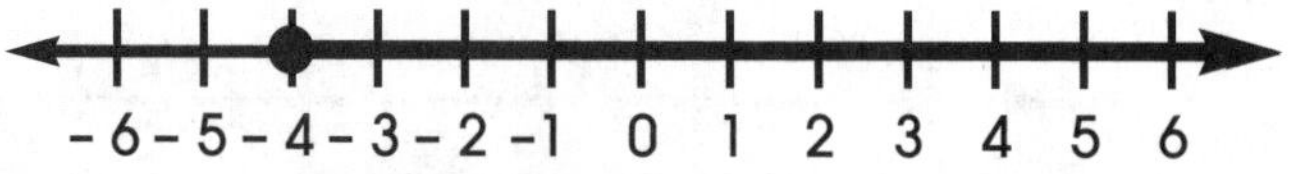

1. $7x - 1 < 20$

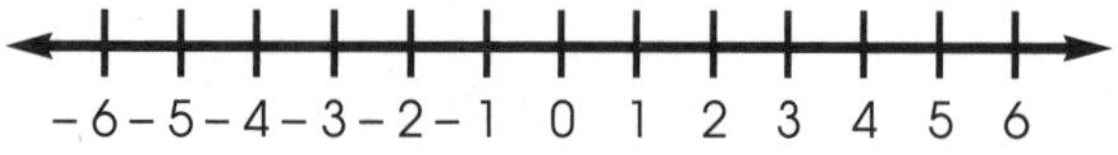

2. $^{-}4 + 2z \ge {^{-}8}$

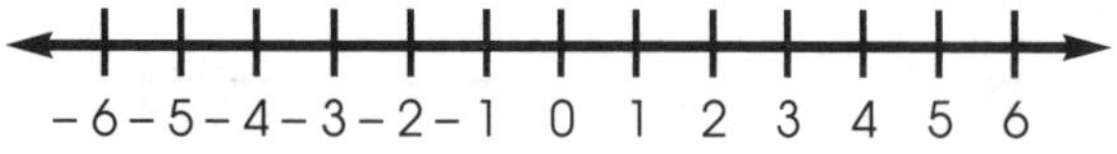

3. $^{-}6x - 9 \ge {^{-}3}$

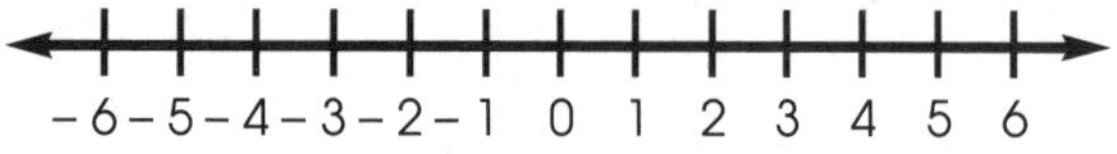

4. $4(2b - 3) \ge 36$

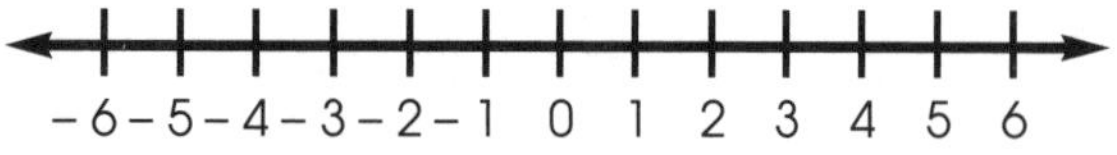

5. $7 < 5x - 8$

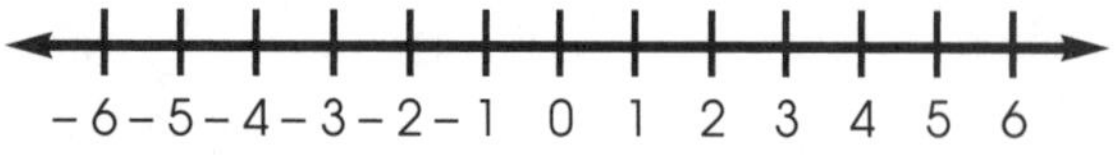

6. $^{-}17 > -7x - 45$

7. $^{-}5(2t - 1) \le 5$

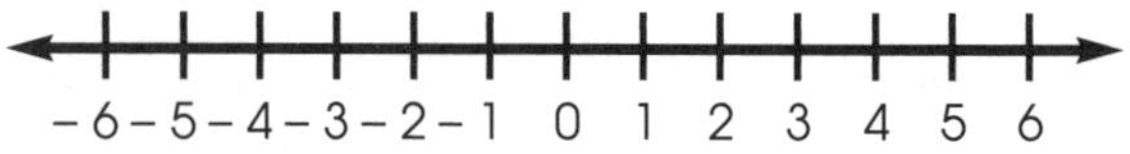

8. $8 - 4x > {^{-}12}$

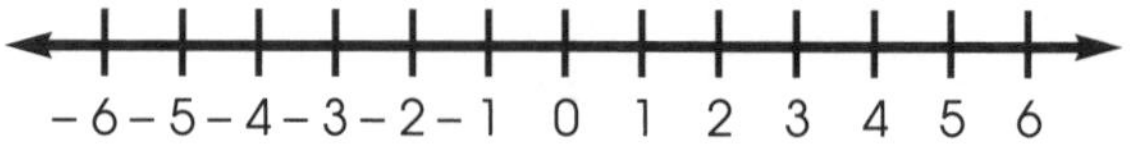

9. $^{-}2(2x - 1) \ge {^{-}9}$

10. $41.56 < 6.3 - {^{-}8.2x}$

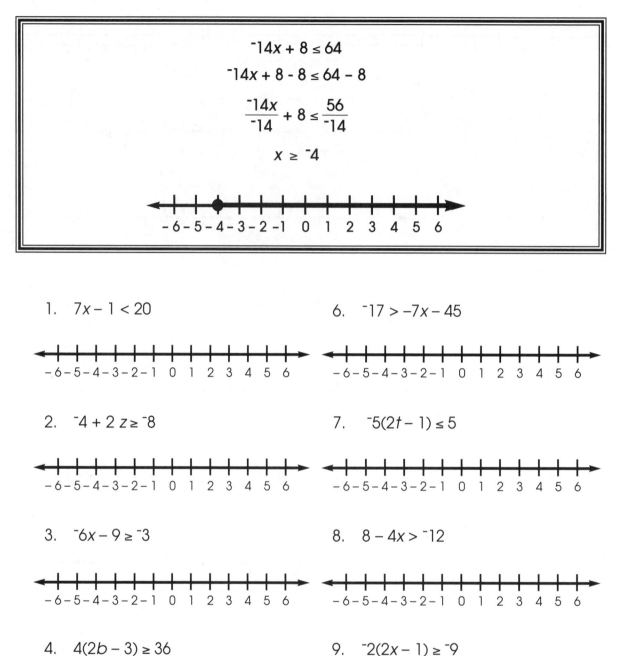

Name ________________________ Date ________________________

Solving Inequalities with Variables on Both Sides

$$^-2a + 11 < a - 1$$
$$^-2a + 2a + 11 < a + 2a - 1$$
$$11 < 3a - 1$$
$$11 + 1 < 3a - 1 + 1$$
$$\frac{12}{3} < \frac{3a}{3}$$
$$4 < a$$

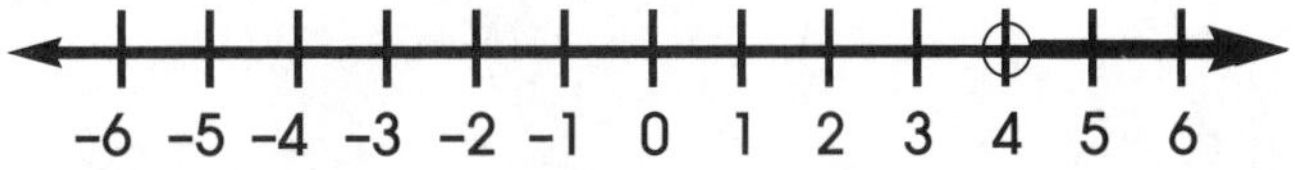

1. $4c + 1 < {}^-(5 + 2c)$

2. $2 - n > 2n + 11$

3. $2(3x - 5) > 2x + 6$

4. $^-2(4y - 21) \leq 12y - 16 + 9y$

5. $n - 3n \geq {}^-4n - 7$

6. $10(x + 2) > {}^-2(6 - 9x)$

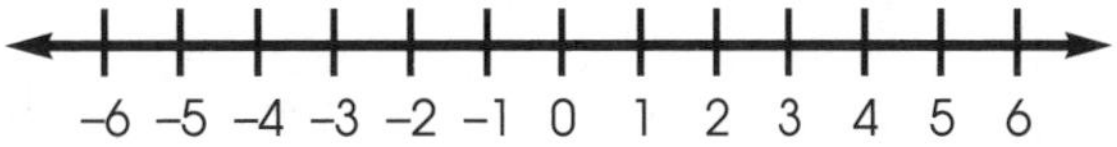

7. $11 + 3({}^-8 + 5x) < 16x - 8$

8. $12\ (2x + 3) \geq 3(9 + 7x)$

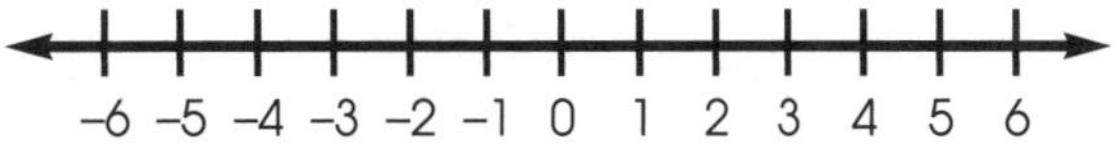

9. $35 - 18x > {}^-8(x + 3x)$

10. $12x + {}^-2(x + 5) < 3x(5 + 2) + 45$

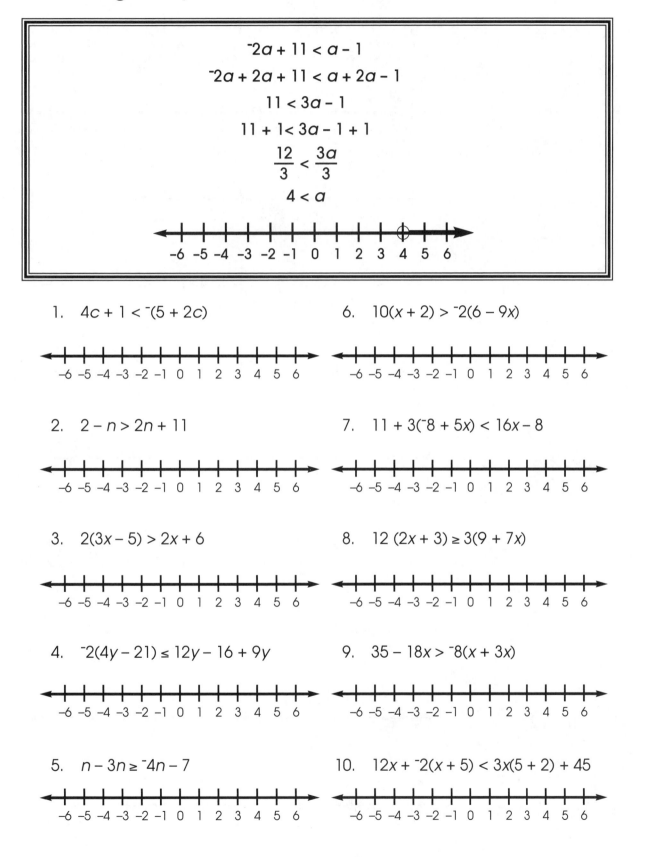

0-7424-1787-5 *Pre-Algebra*

Name ______________________________ Date ______________________________

Mixed Practice: Solving Multi-Step Inequalities

1. $32.4 \geq {}^{-}6c$

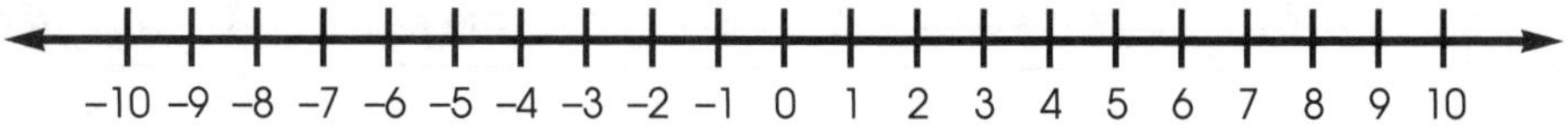

2. $x - {}^{-}15 \leq 9$

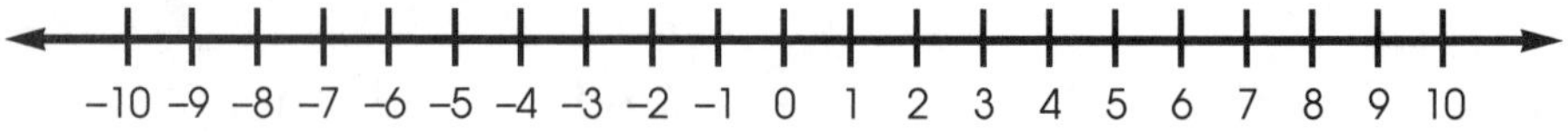

3. $-\frac{2}{3}b > {}^{-}6$

4. ${}^{-}18 + d > {}^{-}11$

5. $6(2z + 3) \leq {}^{-}54$

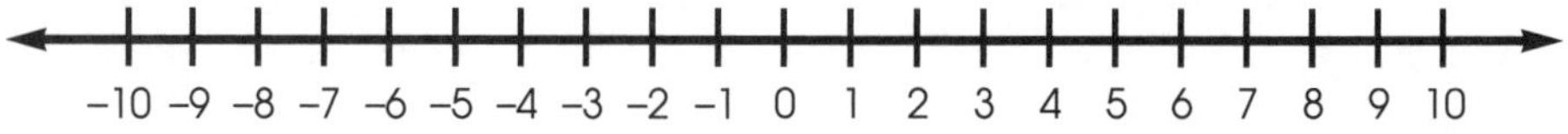

6. $8y - 15 < 27 + 2y$

7. $162 > {}^{-}3a(5 + 1)$

8. ${}^{-}6(5x + 8) \geq 2(8 - 7x)$

9. ${}^{-}40 \leq 8(2t - 2)$

10. $5x(2 - 3) < 3x + 62$

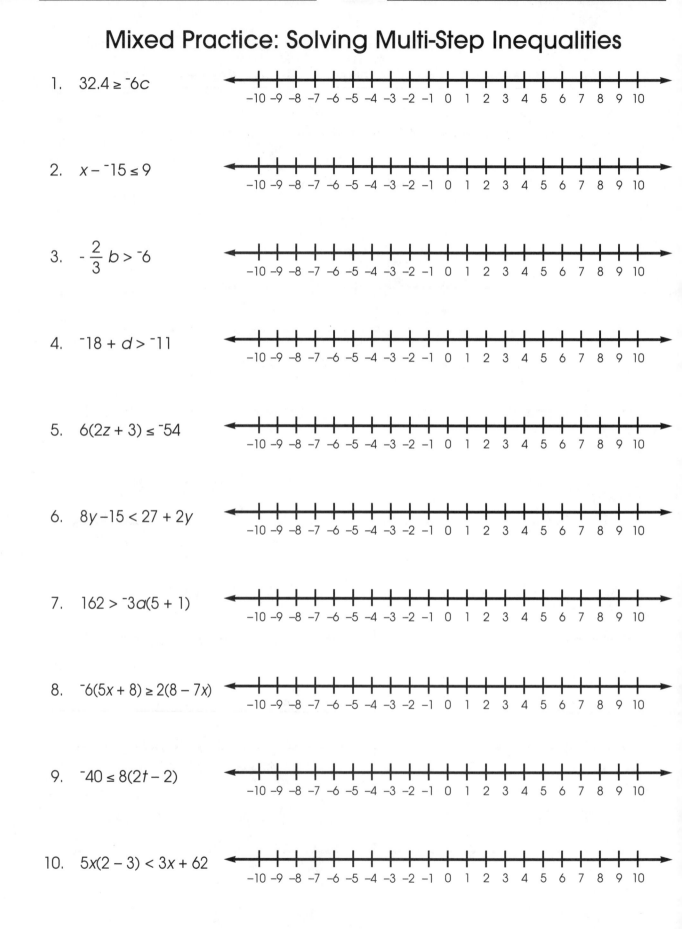

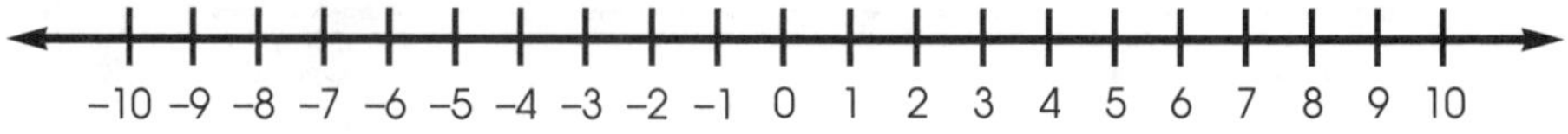

0-7424-1787-5 *Pre-Algebra*

Name ______________________ Date ______________________

More Practice with Inequalities

1. $9x - 8 + x < 16 + 4x$

2. $15y \geq {}^{-}45$

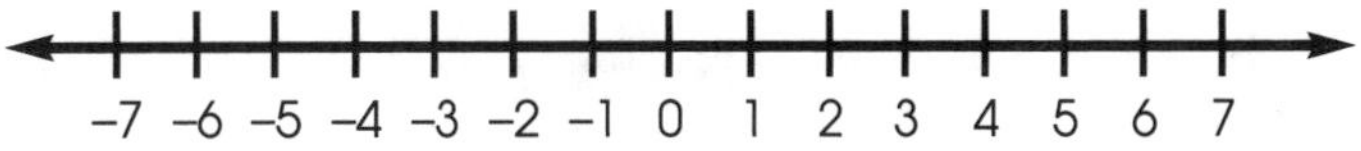

3. $69 > c + 71$

4. $17 + 11n - 13 \leq 4(n + 1) + 2n$

5. $8(2 + x) > 3(x - 3)$

6. ${}^{-}4(3x + 2) \geq 40$

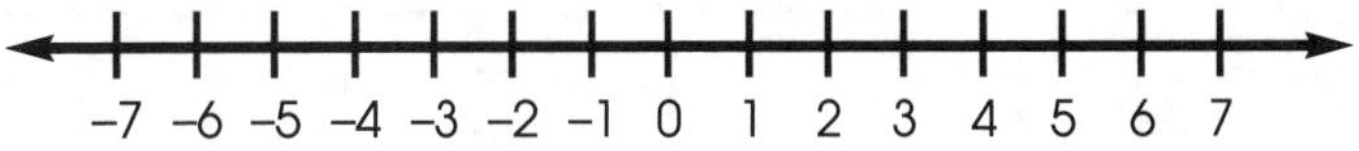

7. $\frac{5}{3} < \frac{2}{3}x - 1$

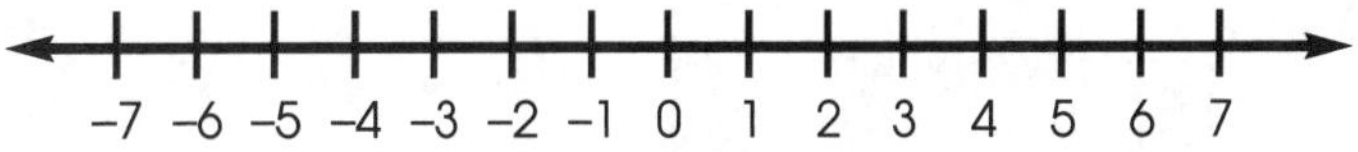

8. $3n - 4(2n - 5) + n + 4 \geq 0$

9. $18c + 11 - 26c < -3c(5 + 1) - 59$

10. $8a - 2(2a + 5) \leq 2a(9 + 1) + 54$

0-7424-1787-5 *Pre-Algebra*

Name ______________________________ Date ______________________________

A Logical Conclusion

Mike, Dale, Paul and Charlie are the athletic director, quarterback, pitcher and goalie, but not necessarily in that order. From these five statements, identify the man in each position.

1. Mike and Dale were both at the ballpark when the rookie pitcher played his first game.

2. Both Paul and the athletic director had played on the same team in high school with the goalie.

3. The athletic director, who scouted Charlie, is planning to watch Mike during his next game.

4. Mike doesn't know Dale.

5. One of these men is a quarterback.

	Quarterback	Goalie	Pitcher	Athletic Director
Mike				
Dale				
Paul				
Charlie				

Name ______________________ Date ______________________

Plotting Points

Connect each of the following ordered points.

$(x, y) = (0, {}^{-}1)$

vertical move ⟹ down one

horizontal move ⟹ no move

"Ancient History"

Start at (0, $^{-}1$)

(1, $^{-}1$)
(1, $^{-}3$)
(3, $^{-}3$)
(3, $^{-}1$)
(5,0)
(8,0)
(7,1)
(9,0)
(8,2)
(5,1)
(4,3)
(3,4)
(2,3)
(1, 4)
(0, 3)
($^{-}1$, 4)
($^{-}2$, 3)
($^{-}3$, 4)
($^{-}4$, 3)
($^{-}5$, 1)
($^{-}8$, 2)
($^{-}5$, 0)
($^{-}3$, $^{-}1$)
($^{-}3$, $^{-}3$)
($^{-}1$, $^{-}3$)
($^{-}1$, $^{-}1$)
(0, $^{-}1$)
End

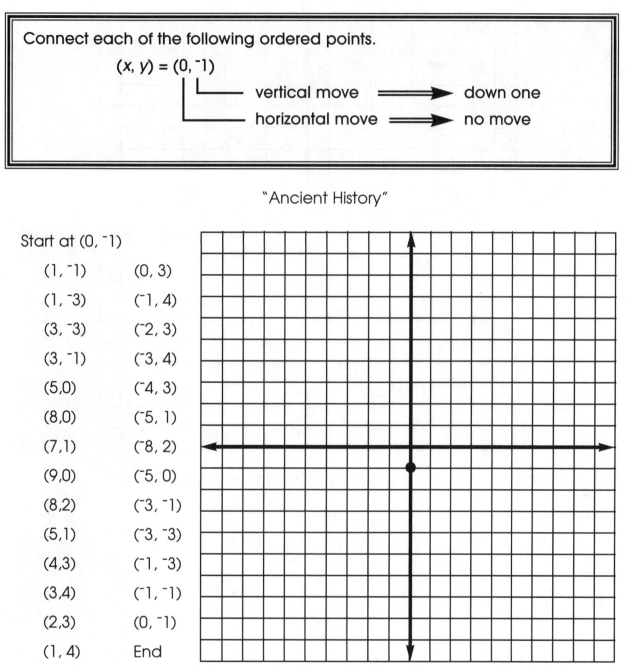

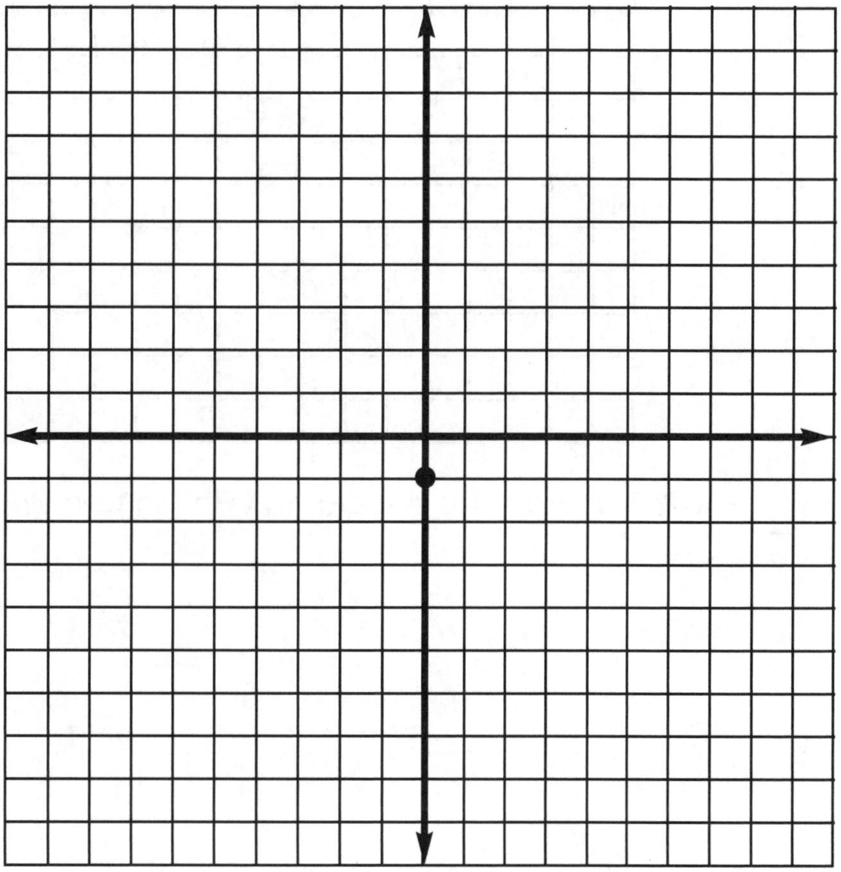

Name ____________________ Date ____________________

Coordinates and Graphing

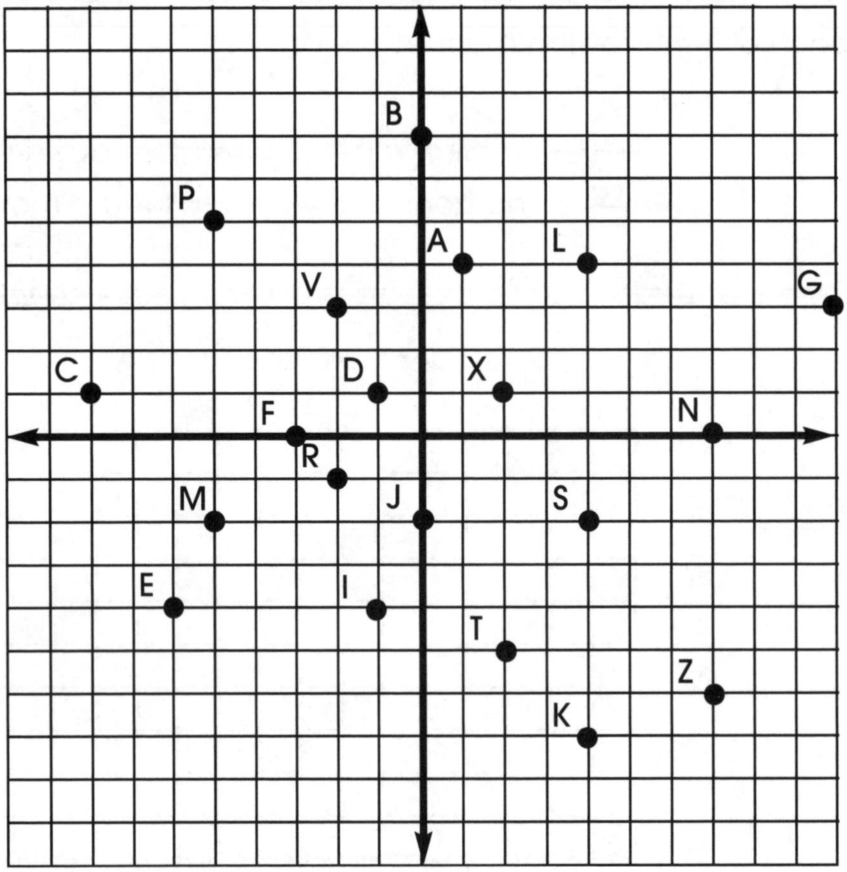

Find the coordinates associated with the following points.

1. A
2. K
3. E
4. P
5. T
6. C
7. B
8. S
9. D
10. N

Find the letter associated with each pair of coordinates.

11. $(2, 1)$
12. $(^-1, ^-4)$
13. $(10, 3)$
14. $(7, ^-6)$
15. $(^-2, ^-1)$
16. $(^-2, 3)$
17. $(^-3, 0)$
18. $(4, 4)$
19. $(^-5, ^-2)$
20. $(0, ^-2)$

0-7424-1787-5 *Pre-Algebra*

Name ______________________ Date ______________________

Solving for y

Solve each equation for y. Then use the given values for x to find the corresponding values for y. Write answers as ordered pairs

$y - 4 = 3x$
$y - 4 + 4 = 3x + 4$
$y = 3x + 4$

Let $x = {}^{-}2, 0, 1$

Solve for y

a. $y = 3 \bullet {}^{-}2 + 4$
$y = {}^{-}6 + 4$
$y = {}^{-}2$
$({}^{-}2, {}^{-}2)$

b. $y = 3 \bullet 0 + 4$
$y = 0 + 4$
$y = 4$
$(0, 4)$

c. $y = 3 \bullet 1 + 4$
$y = 3 + 4$
$y = 7$
$(1, 7)$

1. $y = 5x$ Let $x = {}^{-}3, 0, 2$

Note: This equation is already in the form of $y = ...$

2. $2x + y = 9$ Let $x = {}^{-}1, 0, 5$

3. $-x = y + 3$ Let $x = {}^{-}3, 0, 4$

4. $y = \frac{2}{3}x + 1$ Let $x = {}^{-}4, 0, 3$

5. $8x + y = 1$ Let $x = {}^{-}2, 0, 1$

6. $y - 1 = {}^{-}3x$ Let $x = {}^{-}3, 0, 2$

7. $2 = y - \frac{1}{3}x$ Let $x = {}^{-}9, 0, 6$

8. $7x - y = {}^{-}8$ Let $x = {}^{-}1, 0, {}^{-}3$

Name ______________________ Date ______________________

Graphing Linear Equations by Plotting Points

Solve each equation for y. Then choose 3 values for x and find the corresponding values for y. Graph the 3 ordered pairs and draw the line that contains them.

$$5x + y = {}^{-}1$$
$$5x - 5x + y = {}^{-}1 - 5x$$
$$y = -5x - 1$$

x	y
$^{-}1$	4
0	$^{-}1$
2	$^{-}11$

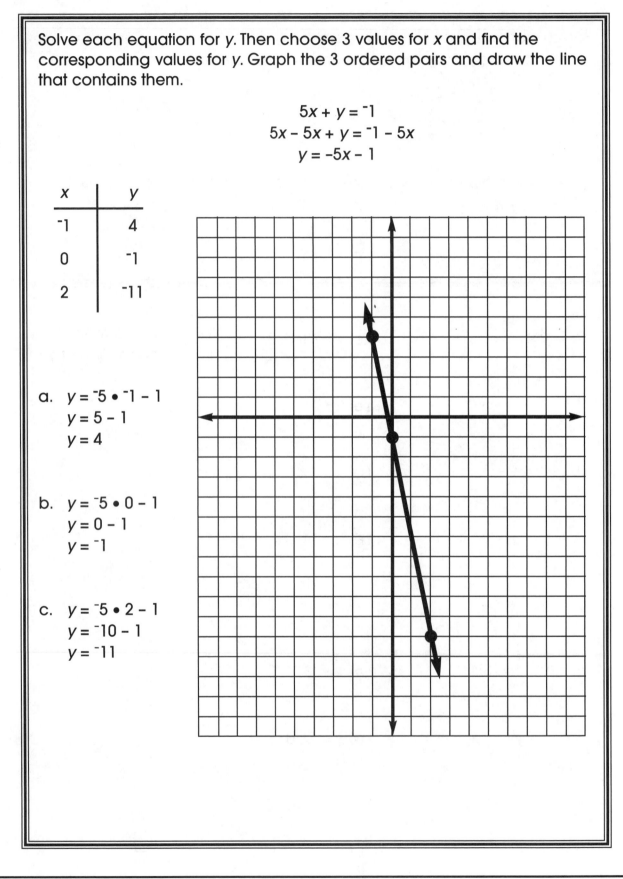

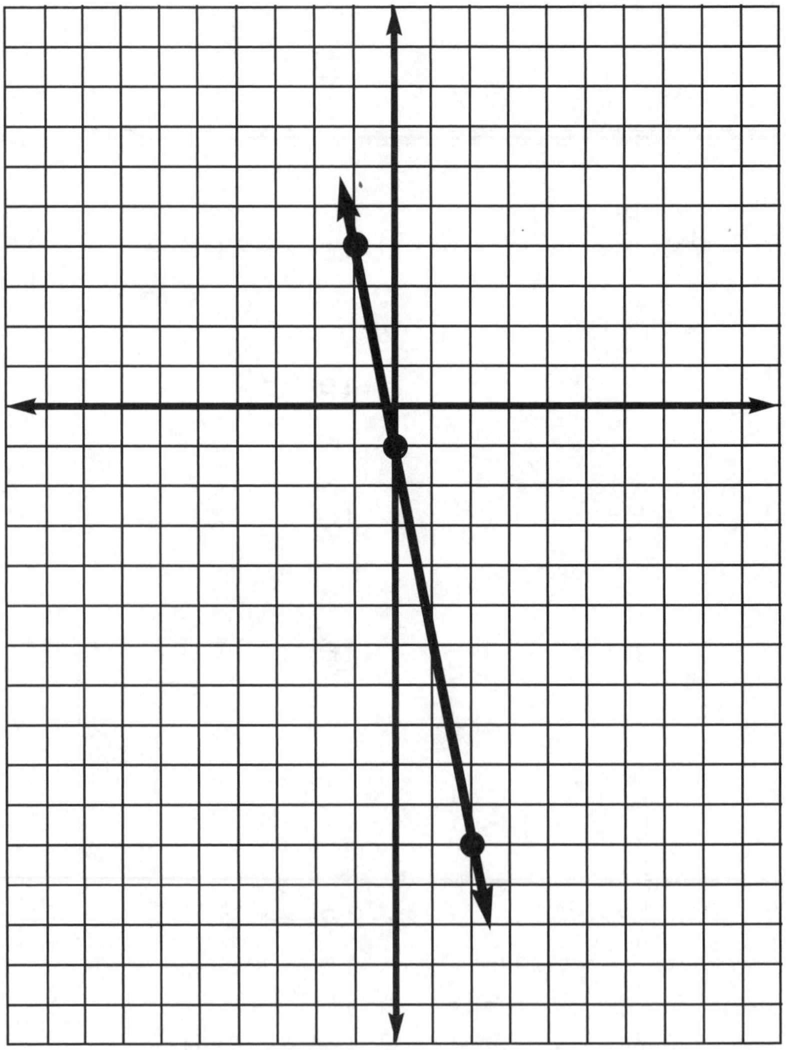

a. $y = {}^{-}5 \bullet {}^{-}1 - 1$
$y = 5 - 1$
$y = 4$

b. $y = {}^{-}5 \bullet 0 - 1$
$y = 0 - 1$
$y = {}^{-}1$

c. $y = {}^{-}5 \bullet 2 - 1$
$y = {}^{-}10 - 1$
$y = {}^{-}11$

Name ______________________ Date ______________________

Graphing Linear Equations by Plotting Points

1. $y = \frac{1}{2}x - 3$

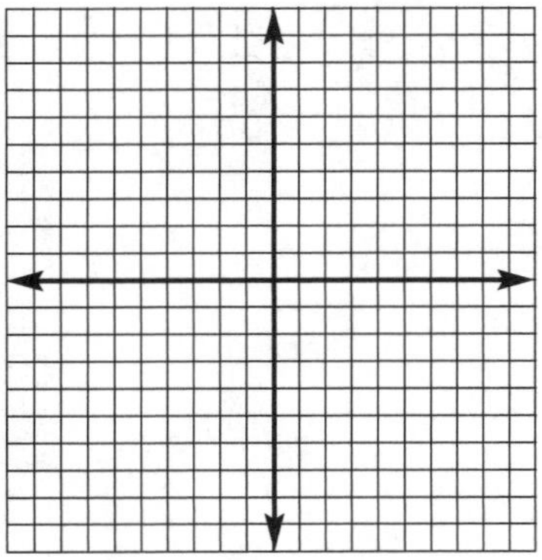

2. $^{-}2x + y = 5$

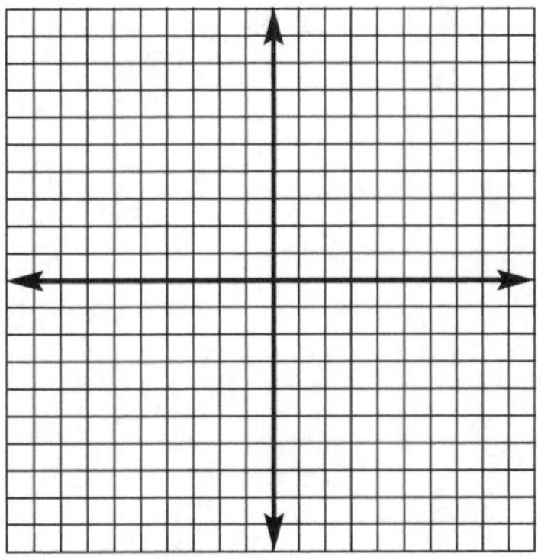

3. $4x + y = {}^{-}7$

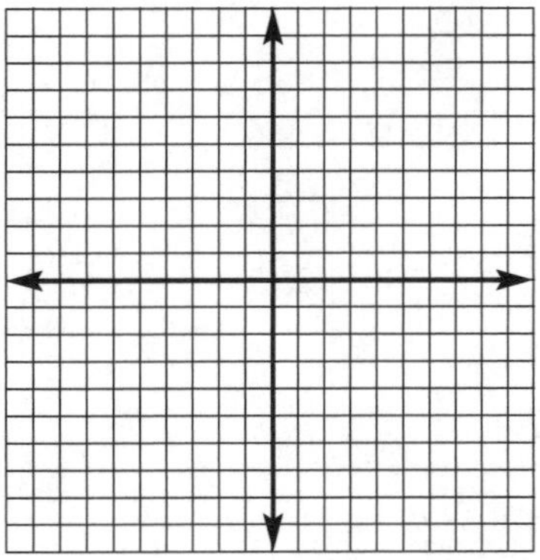

4. $y - 3 = 2x$

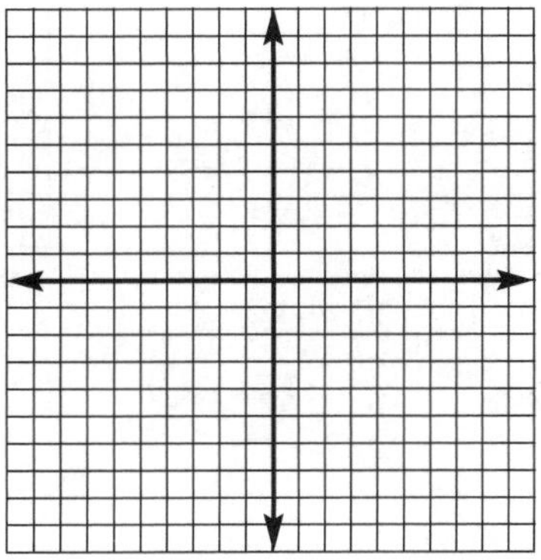

5. $3x + y = 7$

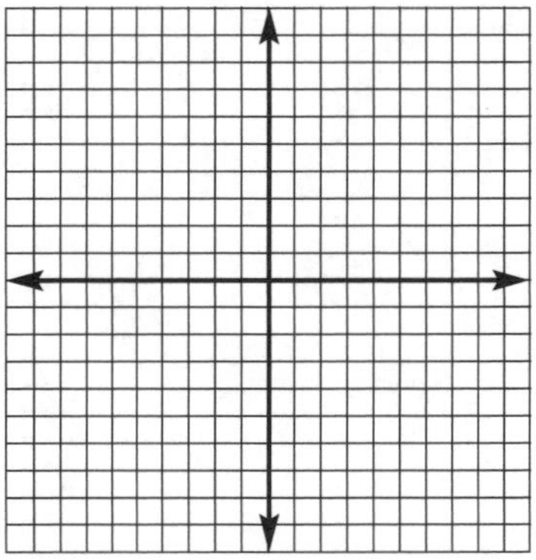

6. $3x - y = {}^{-}2$

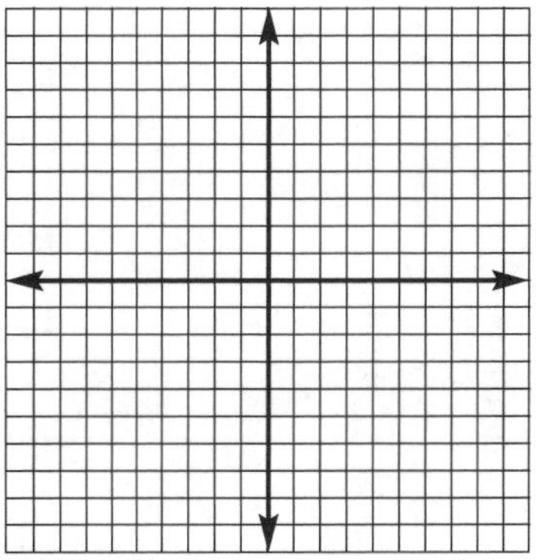

7. $y + 7 = 5x$

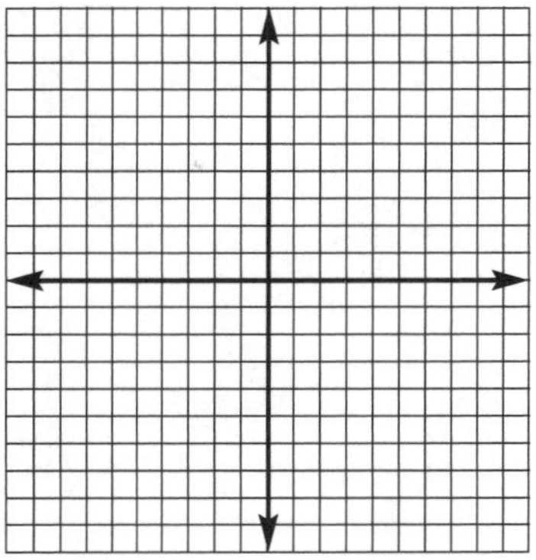

8. $y = \frac{1}{4}x - 2$

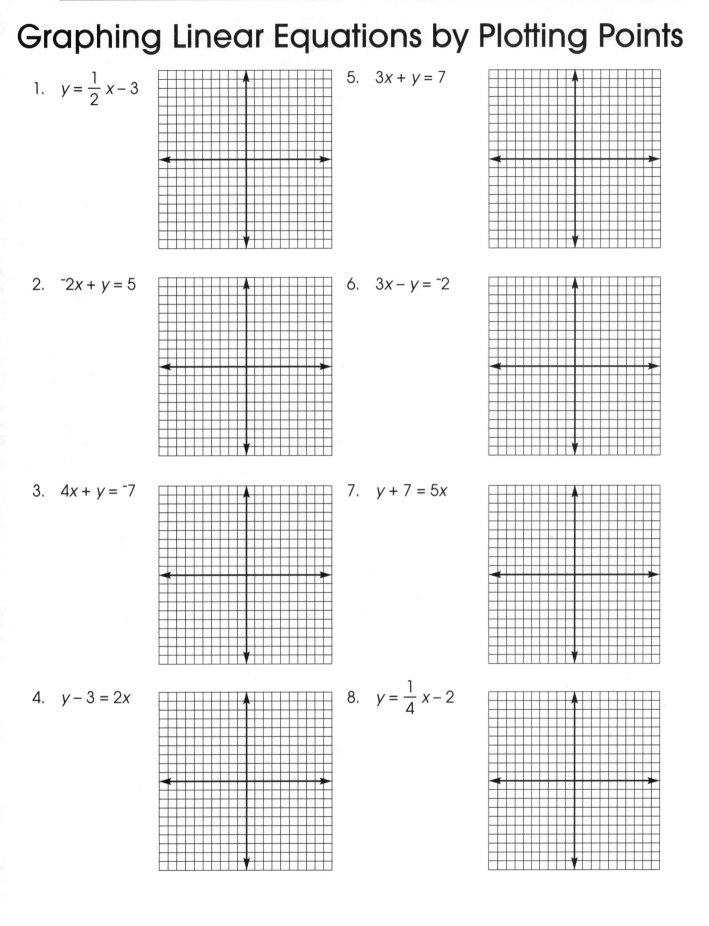

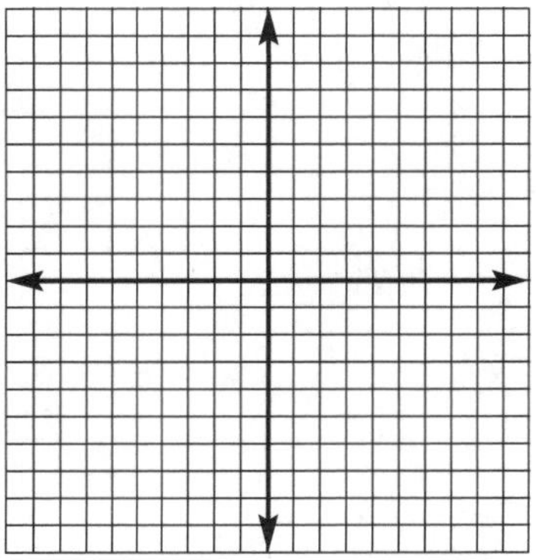

Name ______________________ Date ______________________

Graphing Linear Equations by Plotting Points

9. $\frac{3}{4}x + y = 2$

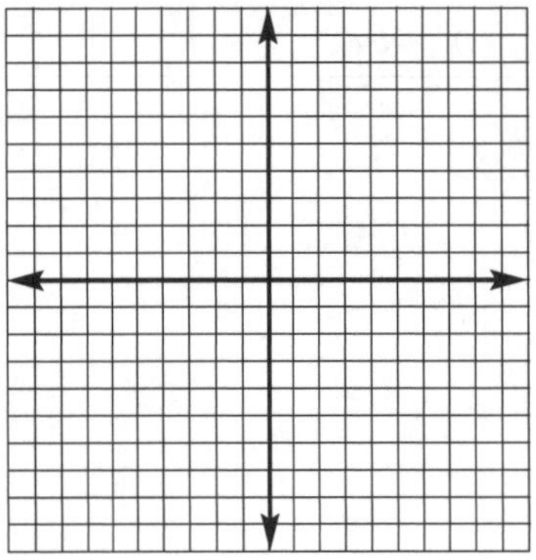

10. $x - y = {}^{-}4$

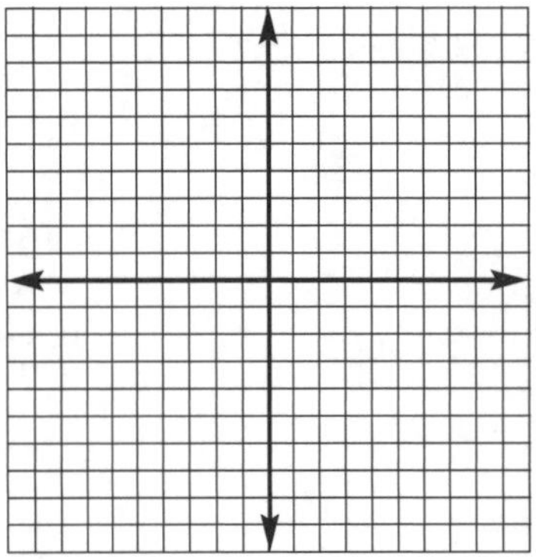

11. ${}^{-}3x + y = {}^{-}4$

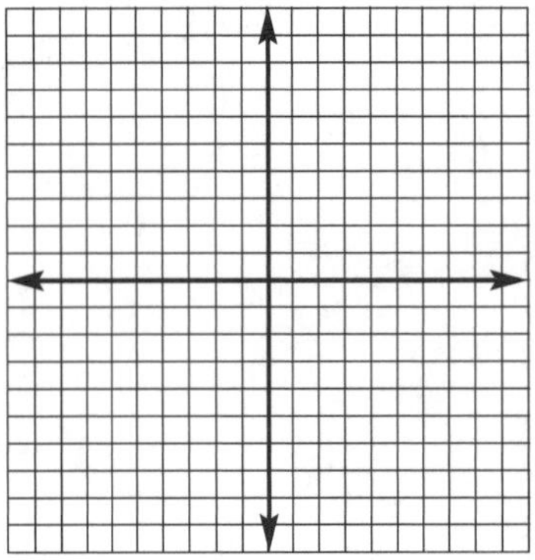

12. $y - x = {}^{-}1$

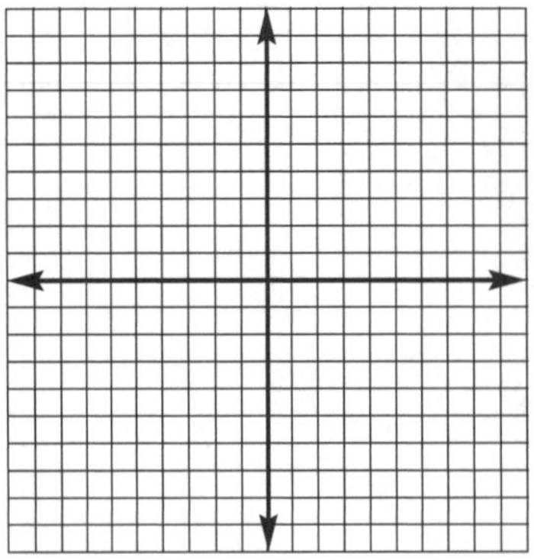

13. $y = -\frac{1}{2}x$

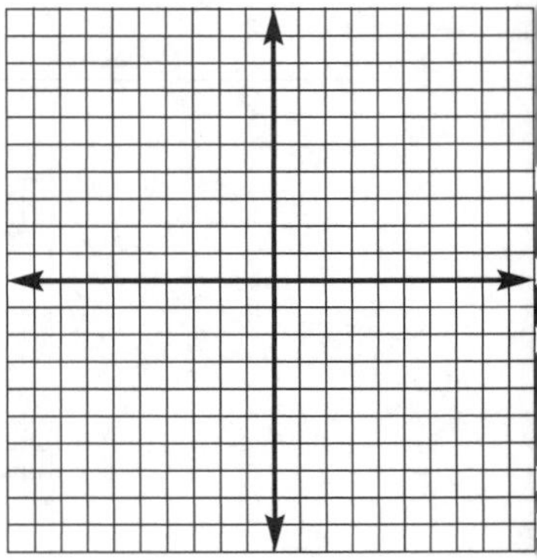

14. $\frac{1}{4}x + y = {}^{-}2$

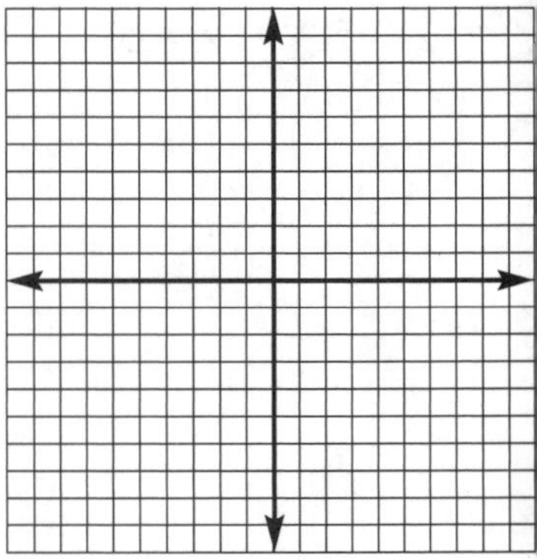

15. $y = {}^{-}4x - 5$

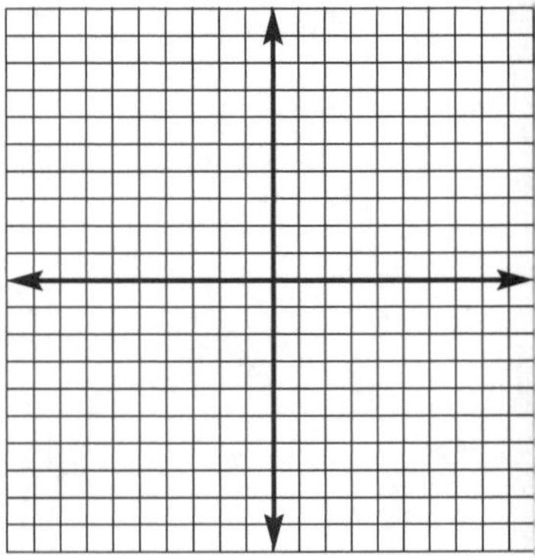

16. $y = {}^{-}2x - 3$

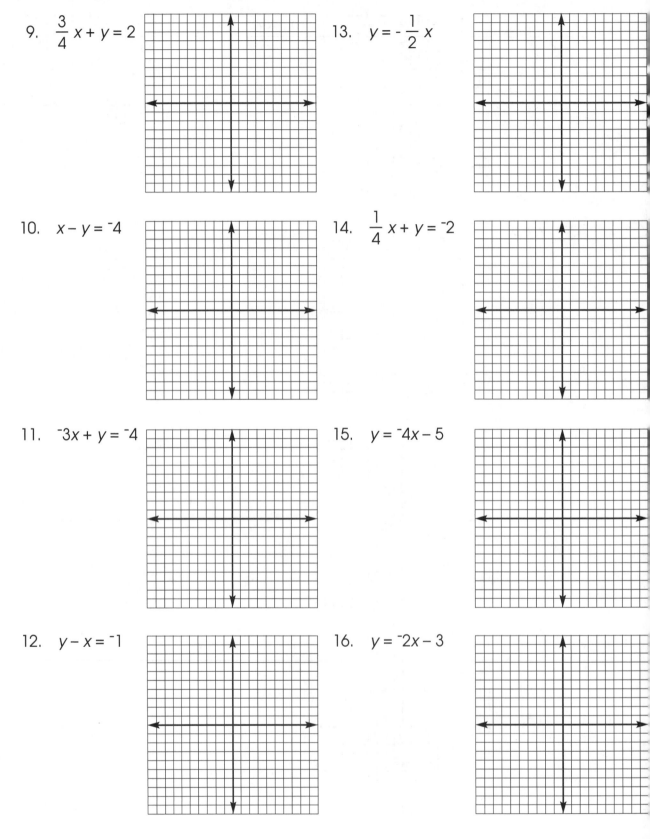

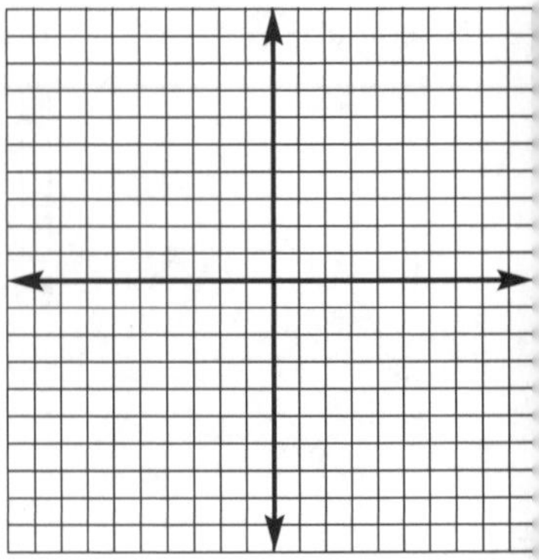

Name ______________________________ Date ______________________________

Finding Slope Using a Graph

Find the slope of the lines passing through the given points.

$$\text{slope} = \frac{\text{change in } y}{\text{change in } x}$$

Choose any 2 points to count the change.

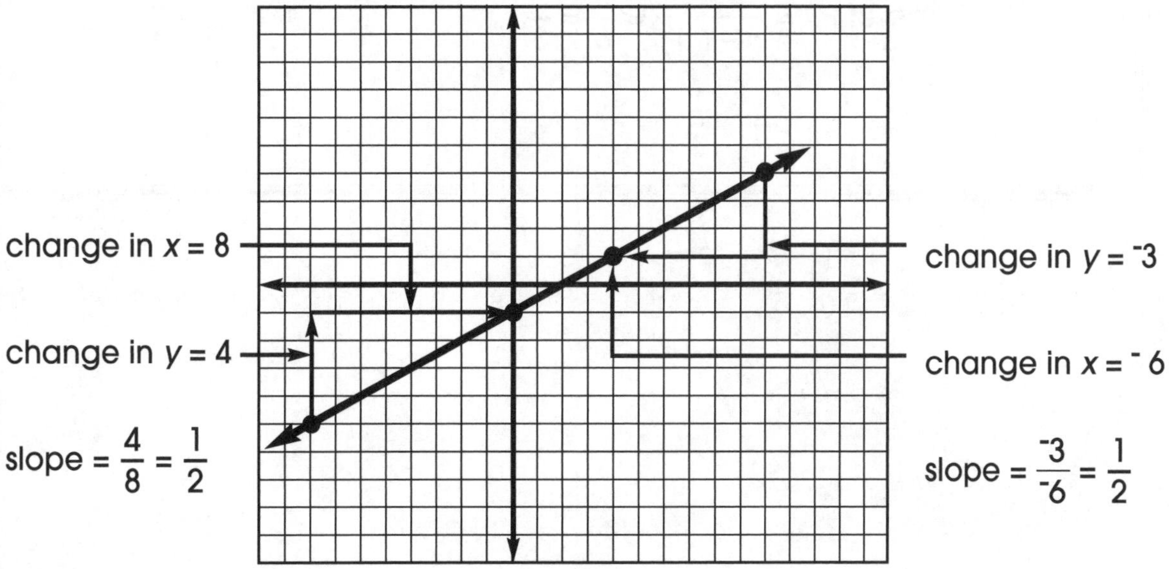

slope is $\frac{1}{2}$

1.

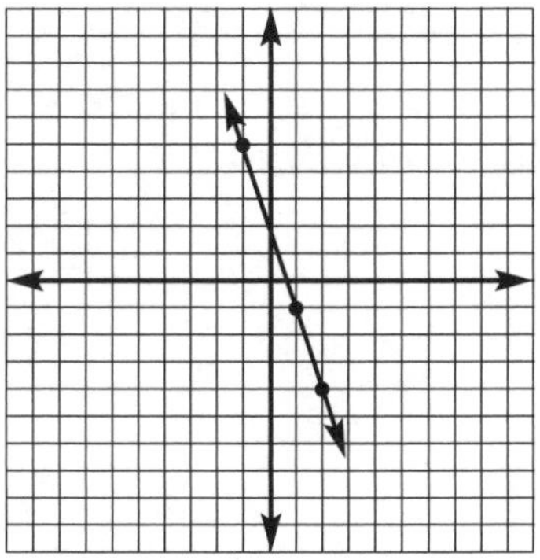

2.

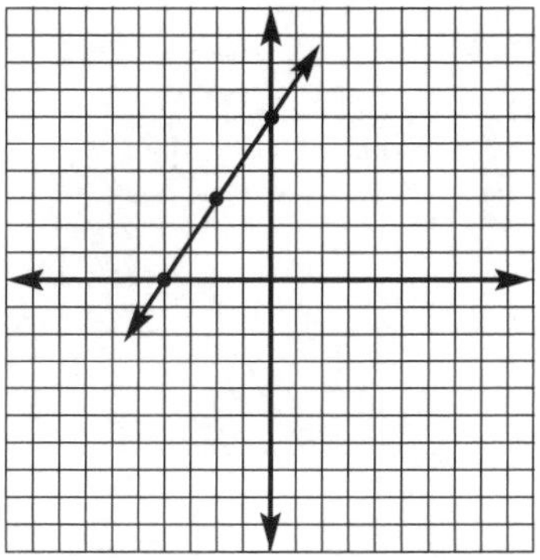

3.

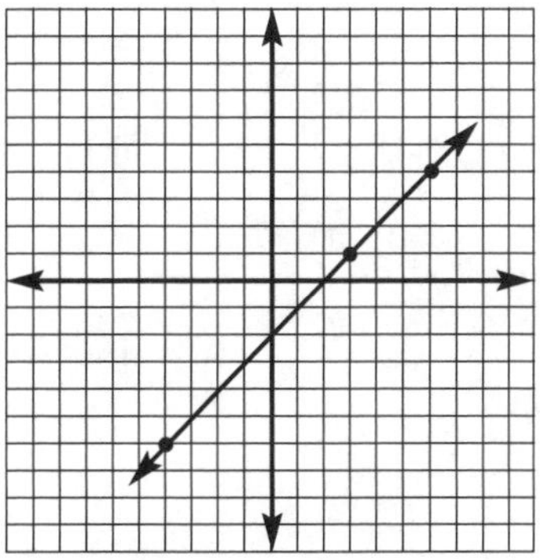

4.

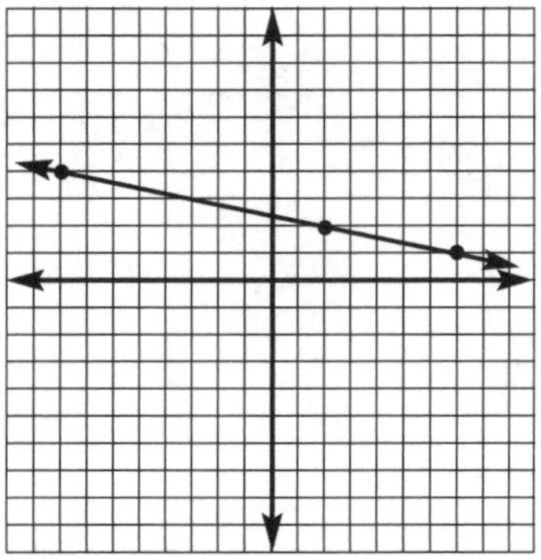

5.

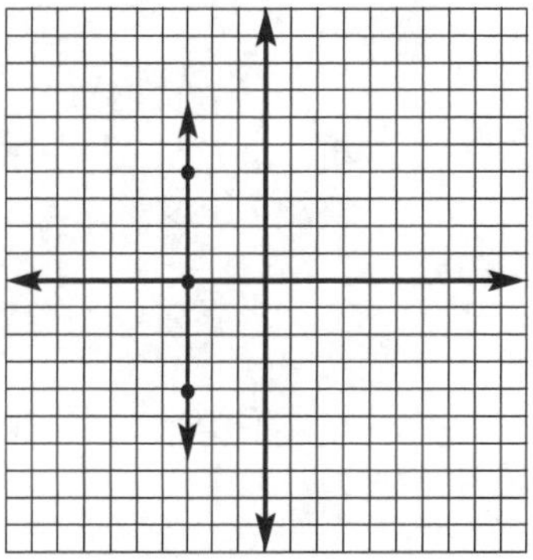

6.

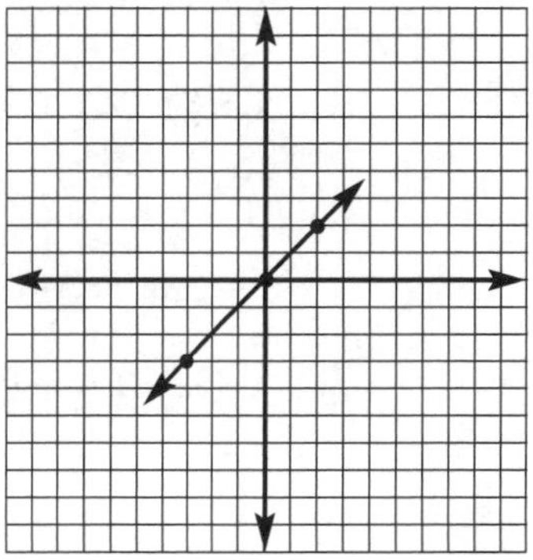

Name ______________________ Date ______________________

Finding Slope Using the Slope Formula

$$\text{slope} = \frac{\text{difference in } y\text{-values}}{\text{difference in } x\text{-values}}$$

P (5, 3) R ($^-1$, 1)

$$\text{Slope of PR} = \frac{3 - 1}{5 - (^-1)} = \frac{2}{6} = \frac{1}{3}$$

$$\text{slope is } \frac{1}{3}$$

1. A ($^-3$, 1) D (4, 5)
2. C (2, 6) F (3, 5)
3. B (0, 8) G (3, 2)
4. J ($^-6$, $^-3$) K ($^-4$, 5)
5. P (9, 4) M (7, 3)
6. Q (0, $^-4$) R (1, $^-6$)
7. L ($^-2$, 6) N (2, $^-3$)
8. S ($^-1$, $^-3$) X (2, $^-6$)
9. T ($^-4$, $^-4$) Z (6, 3)
10. V $(\frac{3}{4}, \frac{3}{2})$ W $(\frac{11}{4}, \frac{5}{2})$
11. U (2, 3) A ($^-2$, 3)
12. C (4, $^-1$) D ($^-2$, 2)
13. Z (3, 5) H (5, 10)
14. J ($^-2$, $^-3$) K (13, 7)

Name ______________________ Date ______________________

Graphing Linear Equations Using Slope

Graph the line that contains the given point and has the given slope.

(2, $^{-}1$), $\frac{2}{3}$

a. Plot point.

b. Locate other points by moving up 2 units and to the right 3 units.

c. Connect the points with a line

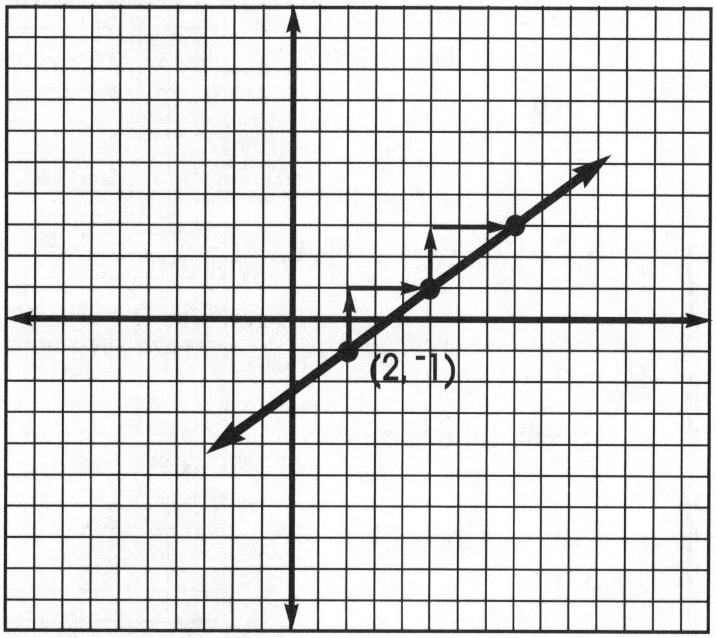

1. ($^{-}5$, $^{-}2$), $-\frac{1}{2}$

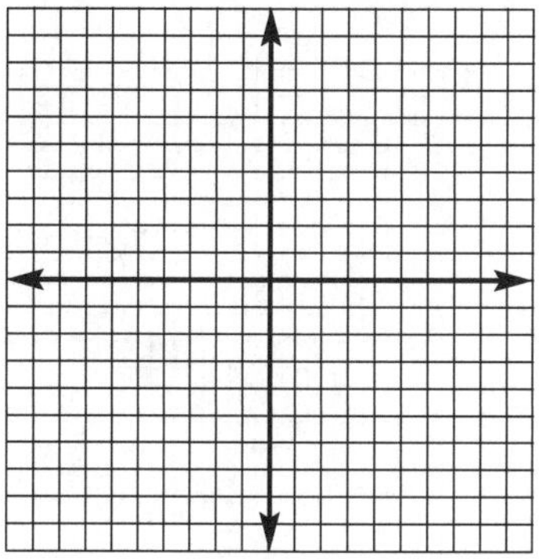

3. (2, $^{-}3$), $\frac{3}{4}$

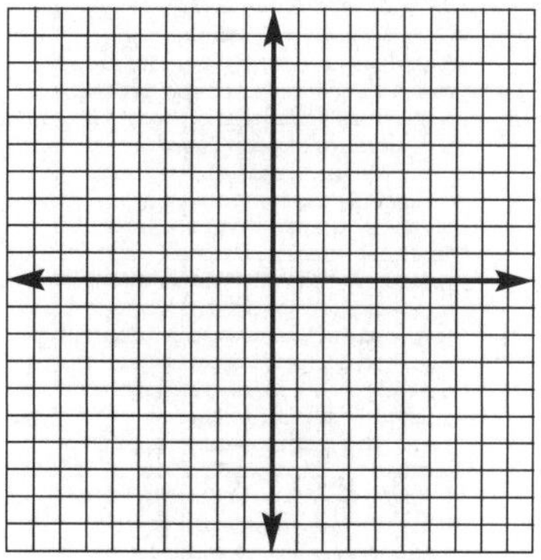

5. ($^{-}1$, $^{-}4$), $-\frac{1}{4}$

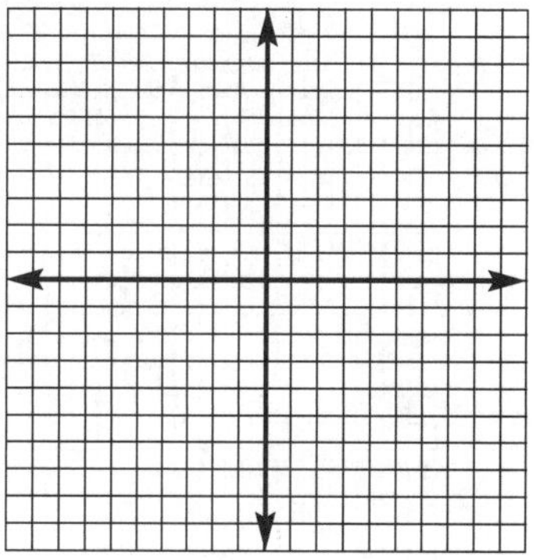

2. (4, 2), 3 (note: $3 = \frac{3}{1}$)

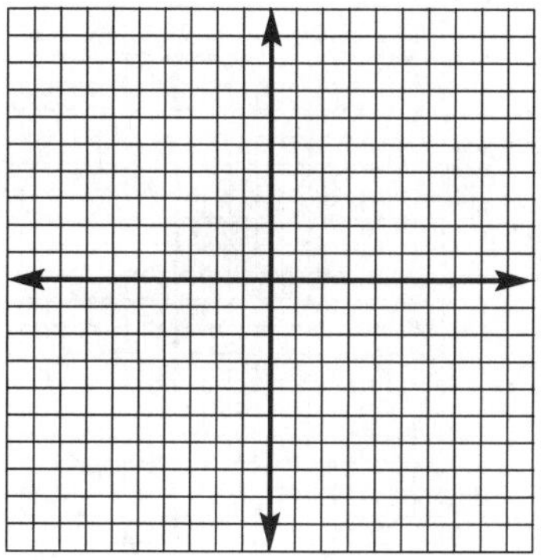

4. (0, 2), $-\frac{5}{2}$

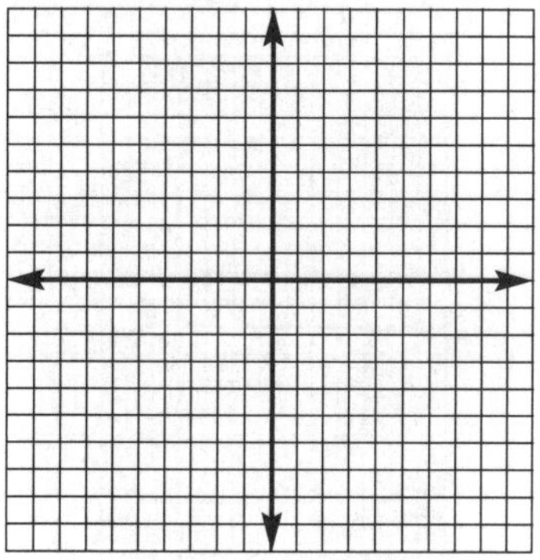

6. (3, $^{-}2$), $^{-}2$

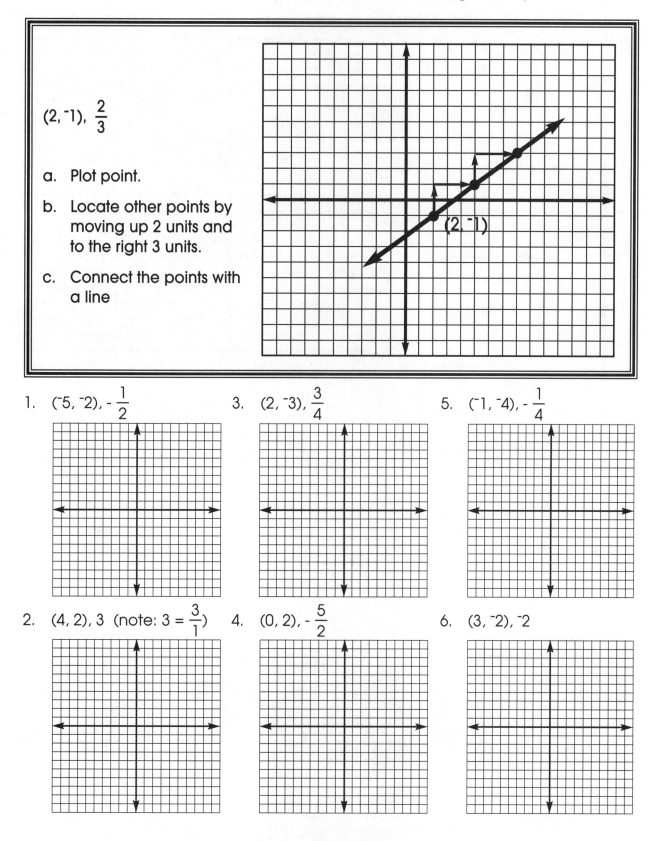

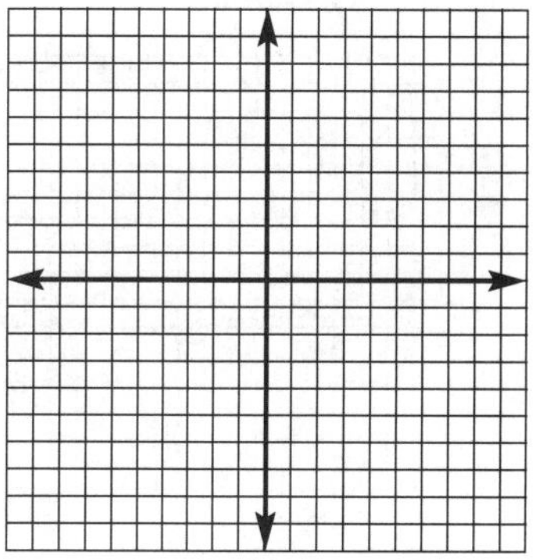

Name ____________________________ Date ____________________________

Graphing Linear Equations Using y-Intercept and Slope

Graph the lines given the equation using the y-intercept and slope.

$y = mx + b$ m = slope
b = y-intercept

$y = \frac{2}{3}x + 2$

m = slope $\frac{2}{3}$

b = y-intercept = (0, 2)

a. Plot y-intercept.

b. Locate other points by using slope.

c. Connect the points with a line

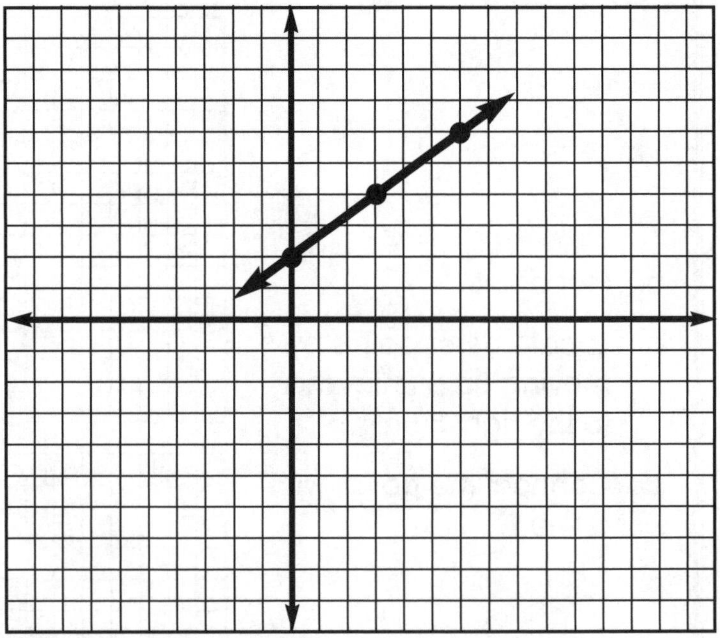

1. $y = \frac{1}{2}x - 1$

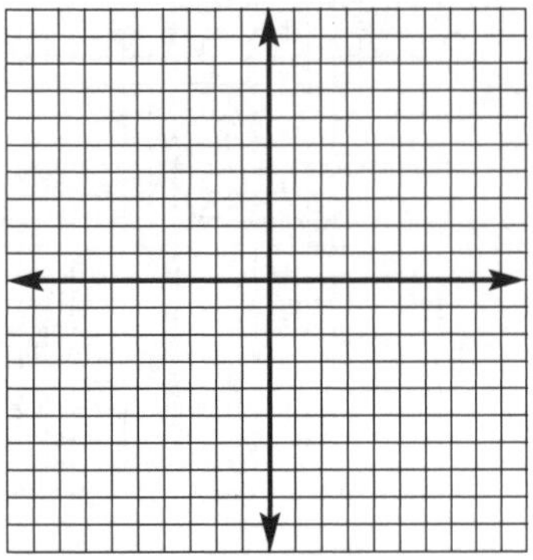

3. $y = -\frac{1}{3}x + 2$

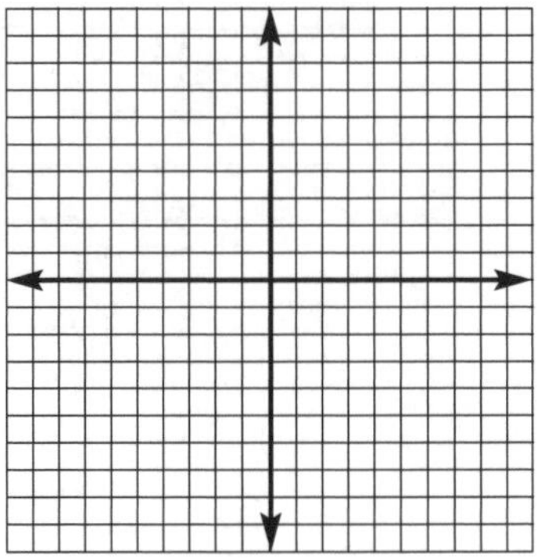

5. $y = -\frac{2}{3}x + 4$

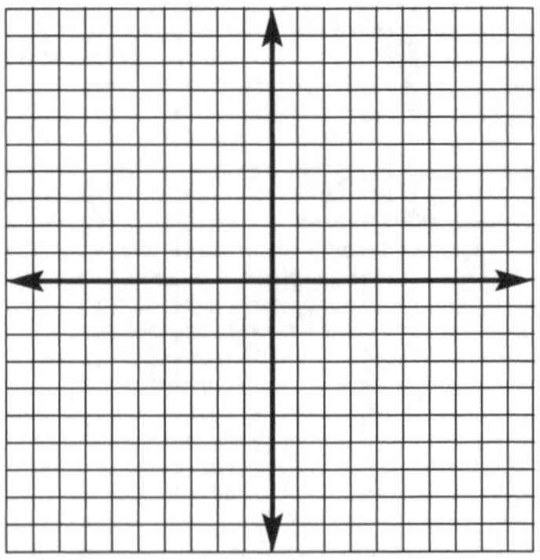

2. $y = 2x + 5$

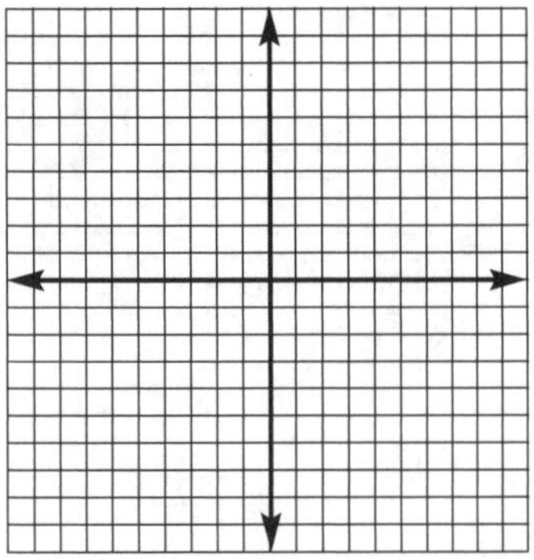

4. $y = {}^{-}3x - 1$

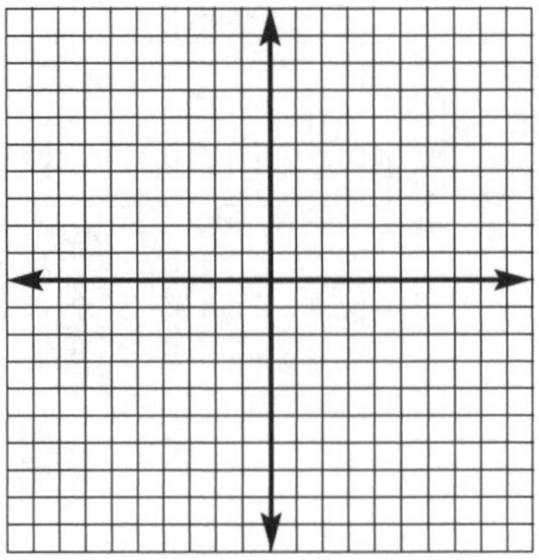

6. $y = x + 3$

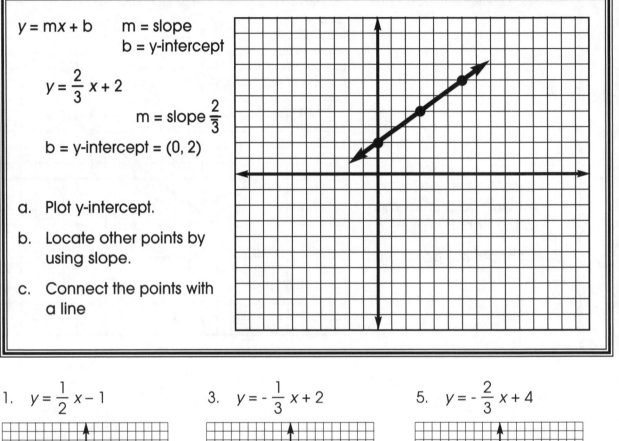

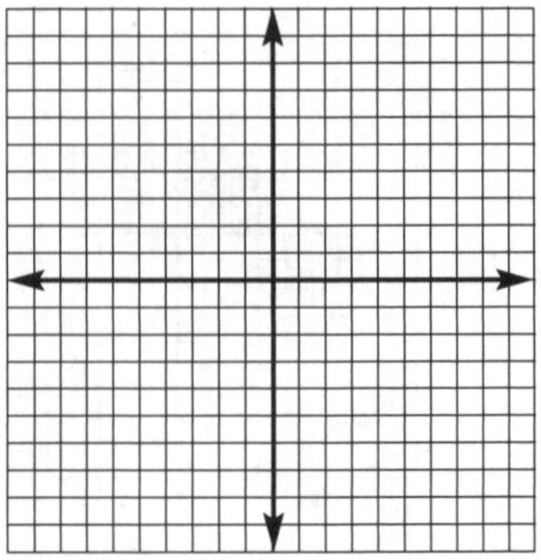

About the Authors

Mary Lee Vivian has helped many secondary students master a variety of mathematical skills during her many years of teaching in the Parkway School District in St. Louis, Missouri. She holds a bachelor of arts degree in mathematics from Central Methodist College and a master's degree from the University of Missouri, St. Louis.

Margaret Thomas is currently a mathematics and science consultant for a major publisher. Her professional experience includes teaching mathematics grades seven through college in Ohio, California, Oklahoma, and Tennessee. For ten years, she served as the Mathematics-Science Coordinator K-12 for Putnam City Schools in Oklahoma City. Margaret is an active member of many professional organizations including NCTM. She currently lives in Indianapolis, Indiana.

Answer Key

7 Adding and Subtracting Fractions

Use the common denominator. Add or subtract the numerators. Reduce to lowest terms.

$\frac{1}{8} + \frac{3}{8} = \frac{4}{8} = \frac{1}{2}$ Add same

1. $\frac{2}{9} + \frac{5}{9} =$ $\frac{7}{9}$
2. $\frac{3}{4} - \frac{1}{4} =$ $\frac{1}{2}$
3. $\frac{9}{15} + \frac{5}{15} =$ $\frac{14}{15}$
4. $\frac{19}{20} - \frac{14}{20} =$ $\frac{1}{4}$
5. $\frac{27}{38} + \frac{13}{38} =$ $1\frac{1}{19}$
6. $\frac{35}{60} - \frac{17}{60} =$ $\frac{3}{10}$
7. $\frac{17}{20} + \frac{23}{20} =$ 2
8. $\frac{25}{13} - \frac{12}{13} =$ 1
9. $\frac{11}{18} + \frac{16}{18} =$ $1\frac{1}{2}$
10. $\frac{17}{48} - \frac{14}{48} =$ $\frac{1}{16}$
11. $\frac{7}{45} + \frac{8}{45} =$ $\frac{1}{3}$
12. $\frac{33}{50} - \frac{17}{50} =$ $\frac{8}{25}$
13. $\frac{16}{33} + \frac{21}{33} =$ $1\frac{4}{33}$
14. $\frac{43}{56} - \frac{19}{56} =$ $\frac{3}{7}$
15. $\frac{12}{42} + \frac{31}{42} =$ $1\frac{1}{42}$
16. $\frac{29}{52} - \frac{13}{52} =$ $\frac{4}{13}$
17. $\frac{15}{18} + \frac{8}{18} =$ $1\frac{5}{18}$
18. $\frac{43}{65} - \frac{28}{65} =$ $\frac{3}{13}$

8 More Adding and Subtracting Fractio

Hint: Remember to re-write fractions.

$\frac{7}{9} - \frac{1}{4} = \frac{28}{36} - \frac{9}{36} = \frac{19}{36}$

36 is the least common multiple

1. $\frac{2}{3} + \frac{5}{9} =$ $1\frac{2}{9}$
2. $\frac{4}{5} - \frac{3}{4} =$ $\frac{1}{20}$
3. $\frac{5}{6} + \frac{7}{12} =$ $1\frac{5}{12}$
4. $\frac{11}{15} - \frac{2}{5} =$ $\frac{1}{3}$
5. $\frac{11}{12} + \frac{5}{8} =$ $1\frac{13}{24}$
6. $\frac{1}{2} - \frac{4}{9} =$ $\frac{1}{18}$
7. $\frac{13}{36} + \frac{5}{12} =$ $\frac{7}{9}$
8. $\frac{7}{8} - \frac{3}{10} =$ $\frac{23}{40}$
9. $\frac{5}{12} - \frac{5}{18} =$ $\frac{5}{36}$
10. $\frac{5}{9} + \frac{3}{8} =$ $\frac{67}{72}$
11. $\frac{5}{12} - \frac{3}{15} =$ $\frac{13}{60}$
12. $\frac{3}{4} + \frac{7}{12} =$ $1\frac{1}{3}$
13. $\frac{8}{19} - \frac{1}{3} =$ $\frac{5}{57}$
14. $\frac{7}{15} + \frac{3}{25} =$ $\frac{44}{75}$
15. $\frac{30}{36} - \frac{5}{18} =$ $\frac{5}{9}$
16. $\frac{4}{5} + \frac{12}{13} =$ $1\frac{47}{65}$

Answer Key

9 — Words to the Wise

Write each sum or difference in lowest terms. Cross out the answers below to reveal the "Words to the Wise."

1. $\frac{4}{9} + \frac{13}{15} = 1\frac{14}{45}$
2. $\frac{5}{6} + \frac{7}{32} = 1\frac{5}{96}$
3. $\frac{13}{15} - \frac{1}{3} = \frac{8}{15}$
4. $\frac{3}{11} + \frac{6}{7} = 1\frac{10}{77}$
5. $\frac{5}{9} - \frac{1}{15} = \frac{22}{45}$
6. $\frac{7}{9} + \frac{1}{6} = \frac{17}{18}$
7. $\frac{9}{10} - \frac{3}{20} = \frac{3}{4}$
8. $\frac{11}{42} + \frac{1}{7} = \frac{17}{42}$
9. $\frac{8}{9} - \frac{1}{12} = \frac{29}{36}$
10. $\frac{7}{12} + \frac{31}{42} = 1\frac{9}{28}$
11. $\frac{11}{12} - \frac{1}{18} = \frac{31}{36}$
12. $\frac{7}{23} - \frac{1}{7} = \frac{26}{161}$
13. $\frac{8}{21} + \frac{36}{49} = 1\frac{17}{147}$
14. $\frac{7}{9} - \frac{1}{4} = \frac{19}{36}$
15. $\frac{11}{30} + \frac{2}{25} = \frac{67}{150}$
16. $\frac{27}{35} - \frac{11}{30} = \frac{17}{42}$
17. $\frac{7}{8} + \frac{13}{14} = 1\frac{45}{56}$
18. $\frac{76}{81} - \frac{22}{63} = \frac{334}{567}$
19. $\frac{1}{3} + \frac{2}{3} = 1$
20. $\frac{23}{45} - \frac{1}{3} = \frac{8}{45}$

~~$\frac{19}{36}$ CAN~~	$\frac{17}{24}$ PUT	~~$\frac{17}{18}$ IT~~	~~$\frac{334}{567}$ PLACE~~	$\frac{7}{8}$ FORTH	~~1 IS~~	~~$1\frac{14}{45}$ WAS~~	~~$1\frac{17}{147}$ WHOLE~~	~~$\frac{29}{36}$ IT~~	$\frac{5}{27}$ HALF	~~$1\frac{5}{96}$ PROPER~~
$\frac{3}{8}$ THE	~~$\frac{26}{161}$ THIS~~	~~$\frac{17}{42}$ ON~~	~~$\frac{31}{36}$ TRY~~	$1\frac{35}{68}$ EFFORT	$\frac{31}{80}$ AND	~~$\frac{8}{15}$ SUM~~	$\frac{9}{30}$ YOU	$\frac{11}{45}$ GET	$\frac{1}{4}$ A	$1\frac{47}{147}$ FRACTION
~~$\frac{8}{45}$ IF~~	~~$\frac{17}{42}$ ARE~~	~~$\frac{22}{45}$ IN~~	$\frac{13}{55}$ OF	~~$1\frac{10}{77}$ TOTAL~~	~~$\frac{67}{150}$ HAS~~	$\frac{3}{5}$ THE	~~$1\frac{45}{56}$ VALUE~~	~~$1\frac{9}{28}$ TO~~	~~$\frac{3}{4}$ ALL~~	$1\frac{7}{47}$ RESULTS

PUT FORTH HALF THE EFFORT AND
YOU GET A FRACTION OF THE RESULTS

10 — Adding and Subtracting Mixed Numb

add

$$3\frac{7}{8} + 5\frac{11}{24} = 3\frac{21}{24} + 5\frac{11}{24} = 8\frac{32}{24} = 9\frac{8}{24} = 9\frac{1}{3}$$

add

1. $1\frac{1}{4} + 2\frac{1}{2} = 3\frac{3}{4}$
2. $5\frac{7}{10} - 1\frac{1}{6} = 4\frac{8}{15}$
3. $8\frac{3}{8} + 9\frac{2}{3} = 18\frac{1}{24}$
4. $6 - 2\frac{8}{11} = 3\frac{3}{11}$
5. $2\frac{1}{16} + 2\frac{1}{3} = 4\frac{19}{48}$
6. $7\frac{7}{8} - 7\frac{5}{12} = \frac{11}{24}$
7. $4\frac{1}{2} + 6\frac{2}{5} = 10\frac{9}{10}$
8. $5\frac{1}{2} - \frac{11}{15} = 4\frac{23}{30}$
9. $1\frac{5}{6} + 4 = 5\frac{5}{6}$
10. $6\frac{7}{9} - 6\frac{1}{2} = \frac{5}{18}$
11. $7\frac{1}{4} + 1\frac{7}{9} + 2\frac{5}{6} = 11\frac{31}{36}$
12. $8\frac{1}{6} - 7\frac{3}{4} = \frac{5}{12}$
13. $5 + 3\frac{3}{11} = 8\frac{3}{11}$
14. $3\frac{5}{8} - 1\frac{6}{7} = 1\frac{43}{56}$
15. $4\frac{3}{7} + 5\frac{5}{14} = 9\frac{11}{14}$
16. $6\frac{3}{12} - 3\frac{9}{36} = 3$

11 — Pair Them Up!

Each problem in the first column has the same answer as a problem in the second column. Solve the problems and determine the matches.

I	1. $7\frac{3}{5} + 2\frac{1}{2} =$	$10\frac{1}{10}$	A. $8\frac{1}{3} + 12\frac{1}{2} =$	$20\frac{5}{6}$
D	2. $10\frac{3}{5} - 4 =$	$6\frac{3}{5}$	B. $2\frac{5}{18} - \frac{11}{24} =$	$1\frac{59}{72}$
E	3. $5\frac{2}{9} + 7\frac{1}{3} =$	$12\frac{5}{9}$	C. $5\frac{2}{9} - 3\frac{7}{9} =$	$1\frac{4}{9}$
G	4. $11\frac{5}{6} - 3\frac{3}{4} =$	$8\frac{1}{12}$	D. $13 - 6\frac{2}{5} =$	$6\frac{3}{5}$
H	5. $4\frac{7}{12} + 4\frac{3}{14} =$	$8\frac{67}{84}$	E. $3\frac{5}{6} + 8\frac{13}{18} =$	$12\frac{5}{9}$
C	6. $8 - 6\frac{5}{9} =$	$1\frac{4}{9}$	F. $17\frac{5}{12} - 4\frac{7}{12} =$	$12\frac{5}{6}$
A	7. $17\frac{14}{15} + 2\frac{9}{10} =$	$20\frac{5}{6}$	G. $7\frac{11}{12} + \frac{1}{6} =$	$8\frac{1}{12}$
B	8. $1\frac{17}{18} - \frac{1}{8} =$	$1\frac{59}{72}$	H. $10\frac{13}{14} - 2\frac{11}{84} =$	$8\frac{67}{84}$
F	9. $6\frac{1}{12} + 6\frac{3}{4} =$	$12\frac{5}{6}$	I. $5\frac{1}{5} + 4\frac{9}{10} =$	$10\frac{1}{10}$
J	10. $8\frac{2}{9} - 6\frac{17}{18} =$	$1\frac{5}{18}$	J. $9\frac{1}{6} - 7\frac{8}{9} =$	$1\frac{5}{18}$

12 — Multiplying Fractions

Multiply numerators. Multiply denominators. Reduce to lowest terms.
Hint: Rewrite mixed numbers as improper fractions.

rewrite

$$2\frac{1}{4} \cdot 1\frac{2}{3} = \frac{9}{4} \cdot \frac{5}{3} = \frac{\overset{3}{\cancel{9}}}{4} \cdot \frac{5}{\underset{1}{\cancel{3}}} = \frac{15}{4} = 3\frac{3}{4}$$

rewrite

1. $\frac{1}{2} \cdot \frac{5}{6} = \frac{5}{12}$
2. $3 \cdot \frac{1}{2} = 1\frac{1}{2}$
3. $\frac{2}{5} \cdot \frac{1}{3} = \frac{2}{15}$
4. $\frac{16}{5} \cdot \frac{25}{27} = 2\frac{26}{27}$
5. $\frac{8}{21} \cdot 2\frac{7}{16} = \frac{13}{14}$
6. $1\frac{5}{7} \cdot 2\frac{1}{4} = 3\frac{6}{7}$
7. $5\frac{7}{8} \cdot 4 = 23\frac{1}{2}$
8. $\frac{5}{7} \cdot \frac{7}{5} = 1$
9. $3\frac{2}{3} \cdot \frac{17}{22} = 2\frac{5}{6}$
10. $\frac{5}{6} \cdot 2 = 1\frac{2}{3}$
11. $8\frac{1}{3} \cdot \frac{3}{4} = 6\frac{1}{4}$
12. $4\frac{1}{4} \cdot 3\frac{1}{5} = 13\frac{3}{5}$
13. $2\frac{1}{6} \cdot \frac{18}{20} = 1\frac{19}{20}$
14. $\frac{21}{35} \cdot 3\frac{4}{7} = 2\frac{1}{7}$
15. $1\frac{3}{5} \cdot 2\frac{3}{16} = 3\frac{1}{2}$
16. $6\frac{3}{4} \cdot 1\frac{5}{9} = 10\frac{1}{2}$
17. $3\frac{1}{3} \cdot 1\frac{3}{18} = 3\frac{8}{9}$
18. $\frac{1}{2} \cdot \frac{6}{11} \cdot \frac{3}{5} = \frac{9}{55}$

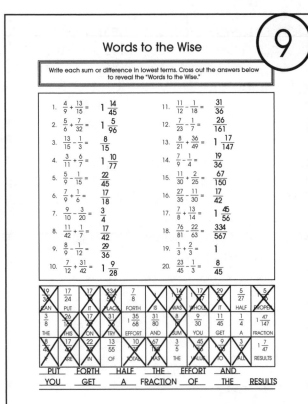

Answer Key

13 Mort's Multiplication

Mort did not understand multiplying mixed numbers when he completed the quiz below. Find and correct the 10 errors Mort made. Explain how to multiply mixed numbers.

FRACTIONS QUIZ — Name: *Mort*

Problem	Correction	Problem	Correction
1. $5\frac{3}{5} \cdot 3\frac{4}{7} = 15\frac{12}{35}$	20	11. $9\frac{1}{3} \cdot 1\frac{5}{7} \cdot \frac{3}{4} = 9\frac{15}{84}$	12
2. $2\frac{1}{12} \cdot 2\frac{2}{15} = 4\frac{4}{9}$		12. $6\frac{8}{9} \cdot 3\frac{6}{7} = 26\frac{4}{7}$	
3. $1\frac{1}{15} \cdot 3\frac{3}{7} = 3\frac{69}{105}$		13. $8\frac{2}{5} \cdot 3\frac{1}{3} = 24\frac{2}{15}$	28
4. $8\frac{2}{9} \cdot 2\frac{7}{8} = 16\frac{7}{36}$	$23\frac{23}{36}$	14. $9\frac{3}{5} \cdot 2\frac{1}{12} = 20$	
5. $16 \cdot 4\frac{1}{4} = 68$		15. $2\frac{1}{2} \cdot 2\frac{8}{9} = 4\frac{4}{9}$	$7\frac{2}{9}$
6. $6\frac{2}{3} \cdot 1\frac{15}{16} = 12\frac{11}{12}$		16. $5\frac{3}{7} \cdot 2\frac{3}{16} = 10\frac{9}{112}$	$11\frac{7}{8}$
7. $5\frac{1}{3} \cdot 4\frac{1}{2} = 20\frac{1}{6}$	24	17. $2\frac{1}{4} \cdot 6 \cdot 1\frac{1}{9} = 15$	
8. $9\frac{1}{3} \cdot 8\frac{1}{10} = 75\frac{3}{5}$		18. $4\frac{1}{2} \cdot 2\frac{2}{5} = 8\frac{1}{5}$	$10\frac{4}{5}$
9. $2\frac{1}{12} \cdot 3\frac{5}{9} = 7\frac{11}{27}$		19. $7\frac{1}{2} \cdot 7\frac{1}{3} = 55$	
10. $3\frac{5}{6} \cdot 8 = 24\frac{5}{6}$	$30\frac{2}{3}$	20. $3\frac{1}{8} \cdot \frac{1}{9} \cdot \frac{9}{10} = 3\frac{1}{80}$	$\frac{5}{16}$

Write mixed numbers as fractions, x numerators, x denominators.

14 Dividing Fractions

Invert and multiply

$$1\frac{1}{2} \div 3\frac{3}{7} = \frac{3}{2} \div \frac{24}{7} = \frac{3}{2} \cdot \frac{7}{24} = \frac{\overset{1}{\cancel{3}}}{2} \cdot \frac{7}{\underset{8}{\cancel{24}}} = \frac{7}{16}$$

rewrite the mixed numbers

1. $\frac{3}{7} \div \frac{1}{2} =$	$\frac{6}{7}$	10. $\frac{7}{8} \div 2\frac{1}{3} =$	$\frac{3}{8}$
2. $\frac{17}{9} \div \frac{8}{9} =$	$2\frac{1}{8}$	11. $9\frac{3}{8} \div 3\frac{3}{4} =$	$2\frac{1}{2}$
3. $6\frac{2}{3} \div 5 =$	$1\frac{1}{3}$	12. $5\frac{1}{6} \div \frac{31}{6} =$	1
4. $1\frac{7}{9} \div 4\frac{2}{9} =$	$\frac{8}{19}$	13. $\frac{7}{8} \div \frac{3}{4} =$	$\frac{1}{16}$
5. $\frac{15}{4} \div \frac{5}{14} =$	$10\frac{1}{2}$	14. $\frac{7}{12} \div \frac{7}{4} =$	$\frac{1}{3}$
6. $\frac{11}{12} \div \frac{13}{8} =$	$\frac{22}{39}$	15. $4\frac{6}{7} \div \frac{1}{3} =$	$14\frac{4}{7}$
7. $4 \div 4\frac{2}{5} =$	$\frac{10}{11}$	16. $5\frac{1}{2} \div \frac{7}{4} =$	$3\frac{1}{7}$
8. $3\frac{1}{4} \div 4\frac{3}{8} =$	$\frac{26}{35}$	17. $2\frac{2}{9} \div 4\frac{2}{6} =$	$\frac{20}{39}$
9. $\frac{6}{15} \div \frac{9}{10} =$	$\frac{4}{9}$	18. $5\frac{5}{12} \div 3\frac{1}{3} =$	$1\frac{5}{8}$

15 Division Magic

In a Magic Square, each row, column and diagonal has the same sum - Magic Sum. Complete the problems and determine the magic Sum.

$\frac{5}{12} \div \frac{1}{2}$ $\frac{5}{6}$	$1\frac{1}{2} \div 1\frac{1}{3}$ $1\frac{1}{8}$	$\frac{5}{6} \div 5$ $\frac{1}{6}$	$\frac{11}{12} \div 2$ $\frac{11}{24}$	$1\frac{1}{2} \div 2$ $\frac{3}{4}$
$6\frac{1}{2} \div 6$ $1\frac{1}{12}$	$\frac{3}{4} \div \frac{9}{4}$ $\frac{1}{3}$	$\frac{5}{6} \div 2$ $\frac{5}{12}$	$2\frac{1}{8} \div 3$ $\frac{17}{24}$	$1\frac{7}{12} \div 2$ $\frac{19}{24}$
$\frac{7}{8} \div 3$ $\frac{7}{24}$	$\frac{6}{7} \div 2\frac{2}{7}$ $\frac{3}{8}$	$\frac{2}{5} \div \frac{3}{5}$ $\frac{2}{3}$	$2\frac{7}{8} \div 3$ $\frac{23}{24}$	$\frac{5}{12} \div \frac{2}{5}$ $1\frac{1}{24}$
$\frac{13}{48} \div \frac{1}{2}$ $\frac{13}{24}$	$\frac{5}{32} \div \frac{1}{4}$ $\frac{5}{8}$	$\frac{2}{3} \div \frac{8}{11}$ $\frac{11}{12}$	$\frac{7}{8} \div \frac{7}{8}$ 1	$\frac{1}{2} \div 2$ $\frac{1}{4}$
$1\frac{1}{2} \div 2\frac{4}{7}$ $\frac{7}{12}$	$1\frac{3}{4} \div 2$ $\frac{7}{8}$	$\frac{7}{18} \div \frac{1}{3}$ $1\frac{1}{6}$	$\frac{1}{3} \div 1\frac{3}{5}$ $\frac{5}{24}$	$\frac{3}{4} \div 1\frac{1}{2}$ $\frac{1}{2}$

Magic Sum = $3\frac{1}{3}$

If every row and column in a Magic Square of problems has the same sum except for the last row and the last column, what do you know?

The problem in the bottom right corner is wrong.

16 Confused Calculations

Cal Q. Late was very confused about fractions when he completed the quiz below. Find and correct the ten errors Cal made.

FRACTIONS QUIZ — Name: *Cal*

Problem	Correction	Problem	Correction
1. $\frac{3}{5} + \frac{1}{3} = \frac{2}{5}$	$\frac{14}{15}$	9. $\frac{3}{4} \cdot \frac{6}{7} = \frac{1}{14}$	$\frac{9}{14}$
2. $\frac{3}{4} + \frac{3}{4} = \frac{6}{8}$	$1\frac{1}{2}$	10. $\frac{1}{3} \cdot \frac{1}{3} = \frac{1}{6}$	$\frac{1}{9}$
3. $4\frac{2}{3} + 6\frac{3}{4} = 10\frac{5}{7}$	$11\frac{5}{12}$	11. $1\frac{2}{3} \cdot 2\frac{1}{2} = 2\frac{1}{3}$	$4\frac{1}{6}$
4. $2\frac{1}{2} + 3\frac{1}{2} = 6$		12. $4\frac{1}{2} \cdot 3\frac{1}{3} = 12\frac{1}{6}$	15
5. $\frac{7}{8} - \frac{2}{3} = \frac{5}{24}$		13. $\frac{3}{4} \div \frac{1}{2} = 1\frac{1}{2}$	
6. $\frac{6}{7} - \frac{2}{7} = \frac{4}{7}$		14. $\frac{2}{3} \div \frac{3}{4} = \frac{8}{9}$	
7. $2\frac{4}{5} - 1\frac{2}{3} = 1\frac{2}{15}$		15. $2\frac{4}{5} \div 1\frac{2}{5} = 2\frac{2}{5}$	2
8. $6\frac{1}{4} - 2\frac{3}{4} = 4\frac{1}{2}$	$3\frac{1}{2}$	16. $5\frac{1}{4} \div 3\frac{1}{2} = 15\frac{1}{8}$	$1\frac{1}{2}$

What rules for computing with fractions would you share with Cal?

Addition: Use a common denominator, add numerators.

Subtraction: Use a common denominator, subtract numerators.

Multiplication: Multiply numerators, multiply denominators.

Division: Invert and multiply.
* Write mixed numbers as simple fractions.

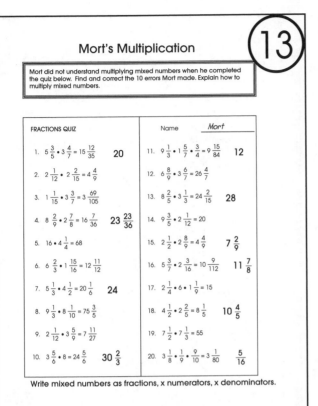

Answer Key

17 ... More Mixed Practice with Fractions

1. $8\frac{1}{15} - 5\frac{11}{20} =$ $2\frac{31}{60}$
2. $3\frac{1}{9} + 8\frac{3}{7} + 1\frac{1}{3} =$ $12\frac{55}{63}$
3. $1\frac{7}{8} \bullet 3\frac{3}{5} =$ $6\frac{3}{4}$
4. $4\frac{4}{5} \div 2\frac{8}{10} =$ $1\frac{5}{7}$
5. $3\frac{5}{12} + 5\frac{1}{4} - 2\frac{7}{20} =$ $6\frac{19}{60}$
6. $(\frac{16}{21} \bullet 3\frac{1}{4}) + 6\frac{1}{3} =$ $8\frac{17}{21}$
7. $5\frac{7}{10} - (\frac{25}{27} \div 3\frac{1}{3}) =$ $5\frac{19}{45}$
8. $(2\frac{15}{24} + 3\frac{11}{12}) \bullet 6\frac{1}{2} =$ $42\frac{25}{48}$
9. $7\frac{3}{12} - 2\frac{8}{9} =$ $4\frac{13}{36}$
10. $1\frac{1}{6} \bullet 3\frac{5}{7} \bullet 2\frac{2}{9} =$ $9\frac{17}{27}$
11. $8\frac{7}{12} + 11\frac{3}{4} =$ $20\frac{1}{3}$
12. $7 - (3\frac{7}{9} \div 4\frac{2}{3}) =$ $6\frac{4}{21}$
13. $2\frac{1}{2} \bullet 3\frac{3}{15} =$ 8
14. $5\frac{2}{9} - 2\frac{17}{18} + 1\frac{2}{3} =$ $3\frac{17}{18}$
15. $(3\frac{6}{8} \div 4\frac{2}{4}) - \frac{13}{16} =$ $\frac{1}{48}$
16. $4\frac{2}{3} \bullet 1\frac{3}{4} \bullet 3\frac{3}{4} =$ $30\frac{5}{8}$
17. $3\frac{4}{15} + 8\frac{3}{45} =$ $11\frac{1}{3}$
18. $12\frac{1}{2} - 7\frac{15}{16} =$ $4\frac{9}{16}$
19. $(1\frac{12}{13} \bullet 7\frac{3}{5}) - 3 =$ $11\frac{8}{13}$
20. $2\frac{1}{8} + (6\frac{2}{3} \div 8\frac{4}{9}) =$ $2\frac{139}{152}$
21. $3\frac{1}{3} \bullet 7\frac{5}{6} \bullet 2\frac{2}{5} =$ $62\frac{2}{3}$
22. $1\frac{15}{16} + 3\frac{7}{24} + 3\frac{11}{12} =$ $9\frac{7}{48}$

18 Problems with Fractions

1. If $1\frac{1}{4}$ pounds of bananas sell for 80¢ and $1\frac{1}{3}$ pounds of apples sell for 90¢, which fruit is cheaper? **bananas 64¢/lb.**
2. A cake recipe calls for $\frac{2}{3}$ teaspoons of salt, $1\frac{1}{2}$ teaspoons baking powder, 1 teaspoon baking soda and $\frac{1}{2}$ teaspoon cinnamon. How many total teaspoons of dry ingredients are used? **$3\frac{2}{3}$ teaspoons**
3. A baseball team played 35 games and won $\frac{4}{7}$ of them.
   How many games were won? **20**
   How many games were lost? **15**
4. During 4 days, the price of the stock of PEV Corporation went up $\frac{1}{4}$ of a point, down $\frac{1}{3}$ of a point, down $\frac{3}{4}$ of a point and up $\frac{7}{10}$ of a point. What was the net change? **down $\frac{2}{15}$**
5. Janie wants to make raisin cookies. She needs $8\frac{1}{2}$ cups of raisins for the cookies. A 15-ounce box of raisins contains $2\frac{3}{4}$ cups. How many boxes must Janie buy to make her cookies? **4 Boxes**
6. A one-half gallon carton of milk costs $1.89. A one-gallon carton of milk costs $2.99. How much money would you save if you bought a one-gallon carton instead of 2 one-half gallon cartons? **99¢**

19 Changing Fractions to Decimals

$\frac{7}{20} \rightarrow 20\overline{)7.00}$ (quotient .35; 6.0, 1.00, 1.00, 0) $\rightarrow \frac{7}{20} = 0.35$ terminating

$\frac{5}{12} \rightarrow 12\overline{)5.00000}$ (quotient .41666; 4.8, 20, 12, 80, 72, 80, 72, 80) $\rightarrow \frac{5}{12} = 0.41\overline{6}$ repeating

1. $\frac{3}{5} =$ 0.6
2. $\frac{11}{25} =$ 0.44
3. $\frac{7}{15} =$ $0.4\overline{6}$
4. $2\frac{1}{9} =$ $2.\overline{1}$
5. $\frac{23}{33} =$ $\overline{.69}$
6. $1\frac{5}{16} =$ 1.3125
7. $\frac{12}{25} =$ 0.48
8. $\frac{1}{3} =$ $0.\overline{3}$
9. $\frac{5}{33} =$ $\overline{0.15}$
10. $2\frac{5}{16} =$ 2.3125
11. $\frac{25}{37} =$ $\overline{0.675}$
12. $3\frac{13}{15} =$ $3.8\overline{6}$
13. $\frac{17}{22} =$ $0.7\overline{72}$
14. $3\frac{11}{12} =$ $3.91\overline{6}$

20 Terminators

Change each of the following fractions into decimal equivalents. Indicate whether the decimal terminates (T) or repeats (R).

Fraction	Decimal	T or R	Fraction	Decimal	T or R
1. $\frac{3}{8}$	0.375	T	11. $2\frac{3}{8}$	2.375	T
2. $\frac{8}{15}$	$0.5\overline{3}$	R	12. $2\frac{15}{37}$	$2.\overline{405}$	R
3. $\frac{27}{32}$	0.84375	T	13. $\frac{67}{90}$	$0.7\overline{4}$	R
4. $\frac{23}{30}$	$0.7\overline{6}$	R	14. $1\frac{19}{33}$	$1.\overline{57}$	R
5. $\frac{4}{7}$	$0.\overline{571428}$	R	15. $\frac{124}{333}$	$0.\overline{372}$	R
6. $5\frac{1}{8}$	5.125	T	16. $5\frac{7}{10}$	5.7	T
7. $1\frac{4}{5}$	1.8	T	17. $2\frac{11}{16}$	2.6875	T
8. $\frac{10}{35}$	$0.\overline{285714}$	R	18. $7\frac{31}{40}$	7.775	T
9. $\frac{9}{15}$	0.6	T	19. $3\frac{9}{16}$	3.5625	T
10. $2\frac{7}{8}$	2.875	T	20. $11\frac{3}{4}$	11.75	T

BONUS: For fractions in lowest terms, what are the prime factors of the denominators that terminate? **2 and 5**

Give a rule for determining whether a fraction will be a terminating or repeating decimal.

Reduce to lowest terms. If the only factors of the denominator are 2 and/or 5, it terminates.

Answer Key

21

Rounding Decimals

Rounding Decimals

Round 8.135 to the nearest tenth.
8.135 → 8.1
less than 5

Round 32.56713 to the nearest hundredth.
32.56713 → 32.57
greater than 5

Round to the nearest whole number.

1. 41.803 = 42
2. 119.63 = 120
3. 20.05 = 20
4. 3.45 = 3
5. 79.531 = 80
6. 8.437 = 8
7. 29.37 = 29
8. 109.96 = 110

Round to the nearest tenth.

9. 33.335 = 33.3
10. 1.861 = 1.9
11. 99.96 = 100.0
12. 103.103 = 103.1
13. 16.031 = 16.0
14. 281.05 = 281.1
15. 8.741 = 8.7
16. 27.773 = 27.8

Round to the nearest hundredth.

17. 69.713 = 69.71
18. 5.569 = 5.57
19. 609.906 = 609.91
20. 247.898 = 247.90
21. 5.535 = 5.54
22. 67.1951 = 67.20
23. 14.0305 = 14.03
24. 6.9372 = 6.94

22

Multiplying and Dividing by 10, 100, e

When multiplying by a power of 10, move the decimal to the right:
34.61 x 10 → move 1 place → 346.1
6.77 x 100 → move 2 places → 677

When dividing by a power of 10, move the decimal to the left:
7.39 ÷ 100 → move 2 place → 0.0739
105.61 ÷ 1000 → move 3 places → 0.10561

1. 4.81 x 100 = 481
2. 37.68 ÷ 10 = 3.768
3. 0.46 x 1,000 = 460
4. 7.12 ÷ 10,000 = 0.000712
5. 5.4 x 10 = 54
6. 27,500 ÷ 1,000 = 27.5
7. 4.395 x 100,000 = 439,500
8. 0.0075 ÷ 100 = 0.000075
9. 2.274 x 10 = 22.74
10. 90,000 ÷ 100 = 900
11. 0.000618 x 1,000 = 0.618
12. 39.006 ÷ 1,000 = 0.039006
13. 16 x 100 = 1600
14. 28.889 ÷ 10,000 = 0.0028889
15. 36.89 x 10,000 = 368900
16. 0.091 ÷ 100 = 0.00091
17. 0.0336 x 100,000 = 3360
18. 1,672 ÷ 100,000 = 0.01672

23

Adding and Subtracting Decimals

13.6 + 7.12 = 13.6 + 7.12 = 20.72

12 − 3.78 = 12 − 3.78 = 8.22

1. 3.5 + 8.4 = 11.9
2. 43.57 + 104.6 = 148.17
3. 15.36 + 29.23 + 7.2 = 51.79
4. 2.304 + 6.18 + 9.2 = 17.684
5. $12.91 + $6.99 = $19.90
6. 0.08 + 19 = 19.08
7. 22.63 + 1.694 = 24.324
8. 362.1 + 8.888 + 0.016 = 371.004
9. 1392.16 + 16.16 = 1408.32
10. 83.196 + 0.0017 = 83.1977
11. 17.6 − 9.3 = 8.3
12. 32.3 − 12.72 = 19.58
13. 23.96 − 19.931 = 4.029
14. $29.98 − $16.09 = $13.89
15. 63.36 − 0.007 = 63.353
16. 16.22 − 0.039 = 16.181
17. 44.44 − 16.1 = 28.34
18. $75.02 − $3.99 = $71.03
19. 575.021 − 65.98 = 509.041
20. 394.6 − 27.88 − 0.0933 = 366.6267

24

More or Less

Compute the sums and differences. Cross out each answer below. The remaining letters spell out an important rule.

1. 6.2 + 0.25 = 6.45
2. 3.3 − 0.33 = 2.97
3. 0.26 + 0.4 = 0.66
4. 8.76 − 5.43 = 3.33
5. 19.9 + 1.1 = 21
6. 9.53 − 5.3 = 4.23
7. 0.22 + 2.2 = 2.42
8. 77.7 − 7 = 70.7
9. 7.8 + 64.2 = 72
10. 9.25 − 2.5 = 6.75
11. 36 + 6.3 = 42.3
12. 37.2 − 32 = 5.2
13. 0.23 + 3.7 = 3.93
14. 28.55 − 20.5 = 8.05
15. 27.8 + 2.2 − 3.5 + 0.5 − 20.5 = 6.5

20 RE	3.33 AL	34 ME	70.7 WA	71 MB	6.75 YS	0.3 ER	6.45 CO	0.66 UN	9 TO	42.3 AD	3.93 DU	8.7 LI	8.05 PT
9.9 NE	2.42 HE	4.4 UP	5.2 PL	4.49 TH	77 EP	72 AC	0.6 OI	21 ES	4.23 TO	9 NT	2.97 AD	6.5 D.	3.07 S.

Write the remaining letters, one letter to space.

REMEMBER TO
LINE UP THE
POINTS

Answer Key

25 Multiplying Decimals

The number of decimal places in a product equals the sum of decimal places in the factors.

(0.7) (0.04) = 0.028
1 + 2 = 3
place places places

1. (0.003) (6) = 0.018
2. (0.051) (0.003) = 0.000153
3. (260) (0.01) = 2.6
4. (9.6) (5) = 48.0
5. (7) (3.42) = 23.94
6. (5.29) (11.3) = 59.777
7. (0.017) (6.2) = 0.1054
8. (0.3) (0.03) (0.003) = 0.000027
9. (1.5) (0.096) (4.3) = .6192
10. (0.05) (0.16) (0.001) = 0.000008
11. (8) (0.217) (0.01) = 0.01736
12. (18) (0.08) = 1.44
13. (16.01) (0.5) (0.31) = 2.48155
14. (1.06) (0.005) = 0.0053
15. (4.802) (11.11) = 53.35022
16. (10.25) (0.331) = 3.39275
17. (5) (1.102) = 5.51
18. (12.8) (0.05) (3.09) = 1.9776

26 Get to the Point

For each multiplication problem, locate the decimal point in the product. Insert zeros if needed.

1. 2.2 x 0.011 = 242 — 0.0242
2. 12.8 x 0.12 = 1536 — 1.536
3. 1.8 x 6.03 = 10854 — 10.854
4. 34.1 x 1.4 = 4774 — 47.74
5. 7.21 x 22.2 = 160062 — 160.062
6. 55 x 0.033 = 1815 — 1.815
7. 6.9 x 11 = 759 — 75.9
8. 6.7 x 0.801 = 53667 — 5.3667
9. 4.04 x 4.04 = 163216 — 16.3216
10. 32.1 x 2.02 = 64842 — 64.842
11. 0.005 x 0.011 = 55 — 0.000055
12. 66.2 x 1.1 = 7282 — 72.82
13. 0.84 x 0.07 = 588 — 0.0588
14. 8.2 x 0.1 = 82 — 0.82
15. 0.6 x 1.7 = 102 — 1.02
16. (5.7) (0.2) (0.07) = 798 — 0.0798
17. (9.8) (2.8) (1.8) = 49392 — 49.392
18. (10.6) (4.3) (0.8) = 36464 — 36.464
19. (0.13) (8.5) (0.5) = 5525 — 0.5525
20. (6.7) (1.2) (0.03) = 2412 — 0.2412

HINT:
The sum of the number of all decimal places in your products equals 64.

27 Dividing Decimals

HINT:
Move the decimal points the number of places needed to make the divisor a whole number.

0.03652 ÷ .88 = 88)036520 = .0415
352
132
88
440
440
0

1. 0.128 ÷ 0.8 = 0.16
2. 2.45 ÷ 3.5 = 0.7
3. 0.5773 ÷ 5.02 = 0.115
4. 39.78 ÷ 0.195 = 204
5. 4.2016 ÷ 5.2 = 0.808
6. 1.45 ÷ 0.08 = 18.125
7. 0.1716 ÷ 5.2 = 0.033
8. 3.906 ÷ 1.2 = 3.255
9. 6.56 ÷ 0.16 = 41
10. 0.0135 ÷ 4.5 = 0.003
11. 0.0483 ÷ 0.21 = 0.23
12. 0.5418 ÷ 0.3 = 1.806
13. 16.83 ÷ 0.11 = 153
14. 0.1926 ÷ 32.1 = 0.006

28 Mixed Practice with Decimals

1. 12.16 – 8.72 = 3.44
2. 119.7 + 11.97 = 131.67
3. (3.4) (8) = 27.2
4. 2960 ÷ 0.37 = 8,000
5. 1.21 ÷ 1.1 = 1.1
6. 7 + 6.91 = 13.91
7. 18.91 – 11.857 = 7.053
8. (1.35) (21.4) = 28.89
9. 21.2 – 9.03 = 12.17
10. 0.7 + 0.02 + 4 = 4.72
11. (0.25) (2.5) (25) = 15.625
12. 95.6 – 87.81 + 12.21 = 20
13. (0.8) (1.3) (0.62) = 0.6448
14. 37.92 ÷ 1.2 = 31.6
15. 0.1007 ÷ 5.3 = 0.019
16. 329.82 + 6.129 = 335.949
17. 893.631 – 11.09 = 882.541
18. 18.332 + 82.82 = 101.152
19. 132.03 ÷ 8.1 = 16.3
20. (16.1) (3.66) = 58.926
21. 1093.62 – 10.993 = 1082.627
22. 6.963 ÷ 2.11 = 3.3

Answer Key

Going Around the Block (29)

Start at 0.5. Move clockwise. Fill the blank spaces with +, −, x , or ÷ to make true math statements. End back at 0.5.

Start →

0.5	×	0.2	=	0.1	÷	0.5	=	0.2	÷	0.8	=	0.25
=												+
0.3												0.75
÷												=
0.15												1
=												−
0.1												0.6
×												=
1.5												0.4
=												×
3												0.3
÷												=
4.5	=	2.5	+	2	=	1.4	+	0.6	=	5	×	0.12

Scientifically Speaking (30)

Scientific notation is used to write very large and very small numbers. A number in scientific notation is the product of a number between 1 and 10 and a power of 10.

Examples: $45,000,000 = 4.5 \times 10^7$ $0.00000625 = 6.25 \times 10^{-6}$

write each measurement in scientific notation; then write the problem letter above the value of the exponent to complete the statement at the bottom of the page.

C	The population of China is greater than 1,250,000,000.	1.25×10^9
E	Scientists at Oak Ridge National Laboratory have sent an electric current of 2,000,000 amperes/cm² down a wire.	2×10^6
E	The diameter of an electron is 0.0000000000011 cm.	1.1×10^{-12}
E	In an election in India, more than 343,350,000 people voted.	3.4335×10^8
E	The Earth's mass is 5,980,000,000,000,000,000,000 metric tons.	5.98×10^{21}
G	The Greenland–Canada boundary is about 1,700 miles long.	1.7×10^3
I	The isotope lithium 5 decays in 0.00000000000000000000044 seconds.	4.4×10^{-22}
I	The isotope tellurium 128 has a half-life of 1,500,000,000,000,000,000,000,000 years.	1.5×10^{24}
M	A microbe strain of H39 has a diameter of 0.0000003 m.	3×10^{-7}
N	A nugget of platinum found in 1843 weighed 340 ounces.	3.4×10^2
N	In 1996 the United States national debt was $5,129,000,000,000.	5.129×10^{12}
O	A Saudi Arabia oil field contains about 82,000,000,000 barrels.	8.2×10^{10}
P	The fastest planet Mercury travels at 107,000 mph.	1.07×10^5
R	Sales of the record "White Christmas" exceeded 30,000,000.	3×10^7
V	In 1973, a vulture flying at 37,000 ft. collided with an aircraft.	3.7×10^4
X	The wavelength of an X ray is about 0.0000000015 m.	1.5×10^9

What the decimal point said about scientific notation:

"It's a $\underset{-7}{M}\ \underset{10}{O}\ \underset{4}{V}\ \underset{-22}{I}\ \underset{2}{N}\ \underset{3}{G}\quad \underset{6}{E}\ \underset{-9}{X}\ \underset{5}{P}\ \underset{-12}{E}\ \underset{7}{R}\ \underset{24}{I}\ \underset{8}{E}\ \underset{12}{N}\ \underset{9}{C}\ \underset{21}{E}$r"

Problems with Decimals (31)

1. Jim's gas credit card bill was $80.97 for June, $41.35 for July and $65.08 for August. What were his total charges for the summer?
$187.40

2. One cup of hot chocolate can be made with .18 ounces of hot chocolate mix. How many cups can be made from a 6.48 ounce canister of mix?
36 cups

3. Karl's car payments are $215.37 per month for the next three years. What will be the total amount he will pay for his car?
$7753.32

4. The dress Sally wants cost $85.15. If the price was reduced by $12.78, how much will she pay?
$72.37

5. Melissa went to the mall and noticed that the price of a coat she wanted was cut in half! The original price was $58.22. What is the sales price?
$29.11

6. Tyler decided that he wanted a dog. He went to the pet store and bought one for $42.95. Tyler also bought three bags of food for $12.55 a bag. How much did Tyler spend altogether?
$80.60

7. Christopher decided to make his grandmother a birdhouse instead of buying her one. The materials for the birdhouse totaled $21.99. the cost of a new birdhouse is $37.23. How much did Christopher save?
$15.24

8. Jim thinks that snow skiing looks like lots of fun. He decided he wants to try it. First he needs equipment. He bought a pair of skis for $129.78, a pair of boots for $62.22, poles for $12.95, a hat for $2.50, a coat for $49.95, ski pants for $27.50 and gloves for $11.25. How much did Jim spend altogether?
$296.15

Changing Decimals to Fractions (32)

Terminating Decimals	Repeating Decimals
$0.25 = \frac{25}{100} = \frac{1}{4}$	$N = 0.\overline{12} = 0.121212...$
$0.132 = \frac{132}{1000} = \frac{33}{250}$	$100N = 12.1212...$ $-\ N = -0.1212...$ $\frac{99N}{99} = \frac{12}{99}$ $N = \frac{4}{33}$ or $0.\overline{12} = \frac{4}{33}$

1. $0.125 = \dfrac{1}{8}$ 7. $0.625 = \dfrac{5}{8}$

2. $0.\overline{6} = \dfrac{2}{3}$ 8. $0.\overline{27} = \dfrac{3}{11}$

3. $0.36 = \dfrac{9}{25}$ 9. $0.3\overline{8} = \dfrac{7}{18}$

4. $0.\overline{46} = \dfrac{46}{99}$ 10. $0.55 = \dfrac{11}{20}$

5. $0.6875 = \dfrac{11}{16}$ 11. $0.5625 = \dfrac{9}{16}$

6. $0.91\overline{6} = \dfrac{11}{12}$ 12. $0.775 = \dfrac{31}{40}$

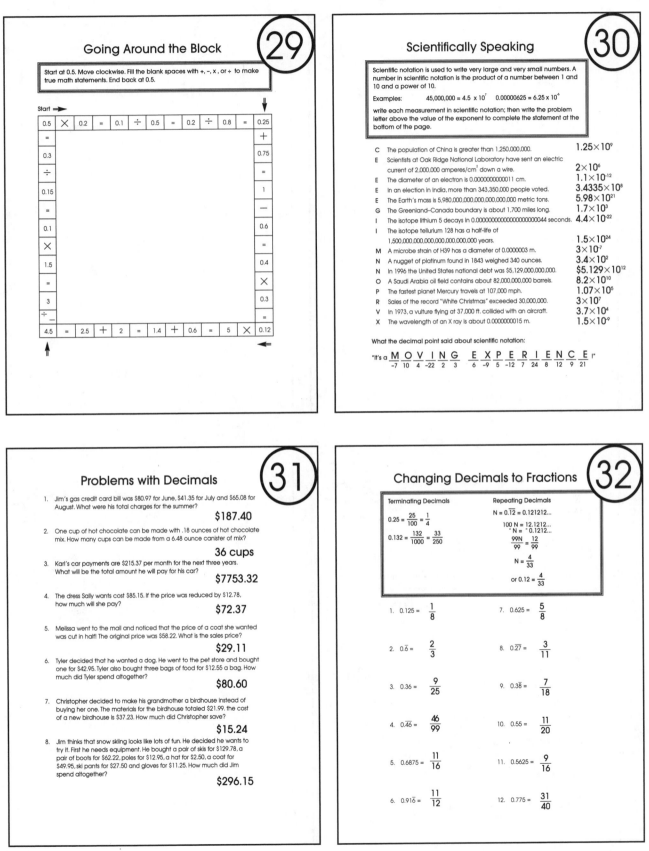

Answer Key

33 Ratios

Write each ratio as a fraction in simplest form.

3 to 12 → $\frac{3}{12} = \frac{1}{4}$ 65 : 35 → $\frac{65}{35} = \frac{13}{7}$

6 out of 40 → $\frac{6}{40} = \frac{3}{20}$

1. 196 to 7 — 28
2. 19 : 76 — $\frac{1}{4}$
3. 18 out of 27 — $\frac{2}{3}$
4. $\frac{3}{8}$ to $\frac{3}{4}$ — $\frac{1}{2}$
5. 0.11 : 1.21 — $\frac{1}{11}$
6. 140 : 112 — $\frac{5}{4}$
7. 18 to 27 — $\frac{2}{3}$
8. 54 out of 87 — $\frac{18}{29}$
9. 112 : 140 — $\frac{4}{5}$
10. 88 to 104 — $\frac{11}{13}$
11. 65 out of 105 — $\frac{13}{21}$
12. 65 : 117 — $\frac{5}{9}$
13. 165 to 200 — $\frac{33}{40}$
14. 168 : 264 — $\frac{7}{11}$

34 Proportions

Solve each proportion.

$\frac{3}{7} = \frac{x}{49}$ $3 \bullet 49 = 7x$

$\frac{147}{7} = \frac{7x}{7}$ $21 = x$

1. $\frac{8}{6} = \frac{m}{27}$ — 36
2. $\frac{z}{3} = \frac{8}{15}$ — $\frac{8}{5}$
3. $\frac{16}{40} = \frac{24}{c}$ — 60
4. $\frac{9}{p} = \frac{5}{2}$ — $\frac{18}{5}$
5. $\frac{1.8}{x} = \frac{3.6}{2.4}$ — 1.2
6. $\frac{4}{5} = \frac{0.8}{y}$ — 1
7. $\frac{x}{2} = \frac{15}{5}$ — 6
8. $\frac{18}{12} = \frac{24}{x}$ — 16
9. $\frac{18}{15} = \frac{6}{x}$ — 5
10. $\frac{121}{x} = \frac{220}{100}$ — 55
11. $\frac{1.6}{x} = \frac{14}{21}$ — 2.4
12. $\frac{x}{168} = \frac{66\frac{2}{3}}{100}$ — 112
13. $\frac{x}{32} = \frac{37\frac{1}{2}}{100}$ — 12
14. $\frac{16}{48} = \frac{x}{100}$ — $33\frac{1}{3}$
15. $\frac{0.12}{.25} = \frac{x}{100}$ — 48
16. $\frac{1.5}{x} = \frac{0.07}{0.14}$ — 3

35 Problems Using Proportions

Three loaves of bread cost \$3.87. How much do 2 loaves cost?

$\frac{\text{number of loaves}}{\text{cost}}$ $\frac{3}{3.87} = \frac{2}{x}$

$3x = 2 \bullet 3.87$

$\frac{3x}{3} = \frac{7.74}{3}$

$x = 2.58$

2 loaves cost \$2.58

1. If 64 feet of rope weigh 20 pounds, how much will 80 feet of the same type of rope weigh? **25 pounds**
2. If a 10 pound turkey takes 4 hours to cook, how long will it take a 14 pound turkey to cook? **5.6 hours**
3. An 18 ounce box of cereal costs \$2.76. How many ounces should a box priced at \$2.07 contain? **13.5 ounces**
4. Mike and Pat traveled 392 miles in 7 hours. If they travel at the same rate, how long will it take them to travel 728 miles? **13 hours**
5. If 2 pounds of turkey costs \$1.98, what should 3 pounds cost? **\$2.97**
6. If 2 liters of fruit juice cost \$3.98, how much do 5 liters cost? **\$9.95**
7. A 12 ounce box of cereal costs \$.84. How many ounces should be in a box marked \$.49? **7 ounces**
8. Janie saw an advertisement for a 6 ounce tube of toothpaste that costs \$.90. How much should a 4 ounce tube cost? **\$.60**

36 Percents

Percent (%) means: per hundred, out of a hundred, hundredths, 2 decimal places

$\frac{3}{4} \rightarrow \frac{3}{4} = \frac{x}{100}$

$300 = 4x$

$75 = x$

$\frac{3}{4} = 75\%$

0.375 → 37.5 hundredths = 37.5%

1. $\frac{4}{5}$ — 80%
2. $\frac{4}{7}$ — 57.14%
3. 0.22 — 22%
4. 2.5 — 250%
5. $\frac{3}{8}$ — 37.5%
6. 0.006 — 0.6%
7. 1.125 — 112.5%
8. $\frac{1}{2}$ — 50%
9. $\frac{9}{40}$ — 22.5%
10. 11.3 — 1130%
11. $\frac{11}{20}$ — 55%
12. 0.086 — 8.6%
13. $\frac{7}{8}$ — 87.5%
14. 16.688 — 1668.8%
15. $\frac{7}{16}$ — 43.75%
16. 621.9 — 62,190%
17. $\frac{5}{16}$ — 31.25%
18. 3.9932 — 399.32%

Answer Key

37 Working with Percents

80% of 30 =

$\frac{80}{100} = \frac{x}{30}$

$100x = 2400$

$x = 24$

1. 20% of 10 = 2
2. 25% of 45 = 11.25
3. 88% of 15 = 13.2
4. $9\frac{1}{2}$% of 20 = 1.9
5. 25% of 39 = 9.75
6. 16% of 90 = 14.4

__% of 30 = 10

$\frac{x}{100} = \frac{10}{40}$

$40x = 1000$

$x = 25$ 25%

1. 60 % of 25 = 15
2. $33\frac{1}{3}$ % of 30 = 10
3. 175 % of 4 = 7
4. 44 % of 75 = 33
5. 40 % of 15 = 6
6. 50 % of 80 = 40

80% of __ = 65

$\frac{50}{100} = \frac{65}{x}$

$50x = 6500$

$x = 130$

1. 20% of 75 = 15
2. 80% of 70 = 56
3. 25% of 76 = 19
4. $33\frac{1}{3}$% of 123 = 41
5. 80% of 20 = 16
6. 30% of 50 = 15

38 Problems with Percents

1. In a group of 60 children, 12 have brown eyes. What percent have brown eyes?
 20%
2. A salesman makes a 5% commission on all he sells. How much does he have to sell to make $1500?
 $30,000
3. A sales tax of $5\frac{3}{4}$ % is charged on a blouse priced at $42. How much sales tax must be paid?
 $2.42
4. A baby weighed 7.6 pounds at birth and $9\frac{1}{2}$ pounds after 6 weeks. What was the percent increase?
 25%
5. A scale model of a building is 8% of actual size. If the model is 1.2 meters tall, how tall is the building?
 15 meters
6. The purchase price of a camera is $84. The carrying case is 12% of the purchase price. Find the total cost including the carrying case.
 $94.08
7. The regular price of a record cost is $15. Find the discount and the new price if there is a 20% discount.
 discount = $3 new price = $12
8. A basketball team played 45 games. They won 60% of them. How many did the team win?
 27
9. A test had 50 questions. Joe got 70% of them correct. How many did Joe get correct?
 35
10. Diet soda contains 90% less calories than regular soda. If a can of regular soda contains 112 calories, how many calories does a can of diet soda contain?
 11.2

39 Can You Decode this Puzzle?

Decipher the code and perform the indicated operations.

.3	$\frac{1}{20}$	2.1
3.1	2.8	$\frac{8}{25}$
4	.1	$\frac{1}{2}$

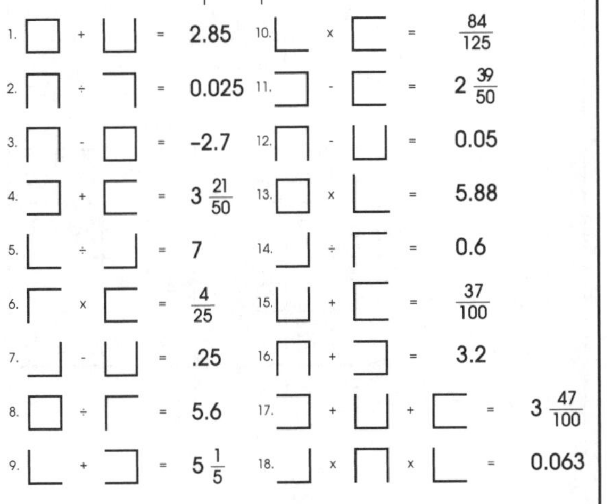

40 Triple Match

Use a ruler to connect each decimal to its fraction equivalent. Then draw a line connecting the fraction to its percent equivalent. Each path (decimal → fraction → percent) will pass through a letter and a number. Write the letter on the blank above the corresponding number at the bottom of the page.

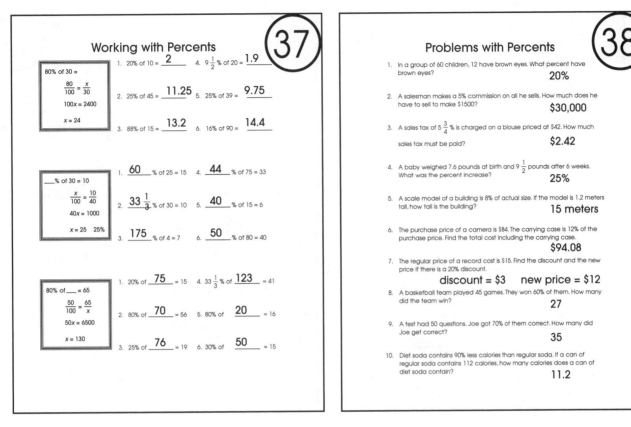

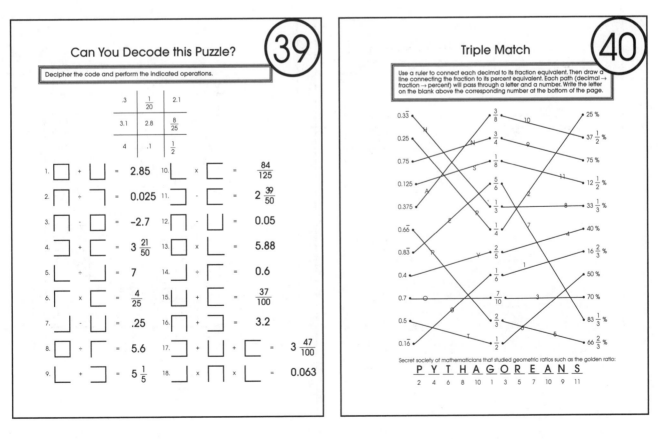

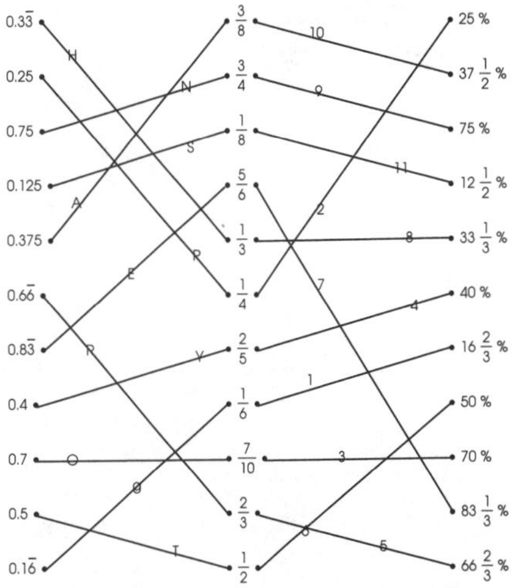

Secret society of mathematicians that studied geometric ratios such as the golden ratio:

P	Y	T	H	A	G	O	R	E	A	N	S
2	4	6	8	10	1	3	5	7	10	9	11

Answer Key

41 Adding Integers (Number Line)

Label each arrow. Write the resulting expression.

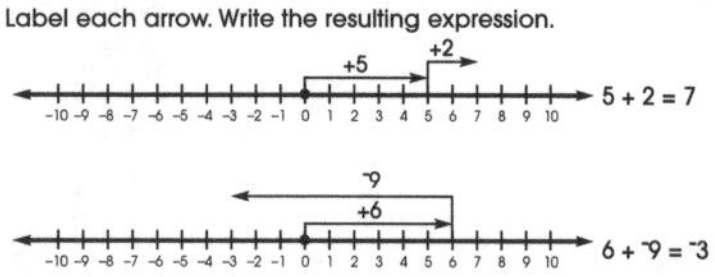

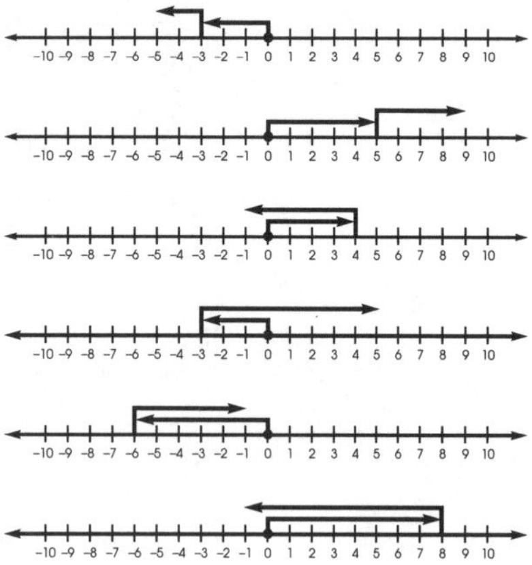

1. -5
2. 9
3. -1
4. 5
5. -1
6. -1

42 Adding Integers with Like Signs

5 + 5 2 positives	=	10 positive
-3 + -12 2 negatives	=	-15 negative

1. 6 + 8 = 14
2. -9 + -23 = -32
3. 25 + 37 = 62
4. -85 + -19 = -104
5. 132 + 899 = 1031
6. -104 + -597 = -701
7. -642 + -33 = -675
8. 88 + 298 = 386
9. -45 + -68 = -113
10. -12 + -18 + -35 = -65
11. 21 + 108 + 111 = 240
12. -62 + -33 + -12 = -107
13. 17 + 39 + 44 = 100
14. -18 + -18 + -18 = -54
15. 19 + 42 + 647 = 708
16. -29 + -108 + -337 + -503 = -977

43 Adding Integers with Unlike Signs

To add integers with different signs:
Use the sign of the number farther from zero.
Find the difference of the two numbers.

(sign) →
18 + -23 = -5
(23 – 18) →

(sign) →
-16 + 19 = +3
(19 – 16) →

1. 21 + -87 = -66
2. -63 + 59 = -4
3. 12 + -12 = 0
4. -28 + 82 = 54
5. -32 + 97 = 65
6. -53 + 74 = 21
7. 132 + -87 = 45
8. 212 + -99 = 113
9. -331 + 155 = -176
10. -413 + 521 = 108
11. 8,129 + -6,312 = 1,817
12. -11,332 + 566 = -10,766
13. 1,627 + -7,193 = -5,566
14. 7,864 + -6,329 = 1,535
15. -10,822 + 6,635 = -4,187
16. 13,894 + -81,139 = -67,245
17. -16,742 + 65,524 = 48,782
18. -56,814 + 73,322 = 16,508
19. 101,811 + -322,885 = -221.074
20. 562,493 + -112,819 = 449,674
21. 116,667 + -912,182 = -795,515
22. -629,922 + 81,962 = -547,960
23. -196,322 + 422,899 = 226,577
24. 467,833 + -36,838 = 430,995

44 Integer Grid

Fill in the blanks so that the last number of each row is the sum of the numbers in that row and the bottom number of each column is the sum of the numbers in that column.

3	-1	5	9	-3	-7	0	4	-8	2
2	6	0	-4	-8	2	-7	1	5	-3
-9	4	-8	1	4	7	0	-3	6	2
4	-8	1	-5	9	-6	2	-6	0	-9
-3	8	2	-6	-3	7	-1	-5	9	8
5	-8	1	-4	7	-1	-5	9	-2	2
-6	0	-7	3	-7	1	5	9	2	0
3	-7	4	-8	2	6	0	4	-9	-5
5	8	-2	6	0	-3	6	-9	-2	9
4	2	-4	-8	1	6	0	4	1	6

Answer Key

45 Subtracting Integers

Re-write each problem as an addition problem and solve.

$6 - 11 = 6 + {}^{-}11 = {}^{-}5$ (add the opposite)

$26 - {}^{-}67 = 26 + 67 = 93$ (add the opposite)

1.	$19 - 23 =$	$^{-}4$	9.	$63 - 72 =$	$^{-}9$
2.	$^{-}8 - 7 =$	$^{-}15$	10.	$^{-}93 - 117 =$	$^{-}210$
3.	$35 - 20 =$	15	11.	$45 - {}^{-}50 =$	95
4.	$^{-}46 - {}^{-}18 =$	$^{-}28$	12.	$^{-}18 - {}^{-}12 =$	$^{-}6$
5.	$^{-}118 - 12 =$	$^{-}130$	13.	$21 - 82 =$	$^{-}61$
6.	$7 - {}^{-}103 =$	110	14.	$^{-}831 - 616 =$	$^{-}1,447$
7.	$211 - 108 =$	103	15.	$^{-}632 - {}^{-}714 =$	82
8.	$^{-}9 - {}^{-}16 =$	7	16.	$1,192 - {}^{-}983 =$	2175

46 More Subtracting Integers

Name ____________ Date ____________

1.	$7 - 13 =$	$^{-}6$	13.	$^{-}23 - {}^{-}96 =$	73
2.	$^{-}17 - 9 =$	$^{-}26$	14.	$^{-}70 - 18 =$	$^{-}88$
3.	$^{-}11 - 7 =$	$^{-}18$	15.	$318 - {}^{-}864 =$	1,182
4.	$^{-}24 - {}^{-}23 =$	$^{-}1$	16.	$^{-}626 - 118 =$	$^{-}744$
5.	$2 - 25 =$	$^{-}23$	17.	$553 - {}^{-}764 =$	1,317
6.	$0 - {}^{-}14 =$	14	18.	$^{-}832 - 1,129 =$	$^{-}1,961$
7.	$^{-}3 - {}^{-}7 =$	4	19.	$6,793 - {}^{-}8,329 =$	15,122
8.	$^{-}8 - {}^{-}27 =$	19	20.	$^{-}7,624 - 11,652 =$	$^{-}19,276$
9.	$^{-}29 - 36 =$	$^{-}65$	21.	$108,719 - {}^{-}96,989 =$	205,708
10.	$^{-}72 - {}^{-}84 =$	12	22.	$^{-}832,629 - {}^{-}163,864 =$	$^{-}668,765$
11.	$63 - 94 =$	$^{-}31$	23.	$^{-}629,299 - 532,106 =$	$^{-}1,161,405$
12.	$77 - {}^{-}27 =$	104	24.	$735,300 - {}^{-}800,919 =$	1,536,219

© Carson-Dellosa Page 46 0-7424-1787-5 *Pre-Algebra*

47 Adding and Subtracting Integers

1.	$^{-}6 + {}^{-}8 =$	$^{-}14$	13.	$^{-}23 - {}^{-}28 =$	5
2.	$^{-}10 - 3 =$	$^{-}13$	14.	$0 - 31 =$	$^{-}31$
3.	$^{-}14 + 20 =$	6	15.	$^{-}40 - 35 =$	$^{-}75$
4.	$31 - {}^{-}9 =$	40	16.	$73 + {}^{-}19 =$	54
5.	$^{-}17 + 9 =$	$^{-}8$	17.	$^{-}231 - {}^{-}231 =$	0
6.	$^{-}8 - {}^{-}27 =$	19	18.	$^{-}107 + {}^{-}293 =$	$^{-}400$
7.	$^{-}33 - 36 =$	$^{-}69$	19.	$52 + {}^{-}41 - 60 =$	$^{-}49$
8.	$19 + {}^{-}32 =$	$^{-}13$	20.	$^{-}85 - {}^{-}106 + 18 =$	39
9.	$112 - {}^{-}52 =$	164	21.	$81 - 165 - {}^{-}75 =$	$^{-}9$
10.	$8 - {}^{-}7 =$	7	22.	$^{-}16 + 312 + {}^{-}621 =$	$^{-}325$
11.	$24 + {}^{-}24 =$	0	23.	$^{-}121 + {}^{-}632 - {}^{-}11 =$	$^{-}742$
12.	$508 - 678 =$	$^{-}170$	24.	$^{-}553 - {}^{-}632 + {}^{-}85 =$	$^{-}6$

48 Multiplying Integers

$(4)\ (4) = 16$ ($+ \cdot + = +$); $({}^{-}8)\ ({}^{-}6) = 48$ ($- \cdot - = +$) — Like Signs → Positive

$({}^{-}5)\ (10) = {}^{-}50$ ($- \cdot + = -$) — Unlike Signs → Negative

1.	$({}^{-}3)\ ({}^{-}6) =$	18	11.	$(31)\ ({}^{-}31)\ (31) =$	$^{-}29,791$
2.	$(14)\ ({}^{-}4) =$	$^{-}56$	12.	$({}^{-}4)\ ({}^{-}18)\ (28) =$	2016
3.	$(25)\ (2) =$	50	13.	$({}^{-}53)\ ({}^{-}14)\ ({}^{-}7) =$	$^{-}5194$
4.	$(20)\ ({}^{-}49) =$	$^{-}980$	14.	$(32)\ (125)\ (11) =$	44,000
5.	$(75)\ (15) =$	1125	15.	$({}^{-}37)\ ({}^{-}18)\ ({}^{-}5)\ (2) =$	$^{-}6,660$
6.	$({}^{-}30)\ ({}^{-}30) =$	900	16.	$(111)\ ({}^{-}63)\ (19) =$	$^{-}132,867$
7.	$({}^{-}17)\ (23) =$	$^{-}391$	17.	$(20)\ ({}^{-}7)\ (35)\ ({}^{-}3) =$	14,700
8.	$({}^{-}218)\ ({}^{-}32) =$	6976	18.	$(16)\ ({}^{-}8)\ ({}^{-}10)\ ({}^{-}1) =$	$^{-}1,280$
9.	$(801)\ ({}^{-}37) =$	$^{-}29,673$	19.	$({}^{-}9)\ ({}^{-}29)\ (32)\ (2) =$	16,704
10.	$({}^{-}89)\ ({}^{-}321) =$	28,569	20.	$({}^{-}18)\ ({}^{-}6)\ ({}^{-}21)\ ({}^{-}30) =$	68,040

Answer Key

49 Dividing Integers

$\frac{^-24}{^-8} = 3$ $\frac{-}{-} = +$ Like Signs → Positive

$^-32 \div 4 = {^-8}$ $- \div + = -$ Unlike Signs → Negative

1. $^-49 \div 7 =$ $^-7$
2. $100 \div {^-4} =$ $^-25$
3. $^-75 \div {^-15} =$ 5
4. $^-84 \div 21 =$ $^-4$
5. $^-120 \div 5 =$ $^-24$
6. $57 \div {^-19} =$ $^-3$
7. $^-288 \div {^-4} =$ 72
8. $804 \div 67 =$ 12
9. $\frac{17}{^-17} =$ $^-1$
10. $\frac{^-72}{^-18} =$ 4
11. $\frac{^-195}{13} =$ $^-15$
12. $\frac{^-23}{^-1} =$ 23
13. $\frac{200}{10} =$ 20
14. $\frac{270}{^-45} =$ $^-6$
15. $\frac{^-343}{7} =$ $^-49$
16. $\frac{^-1125}{^-45} =$ 25

50 Divide and Conquer

Compute. Substitute the values into the problem below.

A. $^-81 \div {^-9} =$ 9

B. $13 \div {^-13} =$ $^-1$

C. $^-60 \div 10 =$ $^-6$

D. $^-88 \div {^-11} =$ 8

E. $^-104 \div 8 =$ -13

F. $^-147 \div {^-21} =$ 7

G. $80 \div {^-5} =$ $^-16$

H. $52 \div 4 =$ 13

I. $^-150 \div {^-6} =$ 25

J. $\frac{^-102}{17} =$ $^-6$

K. $\frac{^-75}{^-5} =$ 15

L. $\frac{196}{^-14} =$ $^-14$

M. $\frac{1378}{^-26} =$ $^-53$

N. $\frac{^-468}{^-26} =$ 18

O. $\frac{253}{11} =$ 23

P. $\frac{^-465}{^-31} =$ 15

Q. $\frac{^-552}{^-23} =$ 24

R. $\frac{^-1824}{^-48} =$ 38

William I of Normandy conquered England in → → → ↓
(A+B+C+D+E+F) – (G+H) – (I÷(J+K+L)) – M•N + (O+P+Q+R) = 1066

(_+_+_+_+_+_) – (_+_) – (_÷(_+_+_)) – _•_ + (_+_+_+_)

$(9 + {^-1} + {^-6} + 8 + {^-13} + 7) - ({^-16} + 13) - (25 \div ({^-6} + 15 + {^-14})) - {^-53} \cdot 18 + (23 + 15 + 24 + 38)$

51 Mixed Practice with Integers

1. $^-41 + {^-125} =$ $^-166$
2. $79 - 88 =$ $^-9$
3. $^-3 \bullet {^-4} =$ 12
4. $\frac{^-125}{5} =$ $^-25$
5. $19 \bullet {^-24} =$ $^-456$
6. $\frac{^-123}{41} =$ $^-3$
7. $82 + {^-95} =$ $^-13$
8. $27 - {^-46} =$ 73
9. $^-31 - {^-32} =$ 1
10. $\frac{^-825}{^-33} =$ 25
11. $^-34 + 52 + {^-18} =$ 0
12. $14 \bullet {^-12} \bullet 3 =$ $^-504$
13. $\frac{^-185}{5} \bullet -4 =$ 148
14. $76 - 19 + {^-60} =$ $^-3$
15. $17 - {^-12} - 22 =$ 7
16. $100 \bullet {^-4} \bullet 40 =$ $^-16{,}000$
17. $\frac{54}{^-9} + \frac{33}{11} + \frac{24}{8} =$ 0
18. $^-51 \div 17 =$ $^-3$
19. $4 - 8 + {^-9} =$ $^-13$
20. $-\frac{98}{49} \bullet {^-10} =$ 20
21. $(256 \div {^-16}) \bullet {^-3} =$ 48
22. $({^-18} - {^-26} + {^-13}) \bullet {^-2} =$ 10
23. $(202 + {^-196} - 321) \div {^-5} =$ 63
24. $(\frac{^-575}{23} - 18) \bullet {^-11} =$ 473

52 Problems with Integers

1. An elevator started at the first floor and went up 18 floors. It then came down 11 floors and went back up 16. At what floor was it stopped?
   23
2. At midnight, the temperature was 30° F. By 6:00 a.m., it had dropped 5° and by noon, it had increased by 11°. What was the temperature at noon?
   36°
3. Some number added to 5 is equal to $^-11$. Find the number.
   $^-16$
4. From the top of a mountain to the floor of the valley below is 4,392 feet. If the valley is 93 feet below sea level, what is the height of the mountain?
   4299 feet
5. During one week, the stock market did the following: Monday rose 18 points, Tuesday rose 31 points, Wednesday dropped 5 points, Thursday rose 27 points and Friday dropped 38 points. If it started out at 1,196 on Monday, what did it end up on Friday?
   1,229
6. An airplane started at 0 feet. It rose 21,000 feet at takeoff. It then descended 4,329 feet because of clouds. An oncoming plane was approaching, so it rose 6,333 feet. After the oncoming plane passed, it descended 8,453 feet, at what altitude was the plane flying?
   14,551
7. Some number added to $^-11$ is 37. Divide this number by $^-12$. Then, multiply by $^-8$. What is the final number?
   32
8. Jim decided to go for a drive in his car. He started out at 0 miles per hour (mph). He then accelerated 20 mph down his street. Then, to get on the highway he accelerated another 35 miles per hour. A car was going slow in front of him so he slowed down 11 mph. He then got off the highway, so he slowed down another 7 mph. At what speed is he driving?
   37 mph

Answer Key

53 Adding and Subtracting Rational Numb[ers]

$$^{-}3 + {}^{-}2 + 2\frac{1}{2} = {}^{-}5 + 2\frac{1}{2} = {}^{-}4\frac{2}{2} + 2\frac{1}{2} = {}^{-}2\frac{1}{2}$$

1. $^{-}1.6 + 1\frac{7}{10} =$ **0.1**
   (Hint: $1\frac{7}{10} = 1.7$)
2. $0 - 6\frac{1}{2} + {}^{-}3 =$ **$^{-}9\frac{1}{2}$**
3. $\frac{^{-}3}{4} + 5 - \frac{1}{2} =$ **$3\frac{3}{4}$**
4. $9 - 10.2 + {}^{-}8.6 =$ **$^{-}9.8$**
5. $\frac{1}{2} + 1\frac{1}{2} - 1\frac{1}{3} =$ **$\frac{2}{3}$**
6. $6.75 - 3\frac{1}{2} + 2.55 =$ **5.8**
   (Hint: $3\frac{5}{10} = 3.5$)
7. $3\frac{3}{7} - {}^{-}1\frac{1}{7} + \frac{3}{7} =$ **5**
8. $^{-}7 - {}^{-}2\frac{3}{4} + {}^{-}5\frac{1}{4} =$ **$^{-}9\frac{1}{2}$**
9. $7\frac{1}{10} + {}^{-}7.25 - 11.39 =$ **$^{-}11.54$**
10. $^{-}8\frac{1}{4} + {}^{-}3\frac{3}{12} - 7\frac{2}{3} =$ **$^{-}19\frac{1}{6}$**
11. $^{-}5 - 7\frac{1}{8} + {}^{-}3\frac{5}{12} =$ **$^{-}15\frac{13}{24}$**
12. $3\frac{3}{10} + {}^{-}3.38 - 6\frac{6}{10} =$ **$^{-}6.68$**

54 More Adding and Subtracting Rational Numbers

1. $^{-}3\frac{5}{10} + 8 =$ **4.5**
2. $^{-}5\frac{3}{7} + {}^{-}3\frac{3}{14} =$ **$^{-}8\frac{9}{14}$**
3. $6\frac{1}{6} - 6\frac{3}{10} =$ **$-\frac{2}{15}$**
4. $^{-}8 + 15.32 =$ **7.32**
5. $^{-}8\frac{3}{10} - {}^{-}5.9 =$ **$^{-}2.4$**
6. $13 - 5\frac{3}{5} =$ **$7\frac{2}{5}$**
7. $12\frac{1}{9} + {}^{-}5\frac{2}{3} =$ **$6\frac{4}{9}$**
8. $^{-}11.03 - {}^{-}21.6 =$ **10.57**
9. $^{-}7\frac{3}{10} - 16.53 =$ **$^{-}23.83$**
10. $31\frac{8}{9} + {}^{-}27\frac{27}{81} =$ **$4\frac{5}{9}$**
11. $11 - 18.6 + {}^{-}3\frac{3}{10} =$ **$^{-}10.9$**
12. $^{-}5\frac{2}{10} + 16.7 - 3\frac{1}{5} =$ **8.3**
13. $13\frac{1}{3} + {}^{-}12 + {}^{-}7\frac{7}{12} =$ **$^{-}6\frac{1}{4}$**
14. $41.32 + {}^{-}18.7 - 16.21 =$ **6.41**
15. $^{-}18.75 - 5\frac{3}{4} - 7\frac{5}{12} =$ **$^{-}31\frac{11}{12}$**
16. $^{-}15 - 21\frac{1}{7} + 18\frac{2}{49} =$ **$^{-}18\frac{5}{49}$**
17. $7\frac{2}{3} + {}^{-}8\frac{4}{9} - {}^{-}16\frac{1}{6} =$ **$15\frac{7}{18}$**
18. $^{-}31.5 - {}^{-}3\frac{7}{10} + 21 =$ **$^{-}6.8$**
19. $25\frac{1}{5} - 17.3 + {}^{-}11\frac{2}{11} =$ **$^{-}3\frac{31}{110}$**
20. $19.25 - {}^{-}6\frac{3}{4} + 12\frac{5}{12} =$ **$38\frac{5}{12}$**

55 Multiplying and Dividing Rational Numbers

$$^{-}4 \cdot 5 \cdot \frac{1}{2} = {}^{-}20 \cdot \frac{1}{2} = -\frac{\overset{10}{\cancel{20}}}{1} \cdot \frac{1}{\underset{1}{\cancel{2}}} = -\frac{10}{1} = {}^{-}10$$

$$5\frac{1}{4} \cdot 1\frac{2}{7} \div 1\frac{1}{2} = \frac{21}{4} \cdot \frac{9}{7} \div \frac{3}{2} = \frac{\overset{3}{\cancel{21}}}{\underset{2}{\cancel{4}}} \cdot \frac{\overset{3}{\cancel{9}}}{\underset{1}{\cancel{7}}} \cdot \frac{\overset{1}{\cancel{2}}}{\underset{1}{\cancel{3}}} = \frac{9}{2} \text{ or } 4\frac{1}{2}$$

1. $^{-}1\frac{2}{3} \bullet {}^{-}3\frac{1}{5} =$ **$5\frac{1}{3}$**
2. $4\frac{5}{9} \div -\frac{10}{27} =$ **$^{-}12.3$**
3. $4\frac{1}{4} \bullet 3\frac{1}{5} =$ **$13\frac{3}{5}$**
4. $^{-}9\frac{3}{8} \div {}^{-}3\frac{9}{12} =$ **2.5**
5. $-\frac{3}{8} \bullet 4 \bullet \frac{4}{9} =$ **$-\frac{2}{3}$**
6. $^{-}9\frac{3}{5} \div \frac{12}{5} \bullet {}^{-}4 =$ **16**
7. $^{-}4.1 \bullet {}^{-}5.2 \div 4 =$ **5.33**
8. $6.2 \bullet 3 \bullet -\frac{1}{2} =$ **$^{-}9.3$**
9. $({}^{-}2\frac{1}{2})({}^{-}2\frac{1}{2}) \div 0.5 =$ **12.5**
10. $-\frac{6}{7} \bullet -\frac{5}{12} \bullet -\frac{2}{15} =$ **$-\frac{1}{21}$**
11. $5\frac{2}{3} \bullet 9.81 \bullet 0 =$ **0**
12. $12 \bullet 3\frac{1}{4} \bullet {}^{-}2\frac{2}{3} =$ **$^{-}104$**

56 More Multiplying and Dividing Rational Numbers

1. $^{-}9\frac{3}{5} \bullet \frac{5}{12} =$ **$^{-}4$**
2. $-\frac{16}{7} \div \frac{12}{35} =$ **$^{-}6\frac{2}{3}$**
3. $4\frac{1}{2} \bullet {}^{-}2\frac{2}{7} =$ **$^{-}10\frac{2}{7}$**
4. $^{-}5\frac{5}{6} \div 2\frac{1}{3} =$ **$^{-}2\frac{1}{2}$**
5. $^{-}8\frac{1}{3} \bullet {}^{-}2\frac{2}{5} =$ **20**
6. $16\frac{1}{8} \div 14\frac{1}{3} =$ **$1\frac{1}{8}$**
7. $^{-}37.6 \bullet 0.03 =$ **$^{-}1.128$**
8. $^{-}16.188 \div {}^{-}4.26 =$ **3.8**
9. $^{-}1.75 \bullet {}^{-}3.4 =$ **5.95**
10. $^{-}3.45 \div 1\frac{1}{2} =$ **$^{-}2.3$**
11. $^{-}8 \div {}^{-}1\frac{1}{3} \bullet {}^{-}5 =$ **$^{-}30$**
12. $4.498 \div {}^{-}1.73 \bullet {}^{-}1.2 =$ **3.12**
13. $-\frac{5}{7} \div -\frac{1}{14} \bullet -\frac{1}{2} =$ **$^{-}5$**
14. $^{-}6\frac{2}{3} \bullet 2.75 \div {}^{-}1\frac{2}{3} =$ **11**
15. $-\frac{3}{8} \div {}^{-}3 \bullet \frac{4}{5} =$ **$\frac{1}{10}$**
16. $12\frac{3}{8} \bullet {}^{-}2\frac{2}{3} \div 2.5 =$ **$^{-}13.2$**
17. $-\frac{5}{6} \bullet 4\frac{1}{4} \bullet -\frac{3}{5} =$ **$2\frac{1}{8}$**
18. $^{-}3\frac{1}{5} \div 4\frac{2}{5} \div {}^{-}1\frac{1}{7} =$ **$\frac{7}{11}$**
19. $3\frac{3}{5} \bullet {}^{-}1.46 =$ **$^{-}5.256$**
20. $4\frac{2}{3} \div -\frac{6}{7} \bullet \frac{9}{10} =$ **$^{-}4.9$**

Answer Key

57 Order of Operations with Rational Numbers

Order of operations: Perform operations within parenthesis.
Compute exponents.
Multiply or divide in order from left to right.
Add or subtract in order from left to right.

$2 + {}^{-}3 \bullet 5 = 2 + {}^{-}15 = {}^{-}13$

$7 - 6^2 \div 2 \bullet 5 = 7 - 36 \div 2 \bullet 5 = 7 - 18 \bullet 5 = 7 - 90 = {}^{-}63$

1. ${}^{-}28 \div 7 + 2\frac{1}{3} =$ **${}^{-}1\frac{2}{3}$**
2. $\frac{1}{2}({}^{-}16 - 4) =$ **${}^{-}10$**
3. ${}^{-}9 \div {}^{-}3 + 4 \bullet -\frac{1}{4} - 20 \div 5 =$ **${}^{-}2$**
4. $\frac{1}{3}(({}^{-}18 + 3) + (5 + 7) \div {}^{-}4) =$ **${}^{-}6$**
5. $(8\frac{1}{3} + 3\frac{2}{3}) \div 4 - {}^{-}16 =$ **19**
6. $\frac{(80 \bullet \frac{1}{2}) + 35}{{}^{-}10 + 25} =$ **5**
7. $2({}^{-}6(3 - 12) - 17) =$ **74**
8. $\frac{1}{4}(20 + 72 \div {}^{-}9) =$ **3**
9. $3 \bullet 2(4 + (9 \div 3)) =$ **42**
10. $50 \div ((4 \bullet 5) - (36 \div 2)) + {}^{-}91 =$ **${}^{-}66$**

58 Calculator Order

Use a scientific calculator to solve each problem. Turn the calculator around to determine the word answer.

Problem	Solution	Clue	Word
1. 501 x 7	3507	To not win	LOSE
2. $10^3 - 3 \times 131$	607	Type of cabin	LOG
3. $17^2 + 7^2$	338	It buzzes.	BEE
4. 67,077 ÷ 87	771	Sick	ILL
5. 2 • (2 • 1900 + 3 • 23)	7738	It rings.	BELL
6. $2^9 + 2$	514	Not hers	HIS
7. $279^2 - (500 - 4)$	77345	Nautilus ____	SHELL
8. $3^3 \times 100 + 3 \times 115$	3045	Worn on foot	SHOE
9. $22{,}416 \div 2^2$	5604	Big pigs	HOGS
10. 473,720 – 12,345	461375	Snow vehicle	SLEIGH
11. 3 x 5 x 246 +15	3705	Bottom of shoe	SOLE
12. 4,738 – 1,234	3504	Fire equipment	HOSE
13. $60^2 + 4 \times 26$	3704	Center of a donut	HOLE
14. 11 x (60 – 2)	638	To plead	BEG
15. 5787 ÷ 9 x 12	7716	Fish organ	GILL
16. 12,345 + 23,456 – 465	35336	They "honk".	GEESE
17. 8 x 100 + 8 – 1	807	Tennis shot	LOB
18. $50 \times 700 + 3 \times 6^2$	35108	Capital of Idaho	BOISE
19. 50 x 110 + (10 – 3)	5507	Not a win	LOSS
20. $64{,}118 - 80^2$	57718	Ducks' beaks	BILLS

A googol is 10^{100} or 1 followed by 100 zeros.
What number would result in the "calculator word" googol? **706006**

59 Comparing Rational Numbers

Use <, > or = to make you a true sentence.

5.68 ___ 5.7 → 5.68 < 5.70

$^{-}7\frac{3}{10}$ ___ $^{-}7.29$ → $^{-}7.30 < {}^{-}7.29$

1. 2.5 **=** $2\frac{17}{34}$
2. 1.049 **<** 1.49
3. $^{-}0.\bar{3}$ **<** $^{-}0.3$
4. 15.62 **>** 1.562
5. 8156.6 **<** 8166.6
6. $^{-}7\frac{4}{5}$ **=** $^{-}7\frac{24}{30}$
7. $^{-}8\frac{7}{8}$ **<** $^{-}8.857$
8. 329.93 **>** 32.993
9. 982.61 **<** 7662.8
10. $13\frac{5}{8}$ **>** 13.6

$5\frac{1}{2}, 5\frac{3}{5}, 5.4$ → Rewrite → 5.5, 5.6, 5.4 → Descending Order → $5\frac{3}{5}, 5\frac{1}{2}, 5.4$

1. 6.41, 6.411, 6.4111 — **3 2 1**
2. $^{-}2\frac{9}{14}, {}^{-}2\frac{5}{8}, {}^{-}2\frac{4}{7}$ — **3 2 1**
3. $11.6, 11\frac{2}{3}, 11\frac{14}{25}$ — **2 1 3**
4. $^{-}0.030, -\frac{33}{100}, {}^{-}0.003$ — **2 3 1**
5. $7\frac{5}{8}, 7\frac{3}{4}, 7.775$ — **3 2 1**
6. $^{-}10\frac{3}{4}, {}^{-}10.82, {}^{-}10\frac{2}{3}$ — **2 3 1**
7. $3.08, 3\frac{4}{5}, 3\frac{3}{5}$ — **3 1 2**
8. $^{-}1.35, {}^{-}1\frac{1}{8}, {}^{-}1\frac{1}{4}$ — **3 1 2**

60 Flip dᴉɹ⊥

Perform each of the following operations on your calculator. Then flip your calculator and find the "word answer" to the questions.

1. What did Amelia Earhart's father say the first time he saw her fly an air plane?
   0.115 x 3 + 10141 x 5 = **50705.345**
   Flip dᴉɹ⊥ **She solos**
2. What did Farmer Macgregor throw at Peter Rabbit to chase him out of the garden?
   (27 x 109 + 4 – 0.027) 2 x 9 = **53045.514**
   Flip dᴉɹ⊥ **his shoes**
3. What did Snoopy add to his doghouse as a result of his dogfights with the Red Baron?
   7 (3 x 303 + 50) x 8 = **53704**
   Flip dᴉɹ⊥ **holes**
4. What kind of double does a golfer want to avoid at the end of a round of golf?
   4 (1956 x 4 + 153) = **31908**
   Flip dᴉɹ⊥ **BOGIE**
5. What did the little girl say when she was frightened by the ghost?
   0.07 x 0.111 x 5 + 0.00123 = **0.04008**
   Flip dᴉɹ⊥ **BOO HOO**

Answer Key

61 Open Sentences

State the solution for each sentence.

$\frac{1}{2} \cdot {}^{-}10 = x$ $\quad$ $\frac{{}^{-}56}{{}^{-}7} - 4 = z$

$\frac{1}{\not 2_{1}} \cdot \frac{\not{{}^{-}10}^{\,{}^{-}5}}{1} = x$ $\quad$ $8 - 4 = z$

${}^{-}5 = x$ $\quad$ $4 = z$

1. $\frac{18 + {}^{-}6}{2} = a$ **6**
2. ${}^{-}3 \cdot 4 - 6 = c$ **${}^{-}18$**
3. $4.5 - 6.2 = p$ **${}^{-}1.7$**
4. $\frac{{}^{-}3}{8} \cdot {}^{-}4 - 1 = q$ **$\frac{1}{2}$**
5. $\frac{{}^{-}15 + {}^{-}27}{3} = x$ **${}^{-}14$**
6. ${}^{-}8.1 \cdot 4.2 + 16 = g$ **${}^{-}18.02$**
7. $\frac{1}{3} \cdot {}^{-}15 + {}^{-}10 = r$ **${}^{-}15$**
8. $1\frac{3}{5} \div \frac{16}{45} = d$ **4.5**
9. $5 \cdot 7.32 - 18.19 = n$ **18.41**
10. $\frac{3}{4} \cdot {}^{-}16 + 8.12 = z$ **${}^{-}3.88$**
11. $\frac{{}^{-}40 + 15}{5} + 6 = b$ **1**
12. $-\frac{2}{5} \div \frac{4}{15} + {}^{-}2\frac{1}{2} = t$ **${}^{-}4$**

62 More Open Sentences

Using the given value, state whether each problem is true or false.

$28 = r \cdot \frac{1}{4}$, if $r = {}^{-}108$

$28 \stackrel{?}{=} {}^{-}108 \cdot \frac{1}{4}$

$28 \stackrel{?}{=} -27 \Longrightarrow$ False

1. $7 + x = 3\frac{1}{2}$, if $x = {}^{-}3\frac{1}{2}$ **true**
2. $y + 15 \div 6 = {}^{-}1\frac{1}{2}$, if $y = {}^{-}3$ **false**
3. $\frac{f}{13} + {}^{-}3 = 0$, if $f = 69$ **false**
4. $2x - 5.45 = 0.97$, if $x = 3.21$ **true**
5. $8\frac{1}{3} + a = 15\frac{8}{15}$, if $a = 7\frac{2}{5}$ **false**
6. $8 + (z - 32) = {}^{-}10$, if $z = 16$ **false**
7. $11.5 + c = 28\frac{1}{4}$, if $c = 16\frac{3}{4}$ **true**
8. $y(5 + 11) + 8 = 41$, if $y = 2$ **false**
9. $3g + 5.26 - 11.9 = 12.64$, if $g = {}^{-}3$ **false**
10. $5 + -\frac{16}{k} = {}^{-}3$, if $k = 2$ **true**
11. $7\frac{1}{9} \div w = \frac{1}{18}$, if $w = 2\frac{17}{32}$ **false**
12. $\frac{3(2q - q)}{8} + 29 = 32$, if $q = 8$ **true**
13. $\frac{16.8 - 91.6}{m}$ 37.4, if $m = 2$ **false**
14. $11\frac{1}{4} - f = 5\frac{1}{16}$, if $f = 16\frac{5}{16}$ **false**

63 Evaluating Expressions

Evaluate the following, if $a = \frac{1}{2}$, $x = 4$ and $y = {}^{-}2$

$5x(2a - 5y) = 5 \cdot 4\,(2 \cdot \frac{1}{2} - 5 \cdot {}^{-}2) = 20\,(1 + 10) = 20\,(11) = 220$

1. $4(a - 1) =$ **${}^{-}2$**
2. $4a - 3y =$ **8**
3. $4(x - 3y) =$ **40**
4. $x(a + 6) =$ **26**
5. $6a + {}^{-}12a =$ **${}^{-}3$**
6. $7(x + -y) =$ **42**
7. $6a(8a + 4y) =$ **${}^{-}12$**
8. $3x + 2(a - y) =$ **17**
9. $x(ax + ay) =$ **4**
10. $ay + y - 5ax =$ **${}^{-}13$**
11. $xy(2a + 3x - 2) =$ **${}^{-}88$**
12. $4x - (xy + 2) =$ **22**
13. $5y - 8a + 6xy - 7x =$ **${}^{-}90$**
14. $10x(8a + {}^{-}4y) + {}^{-}3y =$ **486**
15. $6xy - 2x(4a - 8y) =$ **${}^{-}192$**
16. $(2a - x)(2x - 6) =$ **${}^{-}6$**

64 Simplifying Expressions

Distributive Property

$3(x + 2y) = 3x + 3 \cdot 2y$
$= 3x + 6y$

1. ${}^{-}7(a + b) =$ **${}^{-}7a - 7b$**
2. $x(y - 4) =$ **$xy - 4x$**
3. $-\frac{2}{3}(c - 12) =$ **$-\frac{2}{3}c + 8$**
4. ${}^{-}8(\frac{t}{2} + 6) =$ **${}^{-}4t + {}^{-}48$**
5. $y({}^{-}16 + 2x) =$ **$2xy - 16y$**
6. $3(2a - 8b) =$ **$6a - 24b$**
7. $2x(3y + {}^{-}6) =$ **$6xy - 12x$**
8. $7({}^{-}5x + 8z) =$ **$56z - 35x$**
9. ${}^{-}5y(6z - 10) =$ **$50y - 30yz$**
10. ${}^{-}3x({}^{-}7 + 8y) =$ **$21x - 24xy$**

Combining Like Terms

$6m - 4m + 3p = (6 - 4)m + 3p$
$= 2m + 3p$

same variable

1. $9y + 6y - 2 =$ **$15y - 2$**
2. $25x - x + 2y =$ **$24x + 2y$**
3. $4a + 8b + 11a - 10b =$ **$15a - 2b$**
4. $13xy + 18xy - 20xy =$ **$11xy$**
5. ${}^{-}2m + 16 - 13m =$ **$16 - 15m$**
6. $4a + 7 + 3a - 8 - 3a =$ **$4a - 1$**
7. $16x + {}^{-}18y + 10x - 7y =$ **$26x - 25y$**
8. $6c - 8ab + 9c - 10 =$ **$15c - 8ab - 10$**
9. $18ab + {}^{-}6a + {}^{-}7b + 26ab + {}^{-}7b =$ **$44ab + {}^{-}6a + {}^{-}14b$**
10. $5x - 3x + 2xy + 31x + {}^{-}18xy =$ **$33x - 16xy$**

Answer Key

65 An Expression by Any Other Name

Simplify each expression. Cross out each box that contains an answer. The remaining words can be restated to make a familiar proverb.

1. $3(a + b) + 2b =$ **$3a + 5b$**
2. $5a + 2a(5 - b) =$ **$15a - 2ab$**
3. $8 - 3(6 - 6a) =$ **$^{-}10 + 18a$**
4. $4a + 6(a + 8) =$ **$10a + 48$**
5. $^{-}2a - 3(b - 4a) =$ **$10a - 3b$**
6. $8(6a + 7b) - 11(2b + 8a) =$ **$^{-}40a + 34b$**
7. $^{-}6(a + 5b) - 3(^{-}7b - a) =$ **$^{-}3a - 9b$**
8. $2(a - b) + 3(a - b) - 4(a - b) =$ **$a - b$**
9. $4a + {^{-}7}(a + 2) =$ **$^{-}3a - 14$**
10. $6(a + 2b) + 8a - 16b =$ **$14a - 4ab$**
11. $3a + {^{-}2}(a + b) =$ **$a - 2b$**
12. $2(3a - 4b) - 6a =$ **$^{-}8b$**
13. $^{-}5(2a - 3b) + 5(3b - 2a) =$ **$^{-}20a + 30b$**
14. $4(11a - 9b) - 7(6a) =$ **$2a - 36b$**
15. $^{-}3(4a - 5b) - (a - b) =$ **$^{-}13a + 16b$**

$10 + 18a$ YOU	~~$^{-}10 + 18a$ ARE~~	~~$a - 2b$ SEE~~	$2a + 36b$ CANNOT	~~$3a + 5b$ LEAD~~	$12a - 8b$ INSTRUCT
$14a + 4b$ AN	~~$14a - 4b$ A~~	$40a + 34b$ ELDERLY	~~$^{-}40a + 34b$ HORSE~~	$3a - 14$ CANINE	~~$2a - 36b$ TO~~
~~$10a + 48$ WATER~~	~~$^{-}3a - 14$ BUT~~	$12a - 8b$ ON	~~$^{-}13a + 16b$ YOU~~	~~$^{-}3a - 9b$ CANNOT~~	$15a - 2b$ FRESH
~~$10a - 3b$ MAKE~~	~~$a - b$ HIM~~	~~$15a - 2ab$ DOWN~~	~~$^{-}20a + 30b$ DRINK~~	$20a - 30b$ PROCEDURES	~~$^{-}8b$ HOME~~

Write the familiar proverb.

You can't teach an old dog new tricks.

Page 65

66 Solving Addition Equations

$$1.8 = {^{-}2.1} + x$$
$$1.8 + 2.1 = {^{-}2.1} + 2.1 + x$$
$$3.9 = 0 + x$$
$$3.9 = x$$

1. $a + {^{-}7} = 8$ **15**
2. $y + 76 = {^{-}93}$ **$^{-}169$**
3. $4 + b = {^{-}14}$ **$^{-}18$**
4. $^{-}33 = z + 16$ **$^{-}49$**
5. $^{-}12 + x = 21$ **33**
6. $2.4 = m + 3.7$ **$^{-}1.3$**
7. $^{-}1\frac{1}{2} + n = {^{-}1}\frac{5}{8}$ **$-\frac{1}{8}$**
8. $^{-}27 = c + 27$ **$^{-}54$**
9. $-\frac{5}{8} + x = -\frac{5}{8}$ **0**
10. $y + {^{-}6.2} = 8.1$ **14.3**
11. $38 = x + {^{-}19}$ **57**
12. $a + {^{-}2}\frac{5}{9} = {^{-}10}\frac{5}{18}$ **$^{-}7\frac{13}{18}$**
13. $^{-}1{,}129 + b = 3{,}331$ **4460**
14. $^{-}3.5 = 7\frac{1}{2} + x$ **$^{-}11$**

67 Solving Subtraction Equations

$$24 = x - {^{-}8}$$
$$24 = x + 8$$
$$24 - 8 = x + 8 - 8$$
$$16 = x + 0$$
$$16 = x$$

1. $k - 36 = 37$ **73**
2. $^{-}22 = y - 8$ **$^{-}14$**
3. $x - {^{-}7} = {^{-}19}$ **$^{-}26$**
4. $30 = b - {^{-}2}$ **28**
5. $a - 18 = {^{-}32}$ **$^{-}14$**
6. $^{-}1.7 = b - 9.3$ **7.6**
7. $^{-}4\frac{1}{3} = q - 3\frac{1}{3}$ **$^{-}1$**
8. $^{-}17 = q - 3$ **$^{-}14$**
9. $p - \frac{3}{5} = \frac{3}{5}$ **$\frac{6}{5}$**
10. $5.62 = m - 6$ **11.62**
11. $x - {^{-}36.5} = {^{-}2.563}$ **$^{-}39.063$**
12. $^{-}1{,}132 = b - 6{,}339$ **5207**
13. $7\frac{3}{4} = a - 16\frac{3}{16}$ **$23\frac{15}{16}$**
14. $z - {^{-}5.75} = {^{-}8}\frac{1}{4}$ **$^{-}14$**

68 Solving Addition and Subtraction Equatio

1. $x + {^{-}3} = -18$ **$^{-}15$**
2. $c - 11 = 43$ **54**
3. $12 + y = 32$ **20**
4. $^{-}26 = d - 7$ **$^{-}19$**
5. $^{-}62 = a + 16$ **$^{-}78$**
6. $q - {^{-}83} = 121$ **38**
7. $t + {^{-}101} = 263$ **364**
8. $w - 454 = {^{-}832}$ **$^{-}378$**
9. $^{-}332 = {^{-}129} + s$ **$^{-}203$**
10. $665 = k - {^{-}327}$ **338**
11. $^{-}8.6 = m + 11.12$ **$^{-}19.72$**
12. $a - -\frac{1}{5} = \frac{3}{20}$ **$-\frac{1}{20}$**
13. $-\frac{3}{4} + z = \frac{7}{18}$ **$\frac{41}{36}$**
14. $b - 17.8 = {^{-}36}$ **$^{-}18.2$**
15. $-\frac{13}{24} = -\frac{5}{16} + c$ **$-\frac{11}{48}$**
16. $102.8 = g - {^{-}66.09}$ **36.71**
17. $f + \frac{3}{5} = \frac{3}{4}$ **$\frac{3}{20}$**
18. $b - \frac{5}{6} = -\frac{7}{8}$ **$-\frac{1}{24}$**
19. $21.21 + p = {^{-}101.6}$ **$^{-}122.81$**
20. $^{-}762.46 = h - 32.061$ **$^{-}730.399$**

Answer Key

69 Solving Multiplication Equations

$4y = {}^-28$
$\frac{4y}{4} = -\frac{28}{4}$
$1y = {}^-7$
$y = {}^-7$

1. ${}^-6a = {}^-66$	11	8. $9a = {}^-3$	$-\frac{1}{3}$
2. ${}^-180 = 12b$	${}^-15$	9. $0.25y = 1.5$	6
3. ${}^-13n = 13$	${}^-1$	10. ${}^-0.0006 = 0.02x$	${}^-0.03$
4. $42 = {}^-14p$	${}^-3$	11. ${}^-11x = 275$	${}^-25$
5. $1\frac{1}{2} = 3x$	$\frac{1}{2}$	12. $45\frac{1}{2} = {}^-14c$	${}^-3\frac{1}{4}$
6. ${}^-5.6 = {}^-0.8x$	7	13. $61.44 = 12z$	5.12
7. $8 = {}^-32b$	$-\frac{1}{4}$	14. ${}^-21y = {}^-756$	36

70 Solving Division Equations

$\frac{x}{4} = {}^-6$
$4 \bullet \frac{x}{4} = {}^-6 \bullet 4$
$x = {}^-24$

1. ${}^-18 = \frac{a}{6}$	${}^-108$	8. $3 = -\frac{1}{8}a$	${}^-24$
2. $\frac{x}{6} = {}^-6$	${}^-36$	9. $\frac{w}{{}^-2} = 0.04$	${}^-0.08$
3. $\frac{y}{{}^-2} = 231$	${}^-462$	10. $\frac{u}{{}^-4} = {}^-14$	56
4. $\frac{1}{5}b = {}^-8$	${}^-40$	11. $\frac{x}{{}^-5.1} = {}^-16$	81.6
5. $\frac{m}{0.6} = 0.3$	0.18	12. $-28 = \frac{a}{13}$	${}^-364$
6. $35 = \frac{x}{{}^-7}$	${}^-245$	13. $\frac{1}{18}c = {}^-31$	${}^-558$
7. $0.12 = \frac{y}{0.12}$	0.0144	14. $\frac{b}{{}^-0.29} = 5.5$	1.595

71 Solving Multiplication and Division Equat

1. ${}^-2p = {}^-38$	19	11. $16 = \frac{n}{{}^-21}$	${}^-336$
2. $\frac{b}{8} = {}^-24$	${}^-192$	12. $0.7h = {}^-0.112$	${}^-0.16$
3. ${}^-85 = 17r$	${}^-5$	13. ${}^-80 = \frac{p}{15}$	${}^-1200$
4. ${}^-32 = \frac{c}{{}^-22}$	704	14. $792 = {}^-33y$	${}^-24$
5. ${}^-13a = 52$	${}^-4$	15. ${}^-5.2 = \frac{m}{30.1}$	${}^-156.52$
6. $\frac{1}{47}d = {}^-26$	${}^-1222$	16. ${}^-11.2x = {}^-60.48$	5.4
7. ${}^-12f = {}^-180$	15	17. $\frac{1}{{}^-26}r = {}^-66$	1716
8. $\frac{1}{0.16}x = 0.7$	112	18. $315 = 21s$	15
9. ${}^-77.4 = 9a$	${}^-8.6$	19. $\frac{z}{0.06} = {}^-7.98$	${}^-0.4788$
10. $-\frac{1}{6}q = {}^-11$	66	20. ${}^-14g = {}^-406$	29

72 Mixed Up Pairs

Solve each equation. Each equation in column A has the same solution as an equation in Column B. Find the pairs.

	Column A		Column B	
B	1. $y + 12 = 8$	${}^-4$	A. $y - 12 = {}^-12$	0
E	2. $\frac{y}{6} = {}^-2$	${}^-12$	B. $2y = {}^-8$	${}^-4$
D	3. ${}^-7y = {}^-84$	12	C. $y - 1 = {}^-7$	${}^-6$
G	4. ${}^-42 = y - 20$	${}^-22$	D. $y - {}^-12 = 24$	12
A	5. $92 + y = 92$	0	E. $\frac{y}{{}^-4} = 3$	${}^-12$
H	6. $9 = 54y$	$\frac{1}{6}$	F. $y + 2 = 11$	9
C	7. ${}^-12 = y - 6$	${}^-6$	G. $y + 11 = {}^-11$	${}^-22$
J	8. ${}^-1 = \frac{y}{20}$	${}^-20$	H. $12y = 2$	$\frac{1}{6}$
F	9. $27 = 3y$	9	I. $\frac{y}{{}^-2} = {}^-10$	20
I	10. ${}^-5 + y = 15$	20	J. ${}^-15 = y + 5$	${}^-20$

Answer Key

73 Solving Equations with Two Operations

$$2y - 7 = {}^{-}29$$
$$2y - 7 + 7 = {}^{-}29 + 7$$
$$2y = {}^{-}22$$
$$\frac{2y}{2} = \frac{{}^{-}22}{2}$$
$$y = {}^{-}11$$

1. $13 + {}^{-}3p = {}^{-}2$	5	7. ${}^{-}7r - 8 = {}^{-}14$	$\frac{6}{7}$
2. $\frac{{}^{-}5a}{2} = 75$	${}^{-}30$	8. $\frac{4y}{3} = 8$	6
3. $6x - 4 = {}^{-}10$	${}^{-}1$	9. $16 + \frac{x}{3} = {}^{-}10$	${}^{-}78$
4. $9 = 2y + 9$	0	10. $\frac{{}^{-}4z}{5} = -12$	15
5. ${}^{-}10 + \frac{a}{4} = 9$	76	11. ${}^{-}22 = 3s - {}^{-}8$	${}^{-}10$
6. $17 = 5 - x$	${}^{-}12$	12. $-\frac{a}{6} - {}^{-}31 = 64$	${}^{-}198$

74 Solving Equations with Negative Variab

$$\frac{{}^{-}k}{6} + 1 = {}^{-}5$$
$$\frac{{}^{-}k}{6} + 1 - 1 = {}^{-}5 - 1$$
$$\frac{{}^{-}k}{6} \bullet 6 = {}^{-}6 \bullet 6$$
$${}^{-}k = {}^{-}36$$
$$k = 36$$

1. ${}^{-}8 - y = 22$	${}^{-}30$	7. ${}^{-}82 = -a$	82
2. $18 = {}^{-}k + 3$	${}^{-}15$	8. $\frac{-b}{3} + 50 = 100$	${}^{-}150$
3. $4 - \frac{x}{5} = {}^{-}16$	100	9. ${}^{-}6 - x\frac{1}{9} = {}^{-}18$	108
4. $-x - 15 = {}^{-}15$	0	10. ${}^{-}3z + 5 = 38$	${}^{-}11$
5. $-z = 11$	${}^{-}11$	11. $-a\frac{1}{2} + 12 = {}^{-}9$	42
6. ${}^{-}28 = \frac{-y}{4} - 12$	64	12. ${}^{-}5y - {}^{-}7 = 52$	${}^{-}9$

75 Magical Equations

Solve each equation. In a Magic Square, the sum of each row, column and diagonal is the same.

1. $x = 8$ $\frac{x}{4} + 5 = 7$	2. $x = 15$ $2x - 20 = 10$	3. $x = {}^{-}8$ ${}^{-}3x - 12 = 12$	4. $x = {}^{-}1$ $-x - 6 = -5$	5. $x = 6$ $2 = 2x - 10$
6. $x = 14$ $3x - 7 = 35$	7. $x = {}^{-}4$ $2 + 5x = {}^{-}18$	8. $x = {}^{-}2$ $4x + 5 = {}^{-}3$	9. $x = 5$ ${}^{-}11x + 10 = {}^{-}45$	10. $x = 7$ $5x - 6 = 29$
11. $x = {}^{-}5$ ${}^{-}4 = \frac{4x}{5}$	12. $x = {}^{-}3$ ${}^{-}2x + 7 = 13$	13. $x = 4$ $\frac{5x}{4} + 2 = 7$	14. $x = 11$ ${}^{-}64 = {}^{-}5x - 9$	15. $x = 13$ $2x + 10 = 36$
16. $x = 1$ $8x - 9 = {}^{-}1$	17. $x = 3$ $12 = 3x + 3$	18. $x = 10$ ${}^{-}4 = \frac{2x}{{}^{-}5}$	19. $x = 12$ $9 + 4x = 57$	20. $x = {}^{-}6$ $\frac{x}{{}^{-}2} + 2 = 5$
21. $x = 2$ $6 = \frac{x}{2} + 5$	22. $x = 9$ $2x - 10 = 8$	23. $x = 16$ $8 = \frac{x}{4} + 4$	24. $x = {}^{-}7$ $5x - 15 = {}^{-}50$	25. $x = 0$ $3x - 9 = {}^{-}9$

The Magic Sum is 20.

76 Solving Equations Using the Distributive Proper

$$4(x - 3) = 20$$
$$4x - 12 = 20$$
$$4x - 12 + 12 = 20 + 12$$
$$\frac{4x}{4} = \frac{32}{4}$$
$$x = 8$$

1. $3(x + 8) = {}^{-}6$	${}^{-}10$	7. $6(2 - \frac{x}{6}) = 1$	11
2. $75 = {}^{-}5(a + 5)$	${}^{-}20$	8. ${}^{-}36 = 6(y - 2)$	${}^{-}4$
3. ${}^{-}8(y - 6) = {}^{-}16$	8	9. ${}^{-}7(r + 8) = {}^{-}14$	${}^{-}6$
4. $20 = 4(\frac{t}{4} - 2)$	28	10. $3(m + 5) = 42$	9
5. $17(x - 2) = {}^{-}34$	0	11. ${}^{-}54 = 3(2 + 5m)$	${}^{-}4$
6. $63 = 9(2 - a)$	${}^{-}5$	12. ${}^{-}3(x - 7) + 2 = 20$	1

Answer Key

77 Solving Equations - Variables on Both Sides

$$5x + 6 = 2x + 5$$
$$5x - 2x + 6 = 2x - 2x + 15$$
$$3x + 6 - 6 = 15 - 6$$
$$\frac{3x}{3} = \frac{9}{3}$$
$$x = 3$$

1. $20y + 5 = 5y + 65$ **4**
2. $13 - t = t - 7$ **10**
3. $^-3k + 10 = k + 2$ **2**
4. $^-9r = 20 + r$ **$^-2$**
5. $6m - 2\frac{1}{2} = m + 12\frac{1}{2}$ **3**
6. $18 + 4.5p = 6p + 12$ **4**
7. $5x - \frac{1}{4} = 3x - \frac{5}{4}$ **$-\frac{1}{2}$**
8. $-x - 2 = 1 - 2x$ **3**
9. $3k + 10 = 2k - 21$ **$^-31$**
10. $8y - 6 = 5y + 12$ **6**
11. $-t + 10 = t + 4$ **3**
12. $4m - 9 = 5m + 7$ **$^-16$**

78 Mixed Practice

1. $4x - 7 = 2x + 15$ **11**
2. $^-4 = {^-4}(f - 7)$ **8**
3. $5x - 17 = 4x + 36$ **53**
4. $3(k + 5) = {^-18}$ **$^-11$**
5. $y + 3 = 7y - 21$ **4**
6. $^-3(m - 2) = 12$ **$^-2$**
7. $18 + 4p = 6p + 12$ **3**
8. $^-8(\frac{a}{8} - 2) = 26$ **$^-10$**
9. $^-3k + 10 = k + 2$ **2**
10. $22 = 2(b + 3)$ **8**
11. $6a + 9 = {^-4a} + 29$ **2**
12. $^-22 = 11(2c + 8)$ **$^-5$**
13. $10p - 14 = 9p + 17$ **31**
14. $^-45 = 5(\frac{2a}{5} + {^-3})$ **$^-15$**
15. $16z - 15 = 13z$ **5**
16. $36 + 19b = 24b + 6$ **6**
17. $144 = {^-16}(3 + 3d)$ **$^-4$**
18. $11h - 14 = 7 + 14h$ **$^-7$**
19. $^-3(\frac{2j}{3} - 6) = 32$ **$^-7$**
20. $^-43 - 3z = 2 - 6z$ **15**

79 Equation Steps

Solve these equations.

1. $^-116 = -a$ **$a = 116$**
2. $6m - 2 = m + 13$ **$m = 3$**
3. $x + 2 = {^-61}$ **$x = {^-63}$**
4. $^-30 = {^-6} - y$ **$y = 12$**
5. $^-5t + 16 = {^-59}$ **$t = 15$**
6. $4a - 9 = 6a + 7$ **$a = {^-8}$**
7. $\frac{^-3b}{8} = {^-36}$ **$b = 96$**
8. $^-40 = 10(4 + s)$ **$s = {^-8}$**
9. $28 - \frac{k}{3} = 16$ **$k = 36$**
10. $^-9r = 20 + r$ **$r = {^-2}$**
11. $114 = 11c - {^-26}$ **$c = 8$**
12. $^-38 = 17 - 5z$ **$z = 11$**
13. $^-5(2x - 5) = {^-35}$ **$x = 6$**
14. $20c + 5 = 5c + 65$ **$c = 4$**
15. $\frac{^-d}{5} - 21 = {^-62}$ **$d = 205$**
16. $\frac{^-15c}{^-4} = {^-30}$ **$c = {^-8}$**
17. $384 = 12({^-8} + 5t)$ **$t = 8$**
18. $3n + 7 = 7n - 13$ **$n = 5$**
19. $^-8 - \frac{y}{3} = 22$ **$y = {^-90}$**
20. $^-5t - 30 = {^-60}$ **$t = 6$**

HINT: The sum of the solutions equals the number of steps in the Statue of Liberty — 354

80 Writing Algebraic Expressions

The product of four and eleven	$4 \bullet 11$
A number increased by six	$x + 6$
The number divided by two	$y \div 2$ or $\frac{y}{2}$
Twice a number decreased by one	$2a - 1$

1. Five less than a number **$x - 5$**
2. Three times the sum of a number and twelve **$3(y + 12)$**
3. Ten more than the quotient of c and three **$10 + \frac{c}{3}$**
4. Two increased by six times a number **$2 + 6x$**
5. Two-thirds of a number minus eleven **$\frac{2}{3}y - 11$**
6. Twice the difference between c and four **$2(c - 4)$**
7. The product of nine and a number, decreased by seven **$9x - 7$**
8. Six times a number plus seven times the number **$6n + 7n$**
9. A number increased by twice the number **$n + 2n$**
10. One-fourth times a number increased by eleven **$\frac{1}{4}x + 11$**
11. The quotient of a number and three decreased by five **$\frac{n}{3 - 5}$**
12. Twelve times the sum of a number and five times the number **$12(n + 5n)$**

Answer Key

81 Solving One-Step Problems

Write an equation and solve

Nine more than a number is 33.
Find the number
$9 + n = 33$
$9 - 9 + n = 33 - 9$
$n = 24$

1. A number decreased by 16 is $^-26$. Find the number.
   $^-10$
2. One-fourth of a number is $^-60$. Find the number.
   $^-240$
3. The product of negative eight and a number is 104. Find the number.
   $^-13$
4. Twice a number is 346. Find the number.
   173
5. A number increased by negative twenty-seven is 110. Find the number.
   137
6. Tim weighs five pounds more than Mitchell. Find Mitchell's weight if Tim weighs ninety-three pounds.
   88
7. The cost of five books is $71.00. What is the cost of each book?
   $14.20
8. The cost of a filter is $4.00. What is the cost of six filters?
   $24.00

82 Solving Two-Step Problems

Write an equation and solve

Ten more than 4 times a number is 6.
What is the number?
$10 + 4n = 6$
$10 - 10 + 4n = 6 - 10$
$\frac{4n}{4} = \frac{^-4}{4}$
$n = {^-1}$

1. Three-fifths of a number decreased by one is twenty-three. What is the number?
   40
2. Seven more than six times a number is negative forty-seven. What is the number?
   $^-9$
3. Nine less than twice a number is thirty-one. What is the number?
   20
4. Three times the sum of a number and five times the number is thirty-six. What is the number?
   2
5. The quotient of a number and four decreased by ten is two. What is the number?
   48
6. Carol is sixty-six inches tall. This is twenty inches less than two times Mindy's height. How tall is Mindy?
   43 inches
7. In February, Paul's electric bill was three dollars more than one-half his gas bill. If the electric bill was ninety-two dollars, what was the gas bill?
   $178

83 Solving Multi-Step Problems

Write an equation and solve

One number is seven times a second number.
Their sum is 112. Find the numbers.
$n + 7n = 112$
$\frac{8n}{8} = \frac{112}{8}$
$n = 14$ and 98

1. One of two numbers is five more than the other. The sum of the numbers is 17. Find the numbers.
   6 and 11
2. The sum of two numbers is twenty-four. The larger number is three times the smaller number. Find the numbers.
   6 and 18
3. One of two numbers is two-thirds the other number. The sum of the numbers is 45. Find the numbers.
   27 and 18
4. The difference of two numbers is 19. The larger number is 3 more than twice the smaller. Find the numbers.
   16 and 35
5. 320 tickets were sold to the school play. There were three times as many student tickets sold as adult tickets. Find the number of each.
   80 adults 240 students
6. The first number is eight more than the second number. Three times the second number plus twice the first number is equal to 26. Find the numbers.
   10 and 2
7. Dan has five times as many $1 bills as $5 bills. He has a total of 48 bills. How many of each does he have?
   8 - $5 bills 40 - $1 bills

84 Graphing Inequalities

$x > 2$ 
$y \le 2$ 

1. $x > 1$ 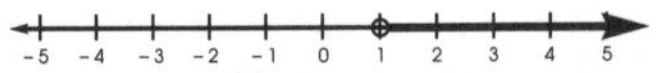
2. $a < {^-1}$ 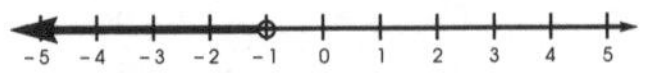
3. $y \le 2$ 
4. $b > {^-4}$ 
5. $p \ge 3$ 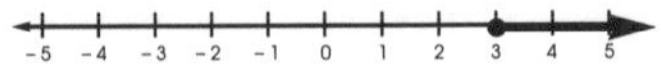
6. $x < \frac{1}{2}$ 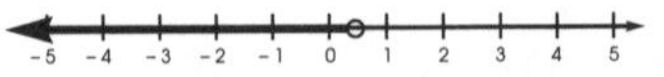
7. $y > {^-1.5}$ 
8. $m \le 4\frac{1}{2}$ 
9. $c \le \frac{^-10}{5}$ 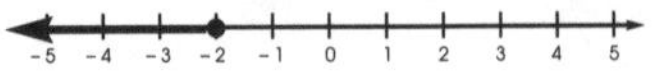
10. $d \ge 3.75$ 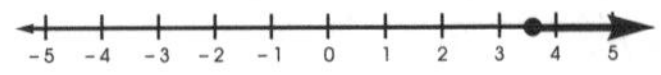

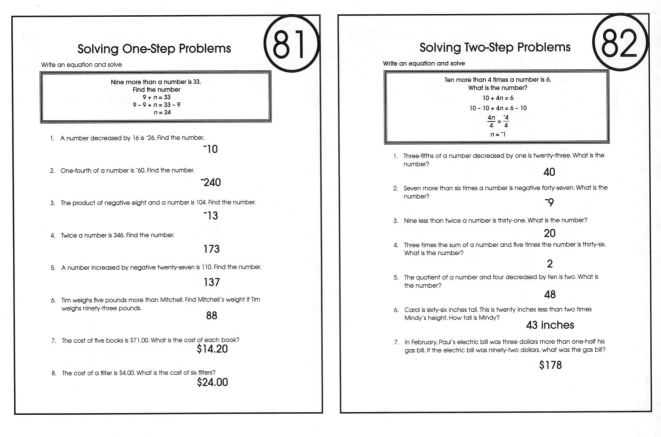

Answer Key

85 Solving Inequalities with Addition or Subtraction

$m + 9 > 5$
$m + 9 - 9 > 5 - 9$
$m > {}^{-}4$

1. $g + 8 > 6$ — $g > {}^{-}2$
2. $d - 7 > {}^{-}3$ — $d > 4$
3. ${}^{-}3 > y + 1$ — $y < {}^{-}4$
4. $a - 3 \le 1$ — $a \le 4$
5. ${}^{-}4 \le 1 + c$ — $c \ge {}^{-}5$
6. $x + \frac{1}{4} \ge 1\frac{1}{2}$ — $x \ge 1\frac{1}{4}$
7. ${}^{-}2.4 < n - 0.6$ — $n > {}^{-}1.8$
8. ${}^{-}20 + m \le {}^{-}24$ — $m \le 4$
9. ${}^{-}7.5 + x \ge {}^{-}9$ — $x \ge {}^{-}1.5$
10. $3\frac{1}{3} \le \frac{2}{9} + c$ — $c \ge 3\frac{1}{9}$

86 Solving Inequalities with Multiplication or Divis[ion]

$\frac{3y}{3} \le \frac{9}{3}$

$y \le 3$

$\frac{40}{{}^{-}10} < \frac{{}^{-}10n}{{}^{-}10}$

${}^{-}4 > n$

$-\frac{5}{2} \bullet -\frac{2}{5}x \ge {}^{-}4 \bullet -\frac{5}{2}$

$x \le 10$

Note: division or multiplication by a negative number switches the sign.

1. $11x > 22$ — $x > 2$
2. ${}^{-}15m \le {}^{-}75$ — $m \ge 5$
3. ${}^{-}1 > \frac{b}{3}$ — $b < {}^{-}3$
4. $1.9x \le {}^{-}7.6$ — $x \le {}^{-}4$
5. $\frac{3}{2}y < 6$ — $y < 4$
6. ${}^{-}26m \ge 13$ — $m \le \frac{{}^{-}1}{2}$
7. ${}^{-}4 \ge \frac{2}{3}x$ — $x \le {}^{-}6$
8. ${}^{-}2c < 2$ — $c > {}^{-}1$
9. ${}^{-}3a \le {}^{-}9$ — $a \ge 3$
10. $-\frac{3}{4}x \ge {}^{-}3$ — $x \le 4$

87 Mixed Practice: Solving One-Step Inequalities

1. $a + 8 > 16$ — $a > 8$
2. ${}^{-}7\frac{3}{5} \ge z - -\frac{1}{15}$ — $z \le {}^{-}7\frac{2}{3}$
3. ${}^{-}28 < {}^{-}4x$ — $x < 7$
4. ${}^{-}28.5 \le c + {}^{-}19.6$ — $c \ge {}^{-}8.9$
5. $\frac{{}^{-}4y}{3} > {}^{-}6$ — $y < 4\frac{1}{2}$
6. $6.3x < 7.56$ — $x < 1.2$
7. $-\frac{b}{3} \ge 3$ — $b \le {}^{-}9$
8. ${}^{-}18.2 < g - 13.7$ — $g > {}^{-}4.5$
9. $b + 3\frac{1}{4} > {}^{-}2\frac{1}{8}$ — $b > {}^{-}5\frac{3}{8}$
10. $\frac{z}{2} \le {}^{-}3$ — $z \le {}^{-}6$

88 Solving Inequalities with More than One Opera[tion]

${}^{-}14x + 8 \le 64$
${}^{-}14x + 8 - 8 \le 64 - 8$
$\frac{{}^{-}14x}{{}^{-}14} + 8 \le \frac{56}{{}^{-}14}$
$x \ge {}^{-}4$

1. $7x - 1 < 20$ — $x < 3$
2. ${}^{-}4 + 2z \ge {}^{-}8$ — $z \ge {}^{-}2$
3. ${}^{-}6x - 9 \ge {}^{-}3$ — $x \le {}^{-}1$
4. $4(2b - 3) \ge 36$ — $b \ge 6$
5. $7 < 5x - 8$ — $x > 3$
6. ${}^{-}17 > -7x - 45$ — $x > {}^{-}4$
7. ${}^{-}5(2t - 1) \le 5$ — $t \ge 0$
8. $8 - 4x > {}^{-}12$ — $x < 5$
9. ${}^{-}2(2x - 1) \ge {}^{-}9$ — $x \le 2\frac{3}{4}$
10. $41.56 < 6.3 - {}^{-}8.2x$ — $y > 4.3$

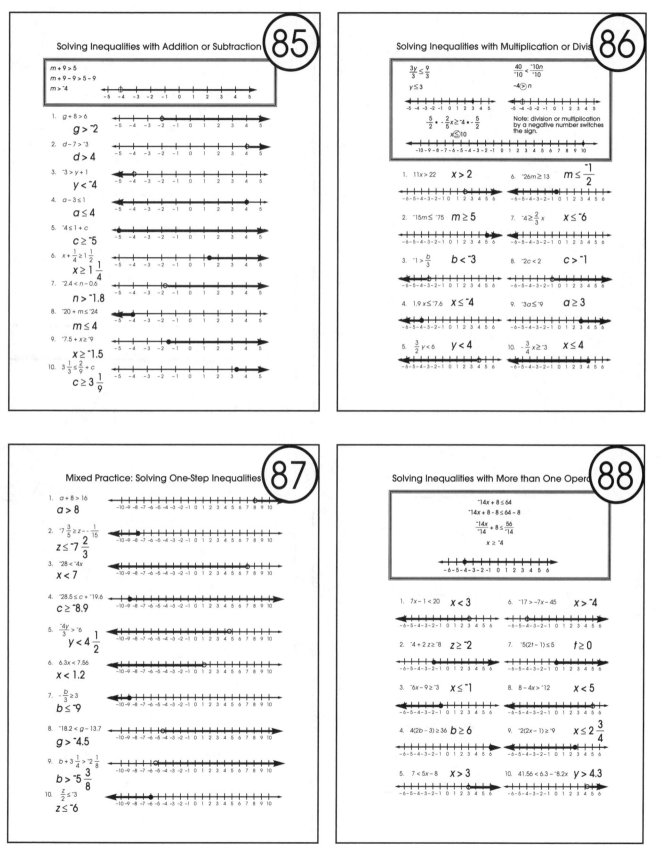

Answer Key

89 Solving Inequalities with Variables on Both Sides

$^{-}2a + 11 < a - 1$

$^{-}2a + 2a + 11 < a + 2a - 1$

$11 < 3a - 1$

$11 + 1 < 3a - 1 + 1$

$\frac{12}{3} < \frac{3a}{3}$

$4 < a$

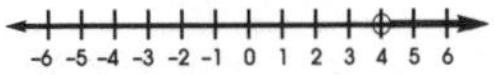

1. $4c + 1 < ^{-}(5 + 2c)$ **$c < ^{-}1$**

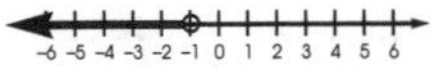

6. $10(x + 2) > ^{-}2(6 - 9x)$ **$x < 4$**

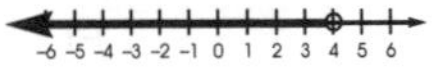

2. $2 - n > 2n + 11$ **$n < ^{-}3$**

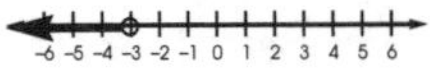

7. $11 + 3(^{-}8 + 5x) < 16x - 8$ **$x > ^{-}5$**

3. $2(3x - 5) > 2x + 6$ **$x > 4$**

8. $12(2x + 3) \geq 3(9 + 7x)$ **$x \geq ^{-}3$**

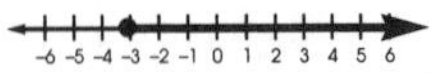

4. $^{-}2(4y - 21) \leq 12y - 16 + 9y$ **$y \geq 2$**

9. $35 - 18x > ^{-}8(x + 3x)$ **$x \geq ^{-}2\frac{1}{2}$**

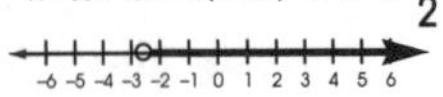

5. $n - 3n \geq ^{-}4n - 7$ **$n \geq ^{-}3\frac{1}{2}$**

10. $12x + ^{-}2(x + 5) < 3x(5 + 2) + 45$ **$x > ^{-}5$**

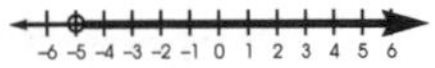

90 Mixed Practice: Solving Multi-Step Inequali[ties]

1. $32.4 \geq ^{-}6c$ **$-5.4 \leq c$**

2. $x - ^{-}15 \leq 9$ **$x \leq -6$**

3. $-\frac{2}{3}b > ^{-}6$ **$b < 9$**

4. $^{-}18 + d > ^{-}11$ **$d > 7$**

5. $6(2z + 3) \leq ^{-}54$ **$z \leq -6$**

6. $8y - 15 < 27 + 2y$ **$y < 7$**

7. $162 > ^{-}3a(5 + 1)$ **$-9 < a$**

8. $^{-}6(5x + 8) \geq 2(8 - 7x)$ **$-4 \geq x$**

9. $^{-}40 \leq 8(2t - 2)$ **$-\frac{3}{2} \leq t$**

10. $5x(2 - 3) < 3x + 62$ **$-\frac{31}{4} < x$**

91 More Practice with Inequalities

1. $9x - 8 + x < 16 + 4x$

2. $15y \geq ^{-}45$

3. $69 > c + 71$

4. $17 + 11n - 13 \leq 4(n + 1) + 2n$

5. $8(2 + x) > 3(x - 3)$

6. $^{-}4(3x + 2) \geq 40$

7. $\frac{5}{3} < \frac{2}{3}x - 1$

8. $3n - 4(2n - 5) + n + 4 \geq 0$

9. $18c + 11 - 26c < -3c(5 + 1) - 59$

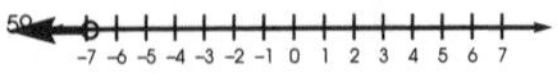

10. $8a - 2(2a + 5) \leq 2a(9 + 1) + 54$

92 A Logical Conclusion

Mike, Dale, Paul and Charlie are the athletic director, quarterback, pitc[her] and goalie, but not necessarily in that order. From these five statements, identify the man in each position.

1. Mike and Dale were both at the ballpark when the rookie pitcher played his first game.
2. Both Paul and the athletic director had played on the same team in high school with the goalie.
3. The athletic director, who scouted Charlie, is planning to watch Mike during his next game.
4. Mike doesn't know Dale.
5. One of these men is a quarterback.

	Quarterback	Goalie	Pitcher	Athletic Director
Mike	X			
Dale				X
Paul			X	
Charlie		X		

Answer Key

93 Plotting Points

Connect each of the following ordered points.

(x, y) = (0, -1)
- vertical move ⟹ down one
- horizontal move ⟹ no move

"Ancient History"

Start at (0, -1)

(1, -1)
(1, -3)
(3, -3)
(3, -1)
(5,0)
(8,0)
(7,1)
(9,0)
(8,2)
(5,1)
(4,3)
(3,4)
(2,3)
(1,4)
(0,3)
(-1,4)
(-2,3)
(-3,4)
(-4,3)
(-5,1)
(-8,2)
(-5,0)
(-3,-1)
(-3,-3)
(-1,-3)
(-1,-1)
(0,-1)
End

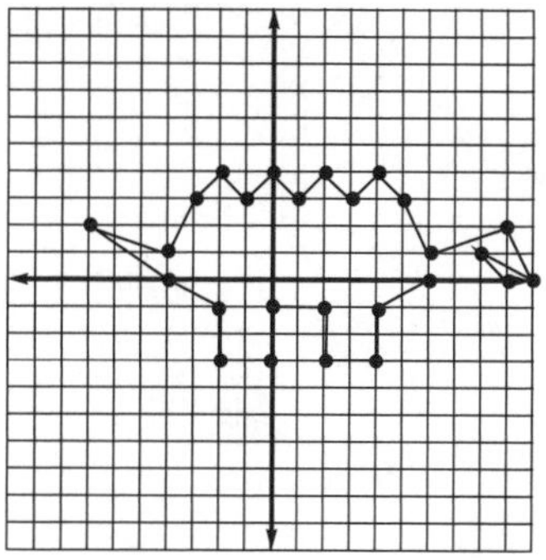

94 Coordinates and Graphing

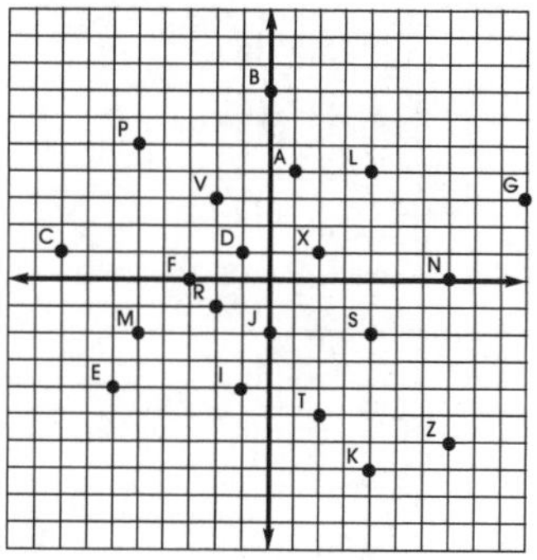

Find the coordinates associated with the following points.

1. A (1, 4)
2. K (4, -7)
3. E (-6, -4)
4. P (-5, 5)
5. T (2, -5)
6. C (-8, 1)
7. B (0, 7)
8. S (4, -2)
9. D (-1, 1)
10. N (7, 0)

Find the letter associated with each pair of coordinates.

11. (2, 1) X
12. (-1, -4) I
13. (10, 3) G
14. (7, -6) Z
15. (-2, -1) R
16. (-2, 3) V
17. (-3, 0) F
18. (4, 4) L
19. (-5, -2) M
20. (0, -2) J

95 Solving for *y*

Solve each equation for *y*. Then use the given values for *x* to find the corresponding values for *y*. Write answers as ordered pairs

$y - 4 = 3x$
$y - 4 + 4 = 3x + 4$
$y = 3x + 4$

Let $x = -2, 0, 1$

Solve for *y*

a. $y = 3 \cdot -2 + 4$
$y = -6 + 4$
$y = -2$
(-2, -2)

b. $y = 3 \cdot 0 + 4$
$y = 0 + 4$
$y = 4$
(0, 4)

c. $y = 3 \cdot 1 + 4$
$y = 3 + 4$
$y = 7$
(1, 7)

1. $y = 5x$ — Let $x = -3, 0, 2$ — Note: This equation is already in the form of $y = ...$
   $y = 5x$ (-3, -15) (0, 0) (2, 10)
2. $2x + y = 9$ — Let $x = -1, 0, 5$
   $y = 9 - 2x$ (-1, 11) (0, 9) (5, -1)
3. $-x = y + 3$ — Let $x = -3, 0, 4$
   $y = -x - 3$ (-3, 0) (0, -3) (4, -7)
4. $y = \frac{2}{3}x + 1$ — Let $x = -4, 0, 3$
   $y = \frac{2}{3}x + 1$ $(-4, -\frac{5}{3})$ (0, 1) (3, 3)
5. $8x + y = 1$ — Let $x = -2, 0, 1$
   $y = -8x + 1$ (-2, 17) (0, 1) (1, -7)
6. $y - 1 = -3x$ — Let $x = -3, 0, 2$
   $y = -3x + 1$ (-3, 10) (0, 1) (2, -5)
7. $2 = y - \frac{1}{3}x$ — Let $x = -9, 0, 6$
   $y = \frac{1}{3}x + 2$ (-9, -1) (0, 2) (6, 4)
8. $7x - y = -8$ — Let $x = -1, 0, -3$
   $y = 7x + 8$ (-1,1) (0, 8) (-3, -13)

96 Graphing Linear Equations by Plotting Po

Solve each equation for *y*. Then choose 3 values for *x* and find the corresponding values for *y*. Graph the 3 ordered pairs and draw the line that contains them.

$5x + y = -1$
$5x - 5x + y = -1 - 5x$
$y = -5x - 1$

x	y
-1	4
0	-1
2	-11

a. $y = -5 \cdot -1 - 1$
$y = 5 - 1$
$y = 4$

b. $y = -5 \cdot 0 - 1$
$y = 0 - 1$
$y = -1$

c. $y = -5 \cdot 2 - 1$
$y = -10 - 1$
$y = -11$

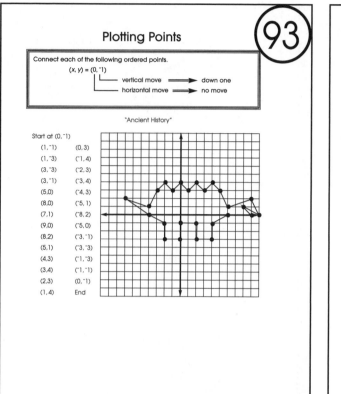

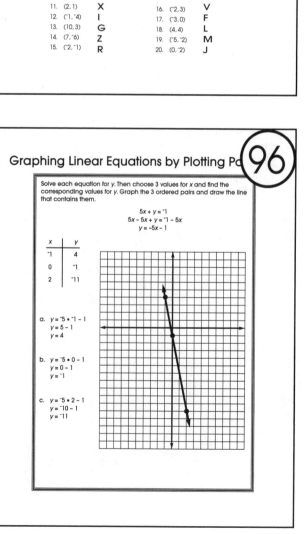

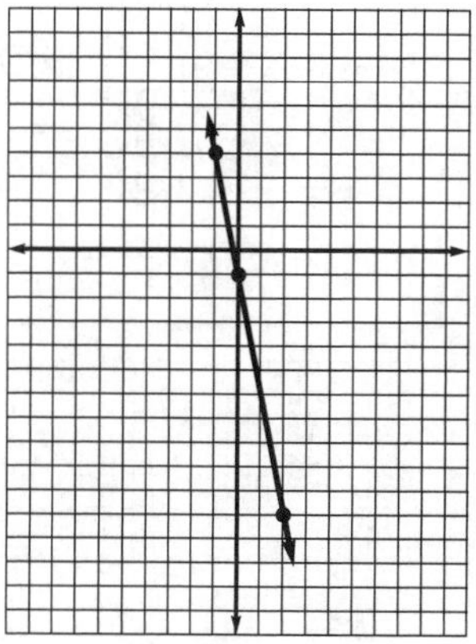

Answer Key

Graphing Linear Equations by Plotting P... (97)

1. $y = \frac{1}{2}x - 3$

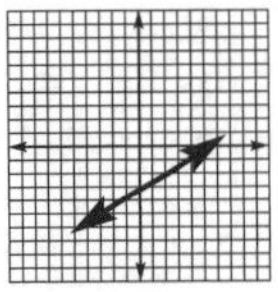

5. $3x + y = 7$

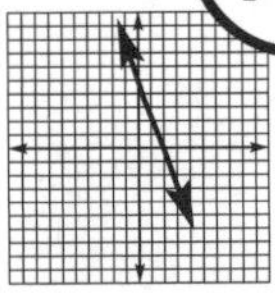

2. $^-2x + y = 5$

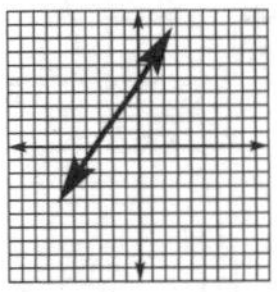

6. $3x - y = {}^-2$

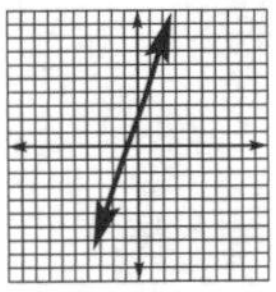

3. $4x + y = {}^-7$

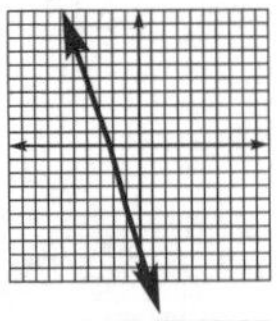

7. $y + 7 = 5x$

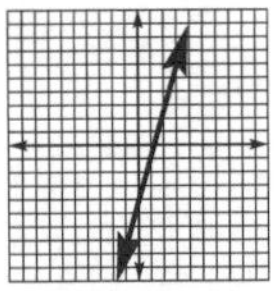

4. $y - 3 = 2x$

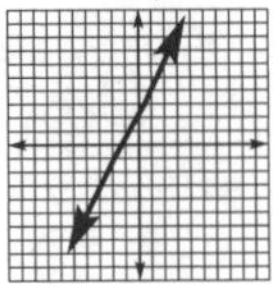

8. $y = \frac{1}{4}x - 2$

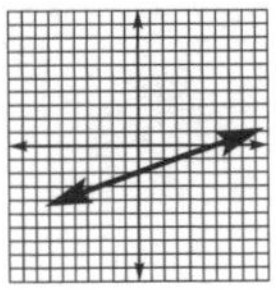

Graphing Linear Equations by Plotting P... (98)

9. $\frac{3}{4}x + y = 2$

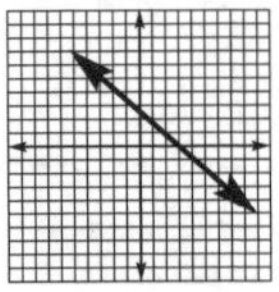

13. $y = -\frac{1}{2}x$

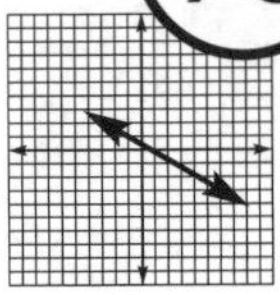

10. $x - y = {}^-4$

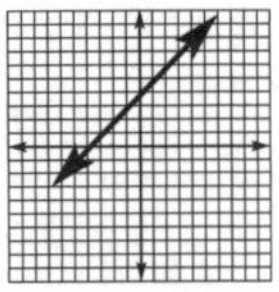

14. $\frac{1}{4}x + y = {}^-2$

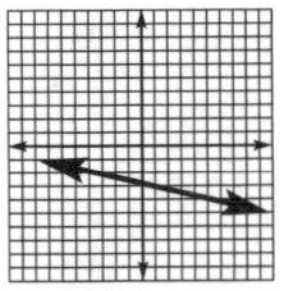

11. $^-3x + y = {}^-4$

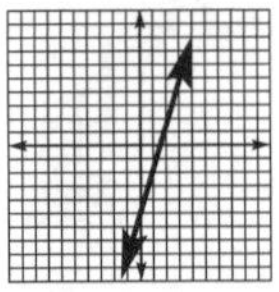

15. $y = {}^-4x - 5$

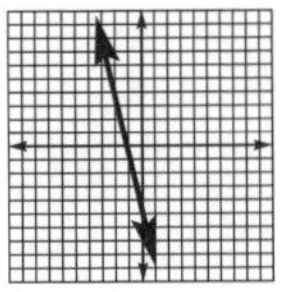

12. $y - x = {}^-1$

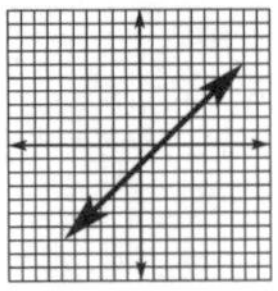

16. $y = {}^-2x - 3$

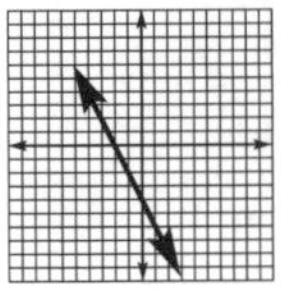

Finding Slope Using a Graph (99)

Find the slope of the lines passing through the given points.

$$\text{slope} = \frac{\text{change in } y}{\text{change in } x}$$

Choose any 2 points to count the change.

change in $x = 8$

change in $y = 4$

slope $= \frac{4}{8} = \frac{1}{2}$

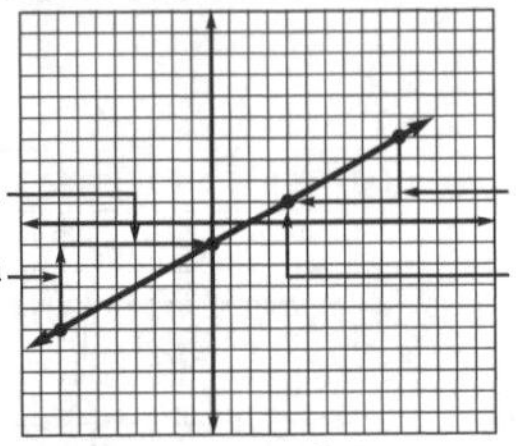

change in $y = {}^-3$

change in $x = {}^-6$

slope $= \frac{^-3}{^-6} = \frac{1}{2}$

slope is $\frac{1}{2}$

1. 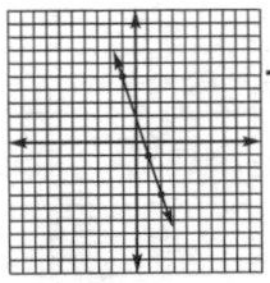 $^-3$

3. 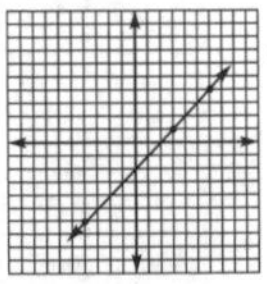 1

5. 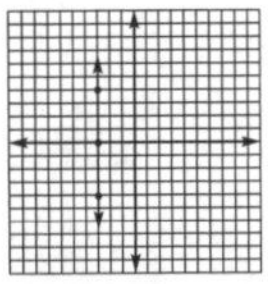 no slope

2. 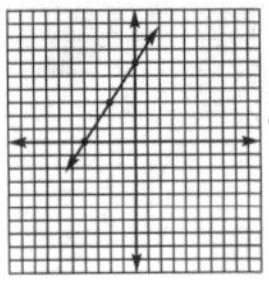 $\frac{3}{2}$

4. 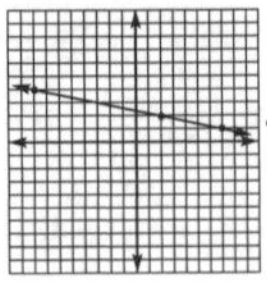 $-\frac{1}{5}$

6. 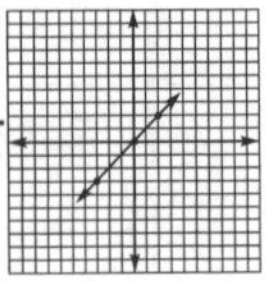 1

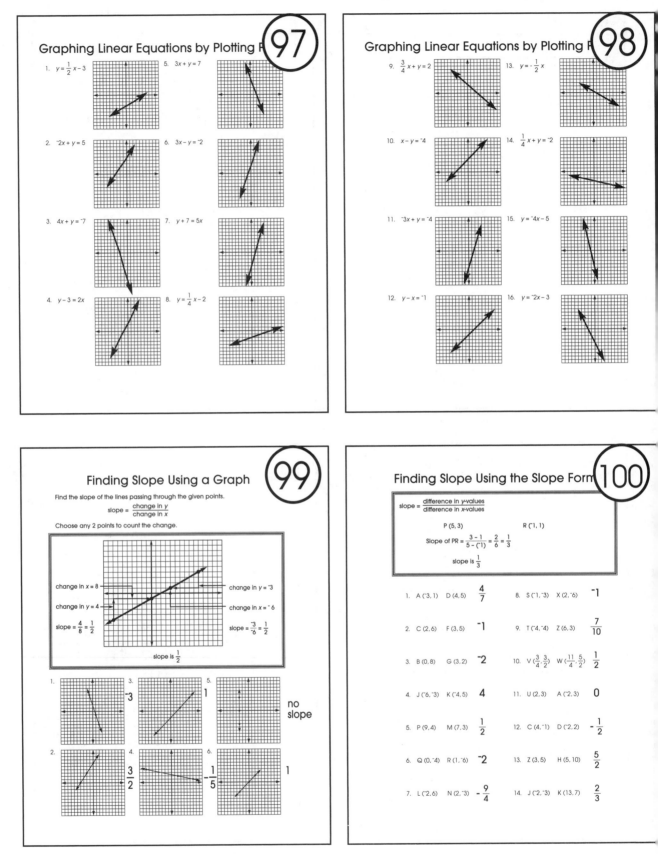

Finding Slope Using the Slope Form... (100)

$$\text{slope} = \frac{\text{difference in } y\text{-values}}{\text{difference in } x\text{-values}}$$

P (5, 3) R ($^-1$, 1)

Slope of PR $= \frac{3 - 1}{5 - (^-1)} = \frac{2}{6} = \frac{1}{3}$

slope is $\frac{1}{3}$

1.	A ($^-3$, 1)	D (4, 5)	$\frac{4}{7}$	8.	S ($^-1$, $^-3$)	X (2, $^-6$)	$^-1$
2.	C (2, 6)	F (3, 5)	$^-1$	9.	T ($^-4$, $^-4$)	Z (6, 3)	$\frac{7}{10}$
3.	B (0, 8)	G (3, 2)	$^-2$	10.	V ($\frac{3}{4}$, $\frac{3}{2}$)	W ($\frac{11}{4}$, $\frac{5}{2}$)	$\frac{1}{2}$
4.	J ($^-6$, $^-3$)	K ($^-4$, 5)	4	11.	U (2, 3)	A ($^-2$, 3)	0
5.	P (9, 4)	M (7, 3)	$\frac{1}{2}$	12.	C (4, $^-1$)	D ($^-2$, 2)	$-\frac{1}{2}$
6.	Q (0, $^-4$)	R (1, $^-6$)	$^-2$	13.	Z (3, 5)	H (5, 10)	$\frac{5}{2}$
7.	L ($^-2$, 6)	N (2, $^-3$)	$-\frac{9}{4}$	14.	J ($^-2$, $^-3$)	K (13, 7)	$\frac{2}{3}$

Answer Key

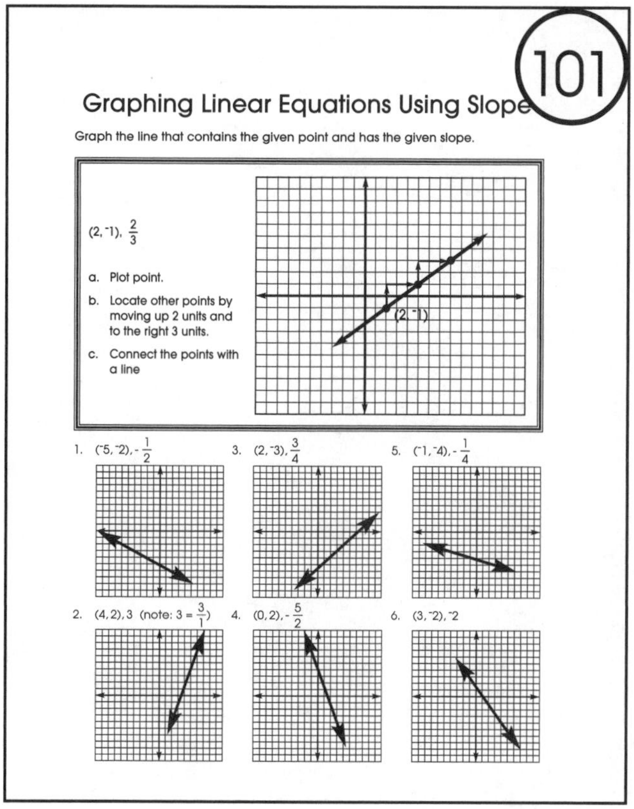

Graphing Linear Equations Using Slope (101)

Graph the line that contains the given point and has the given slope.

(2, ⁻1), $\frac{2}{3}$

a. Plot point.
b. Locate other points by moving up 2 units and to the right 3 units.
c. Connect the points with a line

(2, ⁻1)

1. (⁻5, ⁻2), $-\frac{1}{2}$
2. (4, 2), 3 (note: $3 = \frac{3}{1}$)
3. (2, ⁻3), $\frac{3}{4}$
4. (0, 2), $-\frac{5}{2}$
5. (⁻1, ⁻4), $-\frac{1}{4}$
6. (3, ⁻2), ⁻2

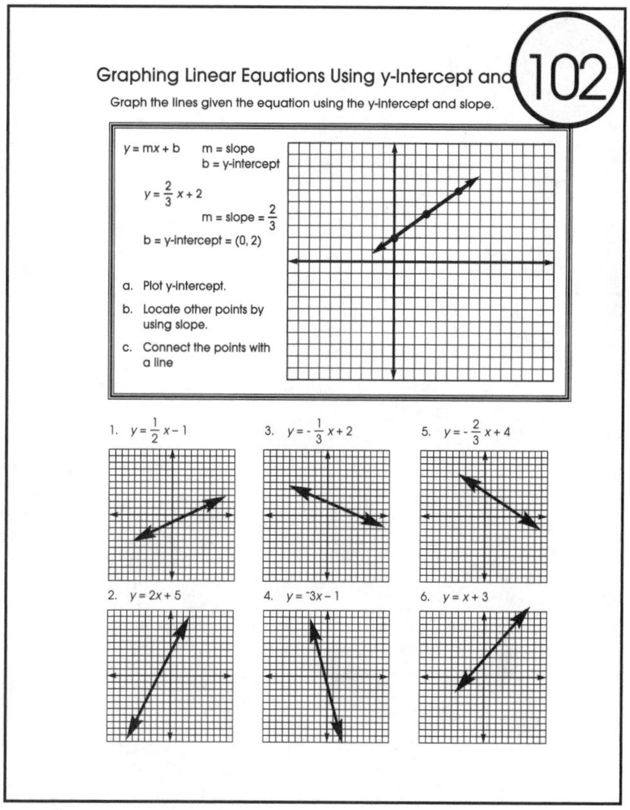

Graphing Linear Equations Using y-Intercept and (102)

Graph the lines given the equation using the y-intercept and slope.

$y = mx + b$ m = slope
b = y-intercept

$y = \frac{2}{3}x + 2$

m = slope = $\frac{2}{3}$

b = y-intercept = (0, 2)

a. Plot y-intercept.
b. Locate other points by using slope.
c. Connect the points with a line

1. $y = \frac{1}{2}x - 1$
2. $y = 2x + 5$
3. $y = -\frac{1}{3}x + 2$
4. $y = {}^{-}3x - 1$
5. $y = -\frac{2}{3}x + 4$
6. $y = x + 3$